4/2362732

WHERE MIRACLES HAPPEN
THE STORY OF
THOMOND PARK

Ronan O'Gara, 2009. (Courtesy *Irish Examiner*)

WHERE MIRACLES HAPPEN
THE STORY OF
THOMOND PARK

CHARLIE MULQUEEN & BRENDAN O'DOWD

The Collins Press

FIRST PUBLISHED IN 2015 BY
The Collins Press
West Link Park
Doughcloyne
Wilton
Cork

© Charlie Mulqueen & Brendan O'Dowd 2015

A CIP record for this book is available from the British Library.

Hardback ISBN: 978-1-84889-255-2
PDF eBook ISBN: 978-1-84889-512-6
EPUB eBook ISBN: 978-1-84889-513-3
Kindle ISBN: 978-1-84889-514-0

Design and typesetting by Fairways Design
Typeset in Garamond
Printed in Poland by Białostockie Zakłady Graficzne SA

Photograph on p. i courtesy of Stephen O'Dowd

CONTENTS

Acknowledgments   vi
Points values explained   vi

Foreword by Edmund Van Esbeck   vii
Introduction   1

1. Beginnings: 1920s to 1940s   6

2. Clifford and Reid   18

3. Overseas Visitors and
Famous Names: 1950s   27

4. Into the 1960s   41

5. 'There is an Isle'   55

6. 'Munster Midgets'   64

7. History at Thomond   69

8. October 1978   80

9. 12 Year Gap Bridged   102

10. 1980s   111

11. 1990s   120

*Half-time at Thomond Park
– Tom Kiernan*   130

12. The Game Goes Open   132

13. Pizza For Life   143

14. A New Millennium   151

15. Chasing The Holy Grail   165

16. 'Just a Field'   174

17. The 'New' Thomond Park   181

18. The Celtic League   198

19. ROG Gets The Drop On The Saints   209

20. Schools Rugby   224

21. Junior Rugby   240

22. Supporters, Soccer, Springsteen
& the Baa-Baas   251

Epilogue by Tony Ward   264

Selected Bibliography   267

Index   268

Acknowledgments

Great rugby people and friends helped to make this book possible. The authors extend sincere gratitude to Denis O'Brien, Michael McLoughlin, Alan English (Editor, *Limerick Leader*) and Tony Leen (Sports Editor and Deputy Editor, *Irish Examiner*). Special thanks to Ciaran McCarthy, Pictures Desk, *Irish Examiner* and Eugene Phelan, Deputy Editor, *Limerick Leader*.

Thanks also to Billy Barry, Des Barry, John Cantwell, Aidan Corr, Michael Cowhey, Marie Dineen, Michael Ellard, Garrett Fitzgerald, John Fitzgerald, Dermot Geary, Sean Geary, Tom Hanley (Order of Malta), Donal Holland, Rory Holohan (PBC), Dan Linehan, Frank Malone, Michael Manning, Dermot McGovern, Andrew McNamara, Matthew and Gerry McNamara, Denis Minihane, Gerry Moore, Peter Mulqueen, Joe Murphy (Michael Punch & Partners), Louis Nestor, Michael Nix, Stephen O'Dowd, Press 22, Charlie Quaid, Don Reddan, Peter Scott, Owen South, Stan Waldron, and designers Sarah Farrelly of Artmark and Glen McArdle of Fairways Design.

To the various rugby clubs throughout Munster and Ireland and to all those from far afield – New Zealand, South Africa, Australia, France and Britain – for their cooperation, our appreciation.

Points values explained

Because scoring values have changed many times over the eighty years since the opening of Thomond Park, the following panel will help to explain how results from different eras were arrived at:

1934 (when Thomond Park first opened)
Try = three points
Conversion = two points
Drop goal = four points
Penalty = three points

1948
Drop goal = three points

1971
Try = four points

1992
Try = five points

Foreword Edmund Van Esbeck

Time goes by and with the passage of time many things change. In that respect the splendid new stadium that is now Thomond Park is in sharp contrast to the old ground which, while it served the game well, was no longer fit for purpose.

It is well over sixty years since I first watched a match in Thomond Park and throughout all these years there is one thing that has not changed: the unique atmosphere that pervades the scene at the ground, and the passion and knowledge of the patrons who through the years have made their way to this hallowed stadium which is renowned throughout the rugby world.

The three great powers of the southern hemisphere have all been beaten at Thomond Park: the Springboks, the Australians and, of course, most notable of all, the All Blacks on that memorable day: 31 October 1978. Those of us who were privileged to be there on that occasion, and the thousands who weren't but wish they had been, will never forget that day when Munster humbled the All Blacks not alone by winning but by keeping the New Zealanders scoreless. Yes indeed, alone it stands.

As the memories roll in of great Munster Senior Cup matches, interprovincials, Schools' Cup matches and All-Ireland League matches, it was a regular occurrence that the ground would be packed to capacity with the sound of battle coming up from the old stand and the terraces.

It has been, too, the venue for international matches, few though they were, but what really prompted those behind the development of the ground was the advent of the Heineken Cup. Munster's exploits in it were such that the need for major development and a vastly increased capacity became apparent. Great credit is due to those who steered that redevelopment led by Pat Whelan.

That the history of Thomond should be written is absolutely appropriate. This has come about through the initiative of an old friend, Brendan O'Dowd, the former Munster and Bohemians forward, one-time president of the Munster Branch and a former Munster selector. His idea took root and now through the writing skills of another old and valued friend and journalistic colleague, Charlie Mulqueen, it has been brought to fruition. These two men are an ideal combination well fitted to tell a wonderful story of sporting endeavour. There is nobody living who has reported more matches at Thomond Park than Charlie Mulqueen, first in his capacity as rugby correspondent of the *Limerick Leader* and then with the *Irish Examiner*.

In the pages that follow the great matches and players and the magnificent occasions will come to life again for those of us who were privileged to have borne witness to them.

The future generations will, through this book, get a splendid education in precisely what they have inherited in the gem that is Thomond Park, for history gives value to the present hour and its meaning.

Edmund (Ned) Van Esbeck is the esteemed former rugby correspondent of The Irish Times. *He has covered the game with complete authority in every corner of the rugby world and is as much admired and respected nowadays as he was when covering the sport he has loved so deeply for many years.*

Introduction

'The most beautiful thing we can
experience is the miraculous.'

Albert Einstein

For a totally unrated Munster team to defeat the otherwise unbeaten 1978 New Zealand All Blacks by twelve clear points, and hold them scoreless in the process, was widely regarded as nothing less than a miracle – in a rugby context, of course. In 2003 another Munster side needed to score four tries and win by twenty-seven points in a Heineken European Cup match against reigning English champions Gloucester to qualify for the knockout stages. To do exactly as required also entered the realms of the miraculous.

In 2011, Munster trailed Northampton Saints by one point deep into injury time in another Heineken Cup game. Displaying a remarkable combination of patience and skill, they totalled 41 phases over a 7-minute-45-second period of time to get close enough to the opposition posts to set up a drop-goal attempt by Ronan O'Gara. The pass to the out-half needed to be perfect, the ball had to be caught and kicked simultaneously. Perfection required. Perfection achieved. The ball sailed between the posts 40 metres away. Surely the hand of God, as well as the boot of O'Gara, was at work?

Everyone will have their own examples of the phenomenon that is Thomond Park – and maybe theirs are even more remarkable than those we have articulated. The point is – when it comes to Thomond Park, anything is possible.

The majority of visiting teams and supporters who made their initial pilgrimage to Thomond Park, from its opening back in 1934 until the old stand and terraces were finally demolished and spectacularly modernised in 2008, wondered what all the fuss was about. To be perfectly honest, the original was far from an architectural gem and – unless it was a particularly noteworthy occasion – not exactly the kind of place you wanted to be. Those sentiments were not lost on Limerick's own. Indeed, before a ball was ever kicked there in anger,

A rather unflattering view of the 'old' Thomond Park (courtesy Joe Murphy (Michael Punch and Partners) Consulting Engineers) and what it looks like today (courtesy Sportsfile).

Thomond Park was described in the *Limerick Leader* as an 'unsheltered plateau'; some referred to it as 'Pneumonia Park'.

The reality is that, quite simply, Thomond Park was born of necessity. Its purpose during the pioneering years of the 1930s was to protect the future of the game in Limerick, something its predecessor, the Markets Field, was no longer in a position to guarantee. So frills and aesthetics were never a consideration. You accepted that on a cold, windy day it could be more than a little unwelcoming. The old stand served a purpose in that it sheltered up to 1,000 people from the elements, but what about the other 10,000 or so spread around the perimeter of the pitch?

Oh, yes, the pitch … from November to April, a 10-yard-wide strip of bare ground stretched from one 25-yard line to the other not far inside the boundary wall on the stand side of the pitch. When the rains fell, it was as slippery and treacherous as any ice-skating rink, with those caught at the bottom of a ruck happy to escape with their faculties still intact. During the dry, breezy, sunny months of spring, it was rock hard, the skin on many a limb was badly grazed and dust swirled about everywhere.

One South African journalist claimed after the 1951 Munster v Springboks encounter that 'it was a boggy mixture of mud and the droppings of sheep who had grazed there recently'. There was more of that kind of stuff, much more.

And yet and yet … everybody seemed to love Thomond Park. From the youngsters right up to the game's greatest, playing there felt like a privilege, an honour to brag about years later to the grandchildren. The place resounded in a way that few other grounds could rival. And then there were the fans, the diehards, the know-alls, the referees' assistants, call them what you will: Thomond Park offered them the opportunity to express their opinion about friend and foe alike within a few short metres of the action. They did so with relish, fearlessly and inevitably with humour and a touch of originality. (And, you know, they haven't gone away.)

Put all these qualities together and you have the unique atmosphere for which Thomond Park has always been famed. To what should its renown be attributed? The games, the players, the characters, the fans, the sense of fair play, the occasions?

Donal Spring, one of the heroes of 1978, credits the spectators for its unique ethos: 'What's so special about Thomond Park? The crowd.

Simply the crowd. The atmosphere is electric. Of all the places I've played, playing with Munster at Thomond Park is what I've enjoyed most.'

Another of that history-making side, Tony Ward, enthused: 'Everything about the occasion just smacked of raw Limerick and Munster passion.'

Andy Haden, generally recognised as one of the finest of all New Zealand second-rows, recalled several years later: 'For those who saw that game, it was fantastic; for those who played in it, it was even better.'

Few revelled in the Thomond Park atmosphere more than Ronan O'Gara. Looking back a couple of years after his retirement, he stated that: 'playing in Thomond Park was – sometimes words don't do it justice – just incredible. It was basically the crowd that drove Munster. When you performed with 20,000 people behind you, you got the feeling that you could not be beaten. That was what usually happened there.'

Nigel Melville, an outstanding England scrum half who later coached Gloucester in the Heineken Cup at Thomond Park, is one of the ground's greatest admirers: 'It is in another league altogether. Limerick is rugby. Everyone knows who you are and why you're there. The banter is knowledgeable and entertaining.'

Has that changed since 2008 with the advent of the magnificent new, modern stadium? In appearance, you naturally think sweet and sour, chalk and cheese, black and white. Incredibly, though, the atmosphere, when Munster have entertained major visiting clubs like Toulouse or Clermont, Northampton or Saracens, national powers like New Zealand or Australia, is as electric as ever.

The point was hammered home on that memorable November night in 2008 when the All Blacks came to mark the official opening of the stadium. They escaped with a two-point victory but it was the occasion and the sense of pride and emotion among the 26,500 fans that most captured their imagination. All Blacks coach Graham Henry was not known for idle words but he was so impressed that he rejoiced: 'It all showed the spirit of the Munster team and the geographic area it represents. It was nice to have a win but I think the occasion was more important. Our players will have learned a lot playing in that kind of atmosphere.'

Jim Kayes of the New Zealand *Dominion Post* described the atmosphere in Thomond Park that night, particularly when Munster's four New Zealanders performed the haka: 'The noise made the din from 82,000 at Croke Park last week (Ireland v New Zealand) sound like a lullaby. Yet the crowd dropped to an awed silence for the All Blacks' response.'

The people at the BBC aren't easily impressed but even they applauded the spectacular occasion: 'For the All Blacks there would have been no embarrassment in losing to the inspired, electrified, relentless, passionate and ultimately magnificent team of Munster men on this unforgettable autumn night at the legendary Thomond Park.'

The rivalry between Munster and Leinster may have sometimes gone over the top. The 92-times capped Ireland and Leinster second-row Malcolm O'Kelly admitted to reservations before lining out at Thomond Park in 2000 in the Barbarians jersey for the last match of his illustrious career. He was to be pleasantly surprised.

'I never thought I'd get a standing ovation at Thomond Park', he said. 'They're a great crowd and it shows the respect they have.'

This book will attempt to explain the remarkable appeal of Thomond Park Stadium. We hope that its contents will entertain and illuminate the reader's understanding of what has occurred there over the last eighty years and the amazing impact it has had on the lives and careers of the players and spectators who have helped to create its unique atmosphere.

1

Beginnings: 1920s to 1940s

T he Markets Field had never been one of the most salubrious of sporting stadiums. From its foundation as a sporting arena in 1893, its most redeeming physical feature was probably that it lay in the shadow of the imposing spire of St John's Cathedral, but that alone was never going to be enough to prevent the Gaelic Athletic Association (GAA) and the Irish Rugby Football Union (IRFU) from seeking pastures new towards the end of the 1920s.

In spite of its shortcomings, the Markets Field in Garryowen had managed to accommodate Munster hurling and football matches up to that point as well as Limerick's major rugby and soccer games (it was also the headquarters of greyhound racing in the mid-west from 1932 until 2010 when the move was made to the old Limerick racecourse at Greenpark). Coping with the demands of Munster senior hurling championship matches on or off the field was proving more and more problematical while Limerick was also losing out on interprovincial rugby games because Leinster and Ulster refused to play at the Garryowen venue.

The GAA were first to bite the bullet. In October 1926, they purchased a 12-acre farm at Coolraine on the Ennis Road. Two years later they were playing junior matches there and by 1932 a successful fund-raising campaign to level the pitch, provide sideline seating and the erection of a boundary wall was under way. The many staunch rugby people who ran their sport in the city and surrounds watched all of this and thought: 'if the GAA can do it, so, too, can we.'

The matter of a new rugby ground for Limerick was raised at a meeting of the county council in 1931 when the chairman, John McCormack, read a letter from Messrs F. W. Fitt and Co. solicitors, Lower Mallow Street, applying on behalf of the Munster Branch of the IRFU for the purchase of 7 acres of the Fair Green for the purpose of a football ground. They believed the Branch would be prepared to make an offer on terms advantageous to the council.

Mr McCormack was of the opinion that the application should be considered, pointing out that 'the city was losing representative rugby matches in the absence of a suitable football ground'. He was supported by the county surveyor who stressed that 'the city has during the past few years been deprived of interprovincial matches because we don't have a suitable ground. They now go to Cork because Ulster and Leinster will not play in the Markets Field.' A committee composed of Messrs E. J. Mitchell, J. Canty, D. J. Madden, M. Colbert and G. Hewson was appointed to meet the representatives of the Munster Branch to discuss the subject and report to the council.

However, that appears to have been the end of the Fair Green proposal. There was a clear preference for the farmland at Hassetts Cross, Thomondgate, known as Foley's Field, and in 1931 the Munster Branch duly completed the purchase of 6½ acres at a cost of £1,150. It was then that Limerick's rugby public demonstrated their love of the game and desire to see it prosper and thrive in north Munster. They were in no way disconcerted that part of the purchase deal of Foley's Field involved the donation by fifty people of £20 each: in fact, twice that number donated twice that amount.

It took a while for the IRFU to appreciate the need for the grounds and the sterling work being done by all in Limerick but eventually they came on board with an extra £1,500 towards the development. With the extra money, the North Munster Branch built a wall around the property with an entrance gate on the old Cratloe Road. Legend has it that a court action needed to be settled to reconcile a dispute over grazing rights and even that the death of a cow delayed the first match actually taking place for another three years. Patience proved a virtue: all was well in the end and the new ground was called Thomond Park because of its location in Thomondgate.

Buoyed by the support of the public and the ever-burgeoning interest in the sport, the North Munster Branch did everything possible to develop the new grounds. The *Limerick Leader* reported that 'the engineer to the Union, Mr Charles Stenson B.E., has prepared an estimate for the fencing of the seven acres which will comprise the enclosure, or to be more correct, the enclosures, for there will be two playing pitches, one for contests and one for practice matches. The plans provide for the erection of a grandstand to accommodate one thousand persons as well as the provision of dressing rooms and other conveniences for the use of teams.'

On 13 December 1933, it was agreed that the contract for the levelling and rolling of the field should be granted to Mr Gerald Griffin, Ballinacurrin, while the fencing was carried out by Messrs D. O'Sullivan and Sons, builders. Jock Morrison, a Scot living in Thomondgate, was appointed groundsman with a brief to bring in topsoil from wherever it could be found and to mark out a main pitch. Inevitably, there were snags and difficulties, most notably that the pitch was not enclosed and there were many unkempt areas.

Furthermore, as is invariably the case with such ventures, more and more cash had to be raised and here again the Munster Branch came up trumps. Before a ball was kicked, they set about acquiring tenant clubs. At the time, there were three senior clubs in Limerick: Garryowen were based at the Markets Field and content to remain there, with Young Munster at the Bombing Field and Bohemians at the Catholic Institute grounds in Rosbrien. Even though Bohs had completed dressing rooms at the Institute in 1929, they took up the offer and became the first Thomond Park tenant club in 1934. Under the agreement, they could train there every Tuesday and Thursday and play a senior club game every second Saturday.

However, we are getting slightly ahead of ourselves. Back to the earliest days of Thomond Park: the first game to be played there was a Munster Senior League tie on 17 November 1934 between Bohemians and Young Munster. Those people who entertained reservations about the development were not slow to raise their objections, with pitch invasions a regular occurrence largely due to the absence of suitable railings around the pitch. Little matters of this nature hardly bothered the Young Munster boys in black and amber who took the points on an 8–0 scoreline thanks to Thomond Park's first-ever try by centre Michael Fitzgerald and another by wing Joe McNeice and a conversion by Eddie Price.

Bohemian RFC, Thomond Park, 1934. Back row (l–r): Dr M. Graham president, R. Ryan, J. Roche, J. W. Stokes, B. McNamara, M. E. Bardon, T. Brockett, P. Power capt., E. Lynch, G. Graham, D. J. O'Malley, hon. secretary; front row (l–r): M. Graham, M. Cussen, P. O'Dwyer, W. T. Jennings, J. Keogh, G. O'Hanlon. (Courtesy Bohemian RFC).

The teams on that historic occasion were:

Young Munster: P. Hickey, J. McNeice, M. Fitzgerald, E. Price, M. Kelly, B. Keane, D. McDonnell, J. J. Connery, A. Moroney, J. Danford, J. O'Brien, W. McKeogh, R. Cantillon, P. Tobin capt., C. St George.

Bohemians: S. O'Sullivan, P. O'Dwyer, W. Jennings, D. Meaney, R. Reilly, J. D. Torrens, A. Harris, T. Hanlon, J. Barry, K. D. O'Sullivan, T. Brockert, P. J. Power capt., M. E. Bardon, G. E. Russell, W. J. Hall.

Both sides contained players of considerable stature. The Young Munster forward Charlie St George was a towering figure central to the club's legendary victories in 1928 in the Munster Senior Cup and Bateman Cup, a prestigious end-of-season tournament contested by the four provincial champions, and he would go on to serve as president of the Munster Branch and as a member of the Irish selection committee. His hostelry in Parnell Street became hugely popular with locals and visitors alike while try scorer Joe McNeice was also appointed president of the Branch. The Bohemians out-half Des Torrens was an outstanding sportsman, making four appearances for Ireland in 1938/39 and was almost certainly deprived of several more caps by the Second World War. He was also a fine golfer who reached the final of the South of Ireland Championship at Lahinch in 1937 only to lose to Mick O'Loughlin over thirty-six holes. M. E. Bardon was also capped by Ireland against England in 1934. Bohemians backs Sean O'Sullivan and Dan Meaney went on to enjoy distinguished careers as referees. Second-row and captain Pat Power worked long years for the game in several capacities including Munster Schools Secretary while Ted Russell was elected Mayor of Limerick and a member of Dáil Éireann.

Many rugby supporters looked on the whole Thomond Park venture with a jaundiced eye and voiced their objections in no uncertain manner when it was chosen for its first Munster Senior Cup game between Bohemians and University College Cork (UCC) on 29 February 1936. 'On Side', the *Limerick Leader* rugby correspondent, wrote that 'this unsheltered plateau is not likely to draw as many spectators as the Markets Field'.

On Monday, 16 August 1937, a meeting of the Munster Branch announced that the erection of a new stand would be completed before the end of October that year; the tender for the building was accepted at £3,600. The stand opened for the first round of the Munster Senior Cup between Young Munster and Cork Constitution on 19 February 1938. It had the capacity to seat 1,000 people and also contained changing rooms and washing facilities. Bohemians were obliged to provide a ton of coal to heat the water in the boiler so that the players could have warm water in the showers and hot tub. However, that was not as straightforward as it might seem because, with the arrival of the war, coal was scarce; it became commonplace for rows and rows of turf to be stacked around the perimeter of the back pitch.

The meeting of Munster and Leinster on Sunday, 11 December marked the official opening of the stand. The respective teams contained some of the most distinguished names in the pre-war game, including Con Murphy, Freddie Moran, Gerry Quinn, Austin Carry, George Morgan and C. R. Graves for Leinster and Munster's

Des Torrens, Stan Walsh, Hugh de Lacy, Charlie Teehan and Dave O'Loughlin.

The large attendance looked forward eagerly to a dynamic home performance on a pitch described by the *Limerick Leader* as being 'in first-class order despite all the rain that fell during the previous days [and that] everything pointed to a close and exciting struggle.' Groundsman Morrison would have been happy with that assessment of his labours. The preview of the game pointed out that Ulster had beaten Leinster to win the interprovincial title for the second year in a row a week earlier and that Leinster had made a number of changes in a bid to rectify matters. They certainly did the trick as tries by C. V. Boyle and Freddie Moran (2) and a conversion by J. Ryan put them a comfortable eleven points ahead before Munster had a late consolation try from E. Ryan. Leinster won 11–3.

Individually, Des Torrens and Dave O'Loughlin were rated Munster's outstanding players with the latter paid this glowing tribute: 'Dave was the hero of the fans. He was here, there and everywhere. In the line-outs, he had the ball almost every time, in the loose he was terrific and if the Irish Five can find seven more forwards with the dynamic force of O'Loughlin, Ireland need not fear that she will play second fiddle to any of the other countries' packs.'

The writer was also impressed by the 'schoolboy half-backs' Walsh and De Lacy: 'They did splendidly in their first big test. De Lacy was excellent when it is considered he was up against one of the most brilliant scrum-halves playing the game today. Walsh is very promising and with more experience of senior football should go further. Torrens was magnificent in attack but even more so in defence. His covering and smothering of his opposite number was a treat to witness.'

However, the selection of a certain J. O'B. Power of Bedford came in for some severe criticism by the *Limerick Leader* man who asked: 'Would it not be wiser in future if the selectors saw such players in action before placing them on representative sides? He came over with a great reputation as a centre. His display did not warrant it.'

Of the Leinster team, full back Con Murphy came in for special mention: 'He looks the likely choice as full back for Ireland. Moran's two tries make him a definite candidate for one of the wing positions. George Morgan is still and will be frequently Ireland's scrum half.'

Leinster: C. Murphy (Lansdowne), F. G. Moran (Clontarf), G. J. Quinn (Old Belvedere), T. Chamberlain (UCD), C. V. Boyle (Lansdowne), A. Carry (Dublin University), G. J. Morgan (Old Belvedere), C. R. Graves (Wanderers), T. Hendon, D. Ryan, J. Ryan (all UCD), S. A. Morrison (Blackrock), R. D. Magill (Old Wesley), D. J. Glenn (Old Belvedere), R. Lyttle (St Thomas Hospital).

Munster: J. Fitzgerald (Cork Constitution), L. O'Connor (Cork Constitution), J. O'B. Power (Bedford), J. D. Torrens capt. (Bohemians), J. J. O'Connor (Blackrock College), S. Walsh (Garryowen and Trinity), H. de Lacy (Garryowen and Trinity), E. Ryan (Dolphin), C. Teehan (UCC), G. F. McDermott (Bohemians), J. McGinn (Cork Constitution), M. Moloney, P. Delaney (both Garryowen), J. Guiney (Bective Rangers), D. B. O'Loughlin (Garryowen).

Beautiful, beautiful Munsters

To be fair, there were teething troubles with the new headquarters of Limerick rugby but the Munster Branch stuck to their guns and Bohs and College duly took to the field for their February 1936 cup clash on another significant day for the game in Limerick and Munster. It was a different sport from the high-scoring games with which we have become familiar in more recent times and once Brendan O'Brien had touched down for the students, they closed up shop and that try was the only score of a typically hard-fought and pulsating Munster Cup tie. Naturally there was a keen sense of disappointment in the Bohemians club, an emotion all the more difficult to assuage given the presence in the College side of Limerick men Joe Laycock, Jim Buckner, Christy Clohessy, Brendan O'Brien, Dave O'Loughlin and Con Moloney.

However, at the time UCC were a team of all the talents and their grasp on the coveted trophy was considered almost inviolate when they qualified for yet another final, in 1938, which was the first to be staged at Thomond Park. The usual Limerick suspects were still available to College along with other notable performers, such as the many-times-capped front-row forward Charlie Teehan. The bookmakers installed them as almost unbackable favourites for the four-in-a-row. Young Munster kept their thoughts to themselves while quietly fancying their chances. After all, they had beaten Cork Constitution by 5–3 in a replay at the Mardyke, the southern headquarters of the game at that time. It was their first victory over the great Cork club in the Munster Cup in Cork and they achieved it with a try by Cyril Lee (who was to play an even more special role in the final), converted by Eddie Price.

They then enjoyed another 5–3 win, this time at the expense of their great Limerick rivals Garryowen, at Thomond Park, thanks to a Micky Kelly try converted by Price. The *Limerick Leader* enthused about a 'match full of thrills with no quarter asked or given, it was clean and vigorous as one has come to expect from these two clubs and the "wasps", with Tommy Hickey an inspiration in the forwards, finishing up the better side and deserving winners.'

In spite of all this, along with the advantage of playing the game not alone in Limerick but at Thomond Park, a venue with which the students would not have been familiar, only those closest to Young Munsters gave them much of a chance. Nevertheless, it was a contest that had captured the public's imagination and the gates had to be closed an hour before kick-off with more than 10,000 inside.

What ensued remains one of the most memorable occasions in the hallowed history of Irish rugby's greatest inter-club cup competition. It may seem unimaginable today but Young Munster won with a drop goal worth four points to a try, three points, by UCC. The all-important four-pointer was contributed by centre Cyril Lee as early as the third minute and this remained the only score of a thrilling first half. A team of UCC's talent was always going to come back and Ben McKenna went over for their try with fifteen minutes still to play. But the conversion was missed and there was to be no further scoring in the tension-packed final moments.

You can only imagine the sense of excitement among the rapturous Young Munster supporters as they turned and looked up to the new Thomond Park stand and awaited the presentation of the trophy. It was only then that the penny dropped. The cup had been left behind in Cork due to a misunderstanding, according to College – or, if you were a Young Munster supporter, because they were so sure of winning that they didn't feel the need to bring it with them. The trophy eventually arrived in Limerick by special car at seven o'clock in the evening and the presentation finally took place in the Athenaeum cinema (later the Royal). Young Munster celebrated a third Munster Cup triumph with their customary style and gusto. The teams in the first Thomond Park cup final were:

Young Munster: J. Hoare, W. Keane, C. Lee, M. Kelly capt., C. Murray, E. Price, M. D. Sheehan, J. Carr, E. Keane, B. Larkin, W. O'Dwyer, P. Hickey, J. Ryan, J. O'Byrne, J. Carr.

UCC: C. Moloney, B. McKenna, B. Collins, C. Crowley, D. Lane, B. O'Brien, R. F. O'Driscoll, D. Riordan, C. Teehan, J. Griffin, D. O'Loughlin, L. Twomey, J. Laycock capt., J. Buckner, R. O'Neill.

Young Munster lost to University College Dublin (UCD) in the final of the Bateman Cup and went down to Bohemians in the first round of the Munster Cup twelve months later. They would not win the cup again for another forty-two years.

Young Munster, Munster Senior Cup winners, 1938. Back row (l–r): P. Deegan secretary, W. O'Dwyer, T. Hickey, B. Larkin, E. Keane, J. Hoare, J. O'Byrne, E. Price, J. McNeice president; front row (l–r): C. Lee, J. Lynn, J. Carr, C. Murray, M. Kelly capt., W. Keane, J. Ryan, James Carr and M. D. Sheehan. (Courtesy Young Munster RFC)

The Second World War and the Army

What is it that gets supporters of Munster and Leinster so energised when it comes to 'derby' matches between the provinces? Even as time moves on and several Leinster men (Felix Jones, Ian Keatley, Andrew Conway and Robin Copeland among them) play for Munster and the likes of Mike Ross, Sean Cronin and Eoin Reddan travel in the opposite direction, the rivalry remains as keen as ever. It extends back to the first meeting of the sides in 1877 and most especially the 1880 game staged on 4 December in Cork. Munster won by a solitary try and as a result under IRFU rules the Munster Branch was entitled to six representatives on the Union's governing body.

In truth, though, it was a rare success for Munster in those days. The teams continued to meet on an annual basis and while the Markets Field was the stage for some of the earlier meetings, it had gradually fallen out of favour and the inevitable switch to Thomond Park occurred in 1938. The clash aroused tremendous interest among the fans and a degree of nervous apprehension among Munster Branch officials, such as president Joe McNeice (Young Munster), D. A. White (Sundays Well) and Jack Quilligan (Garryowen) as they awaited the reaction to the first interprovincial to be staged at the new Limerick ground. As it transpired, they had nothing to worry about and Thomond Park fully justified its lofty new status.

It was an edifice that remained much the same for the next fifty years. There were changing rooms on either side of the showers, an area that also contained a large tub which, we are led to believe, was mainly used by the forwards, while the showers were used by the backs.

The wartime shortage of coal meant that other plans had to be put in place to ensure the boiler was kept active. While the nefarious activities of Adolf Hitler and his cohorts in Germany caused an unbelievable degree of death and chaos and disrupted normal life, Irish sport continued without undue difficulty. In fact, the war led to the formation of an Army XV that was affiliated to the Munster Branch and proved a major force in the competitive arena. The squad was formed under the guidance of Col. T. Feely and many players from Limerick clubs joined as 'The Emergency' was declared. The transfer of the army's Southern Command headquarters to Limerick around this time further strengthened the Army squad.

They called upon several outstanding players as well as famous characters in their ranks, including Pte Paddy ('Whacker') Daly of Richmond and Garryowen; Lt Mossy Curtin, Pte Brendan Morgan, Lt Paddy Griffin, Sgt Davy Ringrose and Con Moloney, Garryowen; Comdt Joe Laycock (UCC and Garryowen); Sgt Sean O'Sullivan and Sgt Donie O'Donovan (Bohemians) and Jimmy Carr (Young Munster). In 1944, the Daly brothers Paddy (Army), Alphie (Young Munster) and Michael (Garryowen) represented three different clubs in the Munster Cup.

Due to the travel restrictions imposed during the war years, the Munster Branch divided the Senior Cup and Senior League into two sections, North and South, with the winners meeting in the respective finals. The Army were noted for the attractive all-round rugby they played and in addition to the All-Army Championship they captured the Limerick Charity Cup and the North Munster section of the Senior League in 1944.

The Army team that won many trophies during the war years and reached the final of the Munster Senior Cup: Insets (l–r): M. Curtin, H. Kelly, Sgt Sheehy; back row (l–r): P. D. Ryan, R. Maddock, F. Dawson, Sgt Carr, Sgt Walsh, P. Griffin, T. Woulfe, Pte McInerney, Pte O'Donovan, unknown; middle row (l–r): F. J. Laycock, Cpl Ryan, B. Morgan, Col T. Feely, Sgt Ringrose, Major P. Curran, D. O'Donovan, C. Moloney, Pte Maher; front row (l–r): S. O'Sullivan, P. Daly. (From *Limerick's Rugby History*)

As the end of hostilities drew near, the Army enjoyed their greatest day in the spring of 1945 when they defeated Garryowen in the semi-final of the cup in front of a massive attendance at Thomond Park. Even though Garryowen prodigy Paddy Reid had emerged as one of the game's biggest prospects and contributed a try, conversion, drop goal and penalty in the first-round defeat of Young Munster, the Army's plans to negate his influence worked to perfection with several of Garryowen's own players very much involved. In fact, Mossy Curtin and Whacker Daly scored the Army tries, Curtin landed a conversion and Garryowen could manage only a drop goal by Reid in reply.

The 1945 semi-final teams at Thomond Park:

Army: Lt J. Carr, Lt M. Curtin, Sgt D. Ringrose, Pte Ryan, Lt Aherne, Pte Barker, Pte P. Daly, Lt C. Carey, Pte B. Morgan, Lt Woulfe, Lt Cusack, Pte O'Connor, Pte Moloney, Sgt Carr, Lt P. Carr.

Garryowen: J. Staunton, F. O'Meara, A. McMorrow, K. McCarthy, C. Carey, P. Reid, H. Leahy, P. O'Dwyer, T. Halpin, F. Dinneen, J. Halpin, M. Walsh, P. O'Sullivan, C. Roche, J. Earlie.

Thomond Park was also the venue for the eagerly awaited final in which the Army took on a powerful Dolphin side that included internationals Jim McCarthy, Bertie O'Hanlon and Dave O'Loughlin under the captaincy of Robin Bolster. The game ended in a three-all draw before Dolphin came out on top in the Mardyke replay. With the end of the war, it represented the Army's last chance of the title and the players returned to their original clubs. Mossy Curtin and Brendan Morgan went on to collect 'peacetime' medals with Garryowen.

2

Clifford and Reid

N ow came an era of some outstanding Irish rugby players with Limerick fortunate to possess two of the greatest, Paddy Reid of Garryowen and Young Munster's Tom Clifford who were born within eight months of each other in the mid-1920s. Reid was one of the finest midfield backs to grace the game in this country while Clifford was a remarkable prop forward good enough to earn a place on the British & Irish Lions team which toured Australia and New Zealand in 1950. Both retain legendary status, Reid mostly for being a member of the Ireland Grand Slam winning team of 1948 and Clifford for his part as the 'life and soul' of the Lions during their six-month trip 'down under'.

Paddy Reid was born on St Patrick's Day 1924 into what was very much a Garryowen family. His father, Willie Reid, his father-in-law, Michael Kelly, and several uncles won Munster Cup medals with the club and when he was still a student at Crescent College, Paddy was already pulling on Garryowen's light-blue jersey. A versatile sportsman, he was as adept with a hurley or more especially a hockey stick in his hands or a soccer ball at his feet. Paddy was also a great communicator. He had no difficulty in calling a spade a spade – nor was he averse to a little bit of mischief or hyperbole.

He enjoyed regaling journalists and other visitors to his home in O'Connell Avenue in Limerick with anecdotes about the early days and particularly the deeds which a gentleman he called 'the Bull' got up to. This individual was, he said, 'a murderer on the field'. Paddy was just fourteen years old when he first shared a Crescent College dressing room with 'the Bull'. And on this day, our hero hit an opponent so hard, Reid declared it was 'the cruellest thing I ever saw in my life'. Afterwards, he plucked up the courage to ask why this foul deed had been perpetrated.

'Paddy, if I didn't hit him, then he'd have hit me,' came the Bull's unapologetic reply.

Things didn't change a whole lot as Reid grew into manhood. Thomond Park was the scene of all the big matches at the northern end of the province and it is without doubt that some of what was accepted as normal at the time would have had yellow and red cards being handed out wholesale today. Nevertheless, Paddy Reid, never a man to hear a harsh word spoken against his native city, went public many years later about a 'rumbustious game against Young Munster. Nine players were put off the field in Thomond Park that day with a full-scale riot to follow. Limerick was mad, crazy. 'Twas savage rugby. We got a terrible beating that same day and, coming off the field, we were being attacked. I didn't go near the fight. I went around the back of the stand to avoid it. But then, [while I was] cycling home on Shelbourne Road, Young Munster supporters were battering me with sods of turf.'

Tom Clifford, a dyed-in-the-wool Young Munster man and not unknown for a mischievous streak of his own, would never have lent any credence to such a claim. At the same time, the respect between the two men was mutual and genuine.

The earliest days of Jeremiah Thomas Clifford could hardly have been in greater contrast to those of Paddy Reid. He was born in the little village of Phippsboro near Ballyporeen, County Tipperary, on 15 November 1923. The inhabitants of this lovely spot in the shadow of the Galtee Mountains might never have heard of rugby football but, as luck would have it, the Clifford family moved to Limerick when Tom was three years of age. They settled in Edward Street in the heart of Young Munster territory. Although he distinguished himself as a hurler at Limerick Christian Brothers School (CBS) and even played League of Ireland soccer with Limerick, once Tom pulled on the black-and-amber jersey at the age of fifteen, his love for his club and dedication to rugby were all enveloping and never wavered.

Which is not to suggest that Tom Clifford didn't know how to enjoy himself! He loved a good pint of Guinness but if anything he enjoyed

Tom Clifford takes to the field during the 1950 Lions tour of New Zealand behind his captain Karl Mullen with another great Irish forward, Bill McKay (centre), also in picture. (Courtesy Tom Clifford)

his grub even more, a point he made in famous fashion as the Lions made the five-week journey to New Zealand on board the luxury liner *Ceramic* in 1950. He quickly scoffed the six-course dinner on the first evening out of port and so decided to tackle each of the eighteen courses on offer the following night.

Cardiff and Wales utility back Billy Cleaver graphically described the occasion in his tour diary: 'We had an excellent dinner of six courses and began to feel the luxury of the travel. Further appreciation of the gastronomic delights was postponed for a couple of days for the majority of the team who went down with seasickness. The notable exception was Tommy Clifford who on the Sunday evening left his legendary imprint on the annals of ocean dining when he said he would have "all the menu".' It was later confirmed that Tommy had indeed gone through the entire card as follows:

Hors d'Oeuvres (various)
Creme de Tomato

Fillets of Sole Tartare
Sweetcorn en croute
Lamb Cutlets Parisienne
Braised York Ham Oporto
French Beans, Boiled and Roast Potatoes
Roast Norfolk Turkey with Cranberry Jelly
Rolled Ox Tongue with Leg of Pork and Apple Sauce
Salad with Mayonnaise Dressing
Plum Pudding with Brandy Sauce
Peach Melba
Dessert Fruit
Coffee
Fromage

Cleaver went on: 'His Irish teammate, Bill McKay, is alleged to have tried to match the Munster man but gave up halfway through, completely bloated. Tom was none the worse for his exploits on board and played in 18 games on the tour, including five of the six Test matches. He became the life and soul of the party, along with fellow prop Cliff Davies of Cardiff and Wales, and never missed a party. Well, he almost missed the final one of the tour on board the *Strathnavar*.'

The great Jack Kyle took up the story: 'We were somewhere in the Bay of Biscay having a final party among ourselves. The call came out for a last rendition of "O'Reilly's Daughter" but Tommy was nowhere to be seen. Suffering the effects of over six months as a Lion he had finally succumbed and taken to his bed. So six of the boys went down to his cabin, lifted him, still in the horizontal position, and carried him into the party. Responding to our musical request, he sat up, sang his favourite song, and then lay back again. We did the only decent thing and carried him back to where we had found him 10 minutes before.'

These days Young Munster play at Tom Clifford Park, the ground named after the club's most famous son.

However, ever before Reid won the Grand Slam or Clifford had toured with the Lions, the whole of Limerick knew all about their capabilities, which is why the Munster Cup final of 1947 between Garryowen and Young Munster attracted huge interest; Thomond Park was bursting at the seams on the big day. It was a game typical of the times, fought with fierce intensity, and the old cliché, 'no quarter either

Programme for the 1948 Munster v Ulster game which resulted in a draw. (Courtesy John Fitzgerald)

asked or given', comes to mind. Free-for-alls broke out among the rival supporters and a player from each side was sent off. As a footballing spectacle, however, it proved an anticlimax of massive proportions. 'N. M.', writing in the *Limerick Leader*, wrote that 'it is becoming very debatable whether cup rugby should be allowed to continue' while his counterpart over at the *Limerick Chronicle* was so unimpressed with the whole thing that he claimed: 'it was a match like tripe without onions, that is just tripe.'

The game failed to produce a try, Reid kicking Garryowen into a six-point lead before Clifford once again demonstrated his remarkable versatility by reducing Young Munster's arrears with a penalty. In fact, the new champions failed to score a try in the course of the competition.

The teams were:

Garryowen: J. Staunton, M. Curtin, P. Reid capt., P. Kelly, J. Nestor, A. McMorrow, S. O'Dea, P. Butler, B. Morgan, S. McNamara, R. Laffan, J. Keyes, C. Roche, T. Reid, P. O'Sullivan.

The Garryowen team captained by Paddy Reid that defeated Young Munster in the 1947 Munster Senior Cup final. Back row (l–r): J. O'Halloran, P. Kelly, J. Staunton, J. Keyes, M. J. Harty president, J. Maher, P. O'Sullivan, M. Curtin, A. McMorrow; middle row (l–r): S. McNamara, C. Roche, P. Reid capt., B. Morgan, T. Reid; front row (l–r): S. O'Dea and J. Nestor. (Courtesy Garryowen FC)

Young Munster: T. Collery, E. Timoney, O. Browne capt., C. Lowe, M Thompson, P. Lysaght, M. Breen, J. Ryan, J. Madigan, S. Byrne, TP. O'Kane, T. Clifford, J. Carr, E. Clancy, D. Heeney.

Paddy Reid was a member of a legendary Irish team that achieved the Grand Slam in the 1948 Five Nations Championship. Captained by Dublin doctor Karl Mullen, they completed the task with a famous victory over Wales at Ravenhill, Belfast, when one of the try scorers was J. C. (Jack) Daly of Cobh and Munster.

Sadly, Tom Clifford never won a Munster Cup medal even though he went on to earn fourteen Irish caps and, of course, star on the 1950 Lions team as well as playing for Young Munster well into his thirties. He was often teased about the absence of a cup win from his CV but he would reply: 'When I see some of those who have them, I know it's not such a bad thing after all.' Tom died on 1 October 1990, a Young Munsterman through and through for every minute of his sixty-seven years.

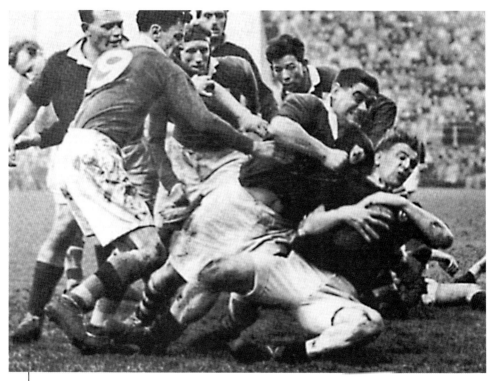

Tom Clifford in action for Ireland against Scotland in 1952. (Courtesy Tom Clifford)

The late 1940s were tough times financially. Reid turned to Rugby League after the Grand Slam year and played for Huddersfield and Halifax (whom he represented in the cup final of 1952 at Wembley Stadium). He made £7 a week plus bonuses before returning to Limerick. League players were ostracised by the Union game and he remained outside the fold until rugby went professional in the 1990s. Paddy Reid was finally forgiven his 'sins' and, having rejoined Garryowen, was their appointment as president of the Munster Branch in 1996/97.

Paddy had departed for Rugby League when it came to the Munster Cup final of 1950 between Garryowen and UCC at Thomond Park. As was invariably the case on these occasions, there was a substantial contrast in age between the college teams and their more experienced rivals. That was so much the case in April of that year that when the students arrived at Limerick railway station, College skipper Jack Horgan recalled in the club's centenary (1974) history how he was asked on arrival at the station: 'Well, Hoggie, what are you doing with the crowd of children you have down to play today?'

Old Crescent R.F.C. (CIRCA 1949)

Probably the first team to represent Old Crescent RFC, Thomond Park, 1949. Back row (l–r): G. Spillane, W. O'Brien, R. Harris, T. Hayes, P. O'Carroll, J. Keane, N. Quaid, A. O'Leary; front row (l–r): J. Rigney, T. Farrell, D. Molony, L. Nestor, A. O'Donovan, G. Wood, G. O'Donovan. Note the crescents on a few jerseys, some going in opposite directions! (Courtesy Louis Nextor)

Horgan went on:

> The 'children' were Bob Hyde, Dick Buckley, Jack Horgan capt., Billy O'Regan, John Hindle, Jimmy Keane, John O'Meara, Leo Dineen, Joe O'Sullivan, Pat Heffernan, Mick Bennett, Noel O'Flynn, Gerald Cussen, Vince Giltenane, Eoin Busteed. Maybe we were children and certainly Garryowen were the favourites, but we did fine. Captain Mick Dowling was the referee and in minutes the alert Mick Bennett saw that the Garryowen forwards were offside in the first ruck and gave them the ball to make it more obvious. I kicked the penalty from the touchline on the 25 and then midway through the half Billy O'Regan kicked a gigantic penalty from two yards inside his own half. Two minutes later all the backs handled and John Hindle scored a fine try that I converted. The half ended

with Billy O'Regan himself scoring a great try. We were jubilant but we took a pounding from Garryowen in the second half before winning 14–8. It was an exciting match well received by the press and the public and made all the more memorable for the sporting manner in which it was played by Sean O'Dea and his men from Garryowen.

3

Overseas Visitors and Famous Names: 1950s

The first match between Munster and a major overseas touring side took place at the Markets Field, Limerick, on 28 November 1905. This New Zealand side, known as 'The Originals', toured these islands winning match after match by wide margins and losing only once – by 3–0 to Wales in controversial circumstances. The Kiwis believed that Bob Deans had scored a perfectly fair try but the referee ruled he was stopped short of the line. So it was no great disgrace for Munster to be overrun by such a powerful side by thirty-three points to nil.

Another forty-two years elapsed before Munster had the opportunity to take on overseas opposition. In 1947, Cork's splendidly atmospheric Mardyke greeted the Australians – or Wallabies – and Munster gave the crowd that poured over the railings and up to the sidelines a lot to cheer about. Paddy Reid converted his own try but the tourists edged home by 6–5. Munster were magnificent that day but as so often in these circumstances, the old cliché 'moral victory' had to be wheeled out to console players and supporters alike.

The Royal Air Force became the first team from outside the country to play a senior representative match at Thomond Park on 2 April 1949. They fielded a very strong side against Munster and waged an interesting battle before going down 6–3 to tries scored by Dom Dineen and Sean McNamara. The *Limerick Leader* man at the game was less than impressed by what he saw. 'At this time of the season when the more dour and rugged cup rugby is being witnessed, it was thought that the game between Munster and the Royal Air Force would be the tonic that most ruggerites needed. But, alas, Thomond Park on Saturday was the scene of one of the most listless and uninteresting exhibitions witnessed for many years by such a large attendance.'

A few Munster players did, however, catch the writer's eye: 'McNamara, completely out of position as a hooker, was a wonderful success and gained a large majority of the set scrums. McCarthy was bobbing up all over the place in his usual energetic manner and was well supported by Dineen and Clifford.'

Munster: Noel Nunan (Cork Constitution), Mick Lane (UCC), Arthur O'Connor (Young Munster), Bertie O'Hanlon (Dolphin), Alfie Nicholson (Dolphin), William O'Regan (UCC), Sean O'Dea (Garryowen), Tom Clifford (Young Munster), Sean McNamara (Garryowen), Pax O'Kane (Young Munster), Archie O'Leary (Cork Constitution), Jim Keyes (Garryowen), Jim McCarthy capt. (Dolphin), Gerald Reidy (Dolphin), Dom Dineen (Bohemian).

Royal Air Force: Flight Lt A. A. Smailes, Wing Commander B. P. Young, Flight Lt R. J. H. Uprichard, R. C. I. L. M. Lumsden, A. C. G. Crerar, Corporal G. R. Tucker, Flight Lt W. T. Hay, Flight Officer C. M. Browse, A/C R. Clark, Flight Lt R Sterling, Pilot Officer G. G. Farley, Corp. E. E. Rossiter, Flight Lt E. L. Horsfall, Squadron Leader R. G. H. Weighill capt., Flight Lt H. K. Rees.

Referee: J. Thompson (Leinster Branch).

Next to visit was the French champion club Lourdes, the first French side to visit Thomond Park. The date was 21 October 1951 when a team captained by the multi-capped French brothers, the great wing forward Jean Prat and his talented brother Maurice in the centre, proved a huge attraction. The game was arranged by Dave O'Loughlin, formerly of UCC, Dolphin and Garryowen, a marvellous forward denied by the war of numerous Irish caps. He was able to field a powerful Garryowen selection that included numerous international players as well as the Australian centre C. J. Windsor.

The teams were:

Garryowen Selected: M. Quaid (Garryowen & Old Crescent), M. Lane (UCC and Ireland), K. Quilligan capt. (Garryowen and Munster), C. J. Windsor (London Irish and Australia), D. Morley (Harlequins and Garryowen), J. Roche (Garryowen and Munster), J. O'Meara (Dolphin and UCC), T. Clifford (Young Munster and Ireland), K. Mullen (Old Belvedere and Ireland), G. Wood (Garryowen and Old Crescent), P. Lawlor (Clontarf and Ireland), S. Healy (Garryowen and Munster), J. S. McCarthy (Dolphin and Ireland), T. Reid (Garryowen and Munster), D. Dineen (Bohemians and Munster).

Lourdes: G. Bernadet, R. Bourdeau, A. Bernadet, M. Prat, M. Martene, A. Labazuy, F. Labazuy, E. Buzy, R. Savrat, D. Saint-Postous, L. Guinle, R. Salzet, J. Manterola, L. Domec, J. Prat capt.

On 11 December 1951, Thomond Park hosted a major touring side for the first time. The South African Springboks boasted the physically strongest squad of players of that era and were unsparing of lighter opponents. The appetite of the Munster public had been whetted by the Lourdes visit so the all-conquering Springboks were assured of a very warm welcome when they came to Thomond Park a few weeks later.

Seventeen years after its opening, those associated with the ground believed everything was going in the right direction. Yes, they would have liked a stand capable of seating many more people and to have had the capital to provide cover on 'the far side' or 'popular side'. The Union purse strings remained tight, however, and the Munster Branch had little or no money, so the capacity remained at around 10,000. When the occasion demanded, though, far greater numbers crammed into every nook and cranny and that is how it was when the Springboks came calling on that fresh, chilly December day.

The local administrators felt they had left nothing to chance in ensuring that Thomond Park measured up to requirements. Ninety-nine per cent of those present gave them the thumbs-up. However, a few months later, a book on the tour, *The Fourth Springboks, 1951/52* by R. K. Stent, was published and painted an entirely different picture. The tourists had comfortably beaten Ireland (a team that included Munster men Mick Lane, John O'Meara, Tom Clifford and Jim McCarthy) by

17–5 on the Saturday before the Thomond Park game and this is where Stent picks up the story.

> Safely past the first two internationals, the Springboks went westward across Ireland to Limerick to meet Munster. They were told to expect a tough match and they got one. Munster, who are of the no-quarter-asked-or-given school, were resolved to improve on their performance against the 1947 Wallabies, whom they led until a minute of the end. Four of the Irish side which had played at Lansdowne Road were in the team – Lane, a wing with the reputation of playing many times for Ireland without ever scoring a try; the scrum half O'Meara; the front-ranker Clifford and the loose forward, McCarthy.
>
> Du Toit captained the Springbok team for the first time and only six of the international side that had beaten Ireland were in this match. The others, by virtue of their experiences in this game, came to be known for the rest of the tour as the Homicide Squad! In this connection, a rather amusing note was struck by the official programme, which all players were asked to sign. On its back, responsibility was disclaimed for 'injury to the holder, sustained from accident or otherwise'.

There was more – much more – to follow.

> The game was one of the poorest of the tour and play at times rose no higher than rough and tumble level. The ground was a boggy mixture of mud and the droppings of sheep who had grazed there recently. It was obvious that Munster's hopes of surprising the Springboks clearly rested on spoiling tactics and it seemed they had briefed a wrecking crew for the purpose. The referee had a difficult game. The Munster loose forwards were inclined to flirt with the offside rule but a worse worry was the robust play early in the match. Fisticuffs have no place in rugby football. Mr Glasgow had a word with both packs in the first fifteen minutes. This did not stop all the trouble but it must be said that the Springbok forwards showed much restraint and no man earned a further rebuke.

We shall see later why the tourists liked the refereeing of Ossie Glasgow from Ulster so much. And, at least, the author of the book saw one good aspect to Munster's performance: 'The work of the international, McCarthy, rose above this plane and he gave an exhibition of loose forward play that was not often excelled by any of the Springboks opponents during the tour.'

Winger Denis Johnstone put the South Africans 3–0 ahead with a try just before the interval and a packed Thomond Park feared the worst as their side turned to face the wind. Instead, they cheered themselves hoarse seven minutes after the restart when a superb kick by out-half Jim Roche brought play into the tourists' 25, John O'Meara, a man more noted for the speed and length of his pass, surprised the defence by nipping around the blind side of a scrum, kicked ahead beautifully and inevitably it was the livewire Jim McCarthy who won the race as the ball rolled over the line. Basie Viviers and Jack Horgan then exchanged penalty kicks leaving the sides level at 6-all before the two incidents that at first delighted the home support and then drove them to despair occurred.

Jim McCarthy was central to the controversy and later described it as follows:

> I was covering behind the backs when Mick Lane gathered a kick ahead and passed to me in our own half. The field was open and off I went with Lane in support. Although I felt I could have made the line myself, I feared the cover was closing in. So, I handed the ball to Lane who was that close and he went over for a try that we were sure would win the match. You can imagine our feelings when the referee Ossie Glasgow, who was back around the halfway line, disallowed the score for a forward pass. The referee was in no position to see what happened.

It says it all when R. K. Stent, a man who brought partisan comment to a new level with his description of the incident, simply wrote: 'The best movement of the match came from the home team when a diagonal kick from Dennis Fry went straight to Lane who beat off Johnstone, passed inside to McCarthy and took a pass back before going over. But the referee ruled a forward pass.' However, he allowed

Munster's Jim McCarthy makes his dash for the line against the Springboks in the 1951 game at Thomond Park. Within a few feet of his target, the great wing forward made sure of a try by passing to his teammate Mick Lane who went over, but referee Ossie Glasgow, seen to the extreme left and seemingly well behind the play, ruled the pass forward. (Courtesy *Cork Examiner*)

that 'Munster now attacked strongly and the Springboks line was menaced by dribbling assaults that carried play twenty and thirty yards at a time.' Alas, the Springboks lifted the siege and won the day with a try by du Rand converted by Viviers. Coming on the heels of the late one-point defeat four years earlier against Australia, this was another heartbreaking setback for Munster against touring teams. There would be several others before the tide turned very dramatically in their favour.

South Africa: A. C. Keevy, M. J. Saunders, M. T. Lategan, S. S. Viviers, D. Johnstone, D. J. Fry, P. A. du Toit, H. J. Bekker, W. Delport, F. E. van der Ryst, B. Myburgh, G. Dannhauser, W. H. M. Bernard capt., J. du Rand, S. Fry.

Munster: P. J. Berkery (Lansdowne), M. Quaid (Garryowen), J. Horgan (UCC), G. C. Phipps (Rosslyn Park), M. F. Lane (UCC), J. Roche (Garryowen), J. O'Meara (UCC), T. Clifford

(Young Munster), D. Crowley (Cork Constitution), D. Donnery (Dolphin), A. O'Leary (Cork Constitution), S. Healy (Garryowen), J. S. McCarthy capt. (Dolphin), G. Reidy (Dolphin), D. Dineen (Bohemians).

Richard Harris

It was around this time, too, that Crescent College, the Jesuit Sacred Heart College located in the heart of Limerick city, was emerging as a serious rugby force. They won their first Munster Schools Senior Cup in 1947 under the captaincy of Paddy Berkery (the full back four years later in that epic 1951 game against South Africa) and did so again in 1949. A member of both teams was a certain Richard Harris, the renowned Limerick-born actor.

Harris was born into a rugby-loving family on the Ennis Road and started playing as soon as he was old enough to kick a ball around with his older brothers: Ivan, Jimmy and Noel, a group of extremely talented

Crescent College, Munster Schools Senior Cup champions, 1947. Back row (l–r): Louis Nestor, Des White, Ivan Harris, Todd Morrissey, Goff Spillane, Tom Hayes, Michael Collins, Jim Roche; middle row (l–r): Gerry Power, Michael Fitzgerald, Paddy Berkery capt, Dermot Molony, Michael Keane; front row (l–r): Richard Harris and John Leahy. (From *The Crescent 100 Year History*)

footballers. Another sibling, Billy, arrived a little later and was equally accomplished. On arrival at the Crescent, Rev. Fr Gerry Guinane SJ, one of the game's shrewdest administrators, quickly realised that the latest member of the Harris family to grace the academy was blessed with considerable rugby ability. The 1949 team was captained by Goff Spillane, an outstanding, red-headed second-row whose vice-captain was Gordon Wood, later to be one of the greats of the Irish game. No matter where in the world his acting career might take him over the years, Harris gladly took time off to regale his audiences about those halcyon schoolboy days.

On the week before Munster played Leicester in the 2004 Heineken Cup final, Harris poured his heart out to England's *Daily Telegraph*. The piece had little to do with his acting career (even though he could have referred to his lead role in *This Sporting Life* which superbly if brutally portrayed the life and times of a Rugby League player). Instead, it was all about his love affair with Rugby Union and Thomond Park.

> I adore Thomond Park which I could see and hear from my bedroom in our house on the Ennis Road. It is the citadel of Munster rugby. We have never lost a European Cup game there in seven years. If Ireland played there we would never lose. Did I ever tell you I scored nineteen tries and one dropped goal on the hallowed turf in various schools and junior games? I can recall every score in intimate detail. My proudest achievement – that and playing alongside Keith Wood's dad Gordon, the Ireland and Lions prop – was the day he [Wood] scored four tries, appearing on the wing, in a cup match against Mungret.
>
> Thomond Park belongs to the heart, not the head. Something to be embraced, or spurned – there can be no middle ground. The essence of the game I know and love is to be found in Limerick. The heroes of Limerick rugby are my heroes. Gladiators, square-jawed warriors who represent us on the battlefield. They are also heroes off the field – men who can drink, sing and talk of great deeds. I am intensely proud of individuals such as Peter Clohessy, Mick Galwey, Anthony Foley and all the boys. Keith Wood, whose father I used to play alongside, is another hero. He lives the rugby life we all dream of.

It was a bitter-sweet day two years ago at Twickenham when we lost to Northampton but the sweet lingers longest. There must have been 30,000 Munster fans in red – an unforgettable and moving sight – and they conducted themselves beautifully. Supporting this rugby team is almost the only way a Munster man can display his allegiance; we have no other comparable sporting or cultural outlet.

Dickie Harris had a love-hate relationship with Garryowen. It was in the light-blue jersey of Garryowen that he picked up his Munster Senior Cup medal in 1952 but he did not play in the final, a situation he found unbearable and one of the reasons that he forever afterwards regarded himself as a Young Munster man!

'Our house was a Garryowen one', Harris wrote in another fascinating interview in *The Irish Times* on 12 May 2012, under the headline 'Thomond Park My True Theatre'.

Garryowen Munster Senior Cup winning team 1952. Back row (l–r): T. Reid, S. Healy, J. Keyes, R. Harris, N. Quaid, A. McMorrow; middle row (l–r): T. O'Loughlin, P. Lawless, W. Quaid, J. Ryan, G. Wood, P. Lysaght, S. McNamara, S. O'Dea, E. Waters; front row (l–r): W. O'Connor hon. treasurer, J. Leahy, W. Reid, P. Quilligan, K. Quilligan capt., M. Quaid president, B. Morgan, T. O'Donovan, Joe Reid. (Courtesy Garryowen FC)

My father rejected any ambition I might have had of playing for Young Munsters. 'Don't set foot in this house again if you wear that black and amber shirt.' Discretion gave way to valour and although I never wore those legendary colours, there were occasions, having played against them, that my body was indelibly tattooed with black and amber.

Parental control lost its control off the field. Charlie St George's pub became not only my haunt but in some ways the lecture hall for my future. Here at nights, sitting after hours before a burning stove, I got my initial education in the theatre. Shaw, O'Casey, Wilde, Shakespeare, Johnson, Yeats were discussed at length and the seeds of nationalism were also sown and eventually Michael Collins joined the hero ranks of Clifford, Reid and Kyle. Reid was a foreigner from Garryowen but his ability was recognised.

Actor Richard Harris and family at Cork Airport, January 1965. (*Irish Examiner*)

Harris admits in the same article that he threw away the chance of a try in a Schools Cup final at Thomond Park when, 'in a moment of directional madness', he ran straight into a goal post. When tackled on the subject on several occasions over the years, he neither confirmed nor denied that he was, in fact, admiring a few young ladies from Laurel Hill in the crowd and waving at them when the fateful collision took place.

Of his own ability, Harris wrote: 'I was a second-row at school but seriously miscast. I should have been a flanker. I loved roving, snaffling tries, putting in big hits – though we called them tackles in those days. I played in two Munster Schools finals and represented Munster Schools and Munster Under-20s – I still wear that very red shirt and intend to be buried in it.'

And if there was still any doubt as to where his heart lay, he finished the piece by writing: 'Last year was a great one for me, winning the

Evening Standard award for the best performance in the English theatre for Pirandello's *Henry IV*, getting a Golden Globe nomination for Jim Sheridan's *The Field* and above and beyond all of that, finally being made a lifetime member of Young Munster Rugby Club.'

Crescent Munster Schools Senior Cup champions, 1949. Back row (l–r): N. Quaid, R. Harris; second row (l–r): T. Dundon, P. O'Meara, G. Murphy, T. Curtin, T. O'Brien, N. Harris; third row (l–r): T. Stack, J. Geary, G. Wood, G. Spillane capt., M. O'Donnell, J. McNamara, J. Ringrose; front row (l–r): F. Coleman and N. O'Brien. (Courtesy The Crescent)

Gordon Wood

If Richard Harris was the rugby character of the time, there is little doubt that the outstanding exponent was Gordon Wood. Born in Limerick's New Street in 1931, the son of a Young Munsterman who served as president of the Munster Branch, he quickly revealed a penchant for most sports. There weren't too many swimming pools around as 'Woody' grew up but he still used the Corbally Baths and the Head Race and other watering holes to become so adept that he won both the long-distance races of the time, the Olo Cup and the Thomond Cup.

It was when he went to secondary school at the nearby Crescent College that Gordon took up rugby and was an immediate success. Fr Guinane recognised that he had the making of an outstanding front-five forward and he was a key member of the Senior Cup winning side in 1949. From there he moved on initially to Old Crescent and then to Garryowen and straight into their senior team combining his skills as a scrummager with considerable agility in the loose. He helped Garryowen to win the Munster Senior Cup in 1952. As always on cup final day, Thomond Park was packed for their clash with UCC who were chasing a hat-trick of titles.

They might well have achieved that ambition were it not for the fact that the older, wiser Garryowen pack and especially the front row, known as 'Morgan, Mac and Wood', was just too strong. The trio in question were Brendan Morgan, Gordon Wood and Sean MacNamara who were outstanding in their own right but even better for the presence behind them of men like Tom Reid, a Lions tourist three years later, and a young Tipperary man, Jack Ryan, who allied all the best qualities of a loose forward with exceptional footballing skills.

All of these players, along with the likes of schools star and later Irish international Tom Nesdale and Con Roche (grandfather of Ireland and Lions scrum half Conor Murray of the modern era), were back in Thomond Park two years later for the final defeat of the holders, Sundays Well. It was also in 1954 that Gordon Wood earned the first of his twenty-nine Irish caps. He remained a regular in the side until 1961, more often than not as part of one of the greatest front rows in the history of Irish rugby. Wood, Ronnie Dawson and Syd Millar achieved one of their most satisfying wins in the green shirt when helping to beat a powerful French team at Lansdowne Road in 1959.

That performance in turn helped greatly to earn places on the Lions tour of Australia and New Zealand for this exalted trio (with Dawson as captain), along with Gordon's great friend Mick English, Tony O'Reilly, Niall Brophy, David Hewitt, Bill Mulcahy and Noel Murphy and later in the tour, Andy Mulligan as a valuable replacement. They are remembered as one of the happiest and most popular Lions tourists both on and off the pitch as they combined merriment and superb football to maximum effect. Woody played in two of the four Tests in New Zealand and even though the series was lost largely due to some parochial refereeing decisions and the accurate boot of the All

Blacks full back Don Clarke, the tour was a huge success and fondly remembered many years later.

The successful 1954 Garryowen captain was Tom Reid who, in fact, was winning his third medal, having also been a member of the 1947 and 1952 teams. Reid was a first cousin of Paddy Reid but there the similarity between the two men seemed to end. Whereas Paddy was relatively small of stature but highly competitive, Tom was very tall for that era, around 6 foot 2 inches, but also very easy-going. He was never one to train much and, interestingly, was probably seen at his best on the 1955 Lions tour of South Africa when he had little choice but to knuckle down.

Thomas Eymard Reid attended Limerick CBS, which had forsaken rugby by the time he arrived in the mid-1940s. He came quickly through the ranks at Garryowen, however, and after impressing for Munster in their 1947 clash with Australia, gradually made his way onto the Irish team, earning the first of his thirteen caps against France in 1954. Selection for the 1955 Lions tour was the highlight of his career and during that trip he struck up a close relationship with a young Dubliner, Tony O'Reilly. Poles apart in age and many other ways, the pair struck up a close relationship. O'Reilly later wrote that Tom saw 'rugby as a little refreshment of the spirit'.

Reid travelled to South Africa expecting to play a secondary role as the captain was another second-row forward, Ulsterman Robin Thompson, while Welshman Rhys Williams had locked down the other spot in the second row. However, when Thompson went down with appendicitis and missed much of the tour, Reid stepped up to the plate and in the eyes of most observers actually strengthened the Lions pack. Vivian Jenkins, the esteemed rugby correspondent of *The Sunday Times*, certainly saw things in that light.

'Tom Reid and Rhys Williams were continually prominent,' he cabled home. 'They were the giants of the piece. They took on the mammoth Springboks second-row men at their own game, pushing like heroes and rising literally to heights previously unattained on tour.'

The *Daily Mail's* authoritative Terry O'Connor believed he understood why Tom was so influential on that tour when the Tests were shared two each. Years later, he wrote: 'If Reid had played in this era, he would have been a fantastic player. But he was never fit although that changed briefly during the 1955 Lions tour. He was an unbelievable man and character.'

Tony O'Reilly delighted in recounting Tom Reid stories. During an official reception on the Lions tour, a group of players were asked to speak about the political situation in Ireland. O'Reilly explained how 'an awkward silence descended on the party until Reid piped up: "Sir, I think nothing of it. I come from Limerick in southern Ireland and I have my own political problems."'

O'Reilly's favourite Tom Reid yarn concerned an Ireland v England game at Twickenham: 'He was playing against England one year and went wandering off outside the Irish dressing room. In the next room, the England captain was exhorting his players to stirring deeds by invoking images of Agincourt and God knows what else. Reid poked his head around the English dressing-room door and said, "would you excuse me, lads, but have any of you got any hairy twine? My laces are broken."'

Speaking himself about the same Twickenham encounter, Tom admitted to a playing colleague, with a perfectly serious expression: 'I had a nightmare last night. I was all alone in the open field at Twickenham with the ball in my hands and I didn't have a clue what to do with it.'

Reid's career effectively came to an end in 1958, an event poignantly described by Peter Bills in *Passion In Exile*, the history of London Irish RFC: 'He went on the Barbarians tour of Canada in 1958 and seemed distracted about things towards the end. When a teammate put his head around his door on the morning of their flight home, expecting Reid to be all packed and ready, the big, genial lock was lying stretched out on the bed, examining the ceiling.

"Come on, get your things, we're leaving on the bus soon", he was told. "I'm not coming, you go without me." "Don't be daft. Get packed." "I tell you, I'm not coming. I've met a woman, I'm in love and I'm staying here forever."

And stay he did, settling in Montreal where he passed away at the age of seventy in 1996.

4

Into the 1960s

The Ginner

Since the late 1920s, there had been what could be fairly described as a cartel of three senior clubs in Limerick: Garryowen, Young Munster and Bohemians. The man largely responsible for the surprise elevation of Old Crescent was the aforementioned Fr Guinane, who arrived to teach at Crescent College in the mid-1940s having served during the war as chaplain to the Royal Ulster Rifles. In a remarkably short space of time, 'the Ginner', as he was known, transformed how rugby was played in the college and helped found the Old Crescent club.

As we have seen, he coached the Crescent team to win the Munster Schools Cup in 1947, an achievement that led to the creation of the Old Crescent club the following September. A mere six years later, they had achieved enough to convince the Munster Branch of their worthiness for senior rugby. As the Old Crescent website honestly acknowledges, 'the Ginner's formidable negotiating skills were more than useful in the process'.

It was often claimed that there was more politicking in Munster rugby than in Leinster House. Fr Guinane was at least as adept as the many others who weren't averse to pulling a stroke that would help their own particular cause or that of their club. It takes a politician to know a politician and Desmond O'Malley, one of Fr Guinane's pupils and later a distinguished government minister for many years, contributed a delightful piece about the reverend gentleman in *The Crescent*, an anthology of the college published in 2009:

Fr J. G. Guinane on a night out with a number of other distinguished rugby administrators. Back row (l–r): J. B. Neiland, Gus O'Driscoll; second row (l–r): J. W. Auchmuty, Ollie Browne; third row (l–r): Pat Carroll, W. W. Gleeson, Tom Collerty, John O'Farrell; front row (l–r): Dom Dineen, Dermot G. O'Donovan, Fr Guinane, and Sean McNamara. (Courtesy *Limerick Leader*)

My arrival in the Crescent coincided with that of Fr Guinane. He made an immediate difference. Crescent won the Munster Senior Cup for the first time in 1947. He was the Declan Kidney of his day. I think he remained in the Crescent for the rest of his life. I remember him best because of the impact he made and the influence he had even if it was not the typical warrior of Ignatius.

The victorious team of 1947 presented him appropriately enough with a Ronson cigarette lighter of the kind that you had to refill constantly with petrol, wicks and a flint. He used it all his life and remarkably never lost it. He left it to me in his will and I presented it to Old Crescent. I hope they still have it. It is a precious heirloom of the Crescent history. By the time I got it, I smoked almost as much as Fr Guinane, but gas lighters had come in by then and they were much more convenient and less messy.

The Ginner would talk incessantly about rugby … his other great topic was the War in which he had served as a Chaplain to the Royal Ulster Rifles. Unfortunately (or perhaps luckily) he broke his two legs jumping off a landing craft on to a Dorset beach a few days before D-Day while practising for landing on a Normandy beach. He maintained his contact with the Royal Ulster Rifles and that explained the consistent support of the Ulster delegates of the IRFU for him. He remained on the committee of the IRFU for nearly twenty years because of the solid support of Ulster and Munster which put Leinster in their place.

The Royal Ulster Rifles held a dinner in the United Services Club in Dublin on the Friday night before the English match every second year … In the mid-1950s, a new young officer who had fought in the Korean War but not in the World War became secretary of the association. He did not know the Ginner. He sent an invitation to the dinner to 'The Reverend and Mrs J. G. Guinane SJ, Sacred Heart Church, The Crescent, Limerick'. Fr Bates and a few of his colleagues did not let him forget that for several years.

The elevation of Old Crescent, one has to suspect, made for a deal of teeth-gnashing across the city at Shannon RFC. After all, they had been around since 1884 and firmly believed if any club was to be elevated, it should be them. However, they did not have long to wait. Club historian of the time, Willie W. ('Whack') Gleeson stated that 'on the proposition of Garryowen', Shannon finally got the call in the 1953/54 season. Not alone that but in 1940 they also became the second tenant club at Thomond Park where they have been ever since. The explosion in their membership numbers also inevitably meant they needed to provide their own grounds at Athlunkard and more recently at Coonagh.

In the mid-1960s, they sought Munster Branch approval to build their own pavilion in its present location, just inside the West Stand gates at Thomond. Bill O'Shea, one of the architectural team, reported that 'some opposition from outside sources was encountered but with a little diplomacy, that was overcome and permission was eventually granted.'

O'Shea continues the story:

> A building committee was appointed of Jack Cowhey, Bill O'Shea, Des Gilligan, Fred Roche, William Lysaght, A. O'Halloran and Donal Gilligan. Work on the great voluntary undertaking began on Monday, 4 July 1966.

At the time, the club had little cash for such a project, nevertheless there was a profusion of all the relevant tradesmen readily available and eager to help out. Volunteers who had never handled a shovel since they had built sandcastles in Kilkee quickly became proficient in their use. Work progressed through the winter of '66 and with the approach of the '66/67 season, meals were organised for the Saturday work force to speed up operations.

An amusing incident can be recalled about one such Saturday meal. A ball hopper who shall be nameless started a rumour that turkey and ham would be on the menu for the coming Saturday. The day was cold with a light covering of frost on the ground. The two regular 'cooks' knew nothing of the rumoured turkey and ham menu. In actual fact, the menu for the day was backbones and potatoes followed by sponge cake and tea with two 'Dannos' (pint bottles of Guinness) each to finish. While the lads were working away outside happy with the thought of the upcoming meal, things in the kitchen were not going at all smoothly.

The gas ring had been borrowed earlier that morning by one of the lads doing a 'Tommer' [i.e. doing work on the side] and the electric cooker which was only temporarily wired kept blowing fuses with the result that the water in the cooking pots was barely warm. The upshot of the affair was that the workers had to make do with a meal of two 'Dannos' and sponge cake. Needless to say, some very pertinent remarks were made about the cooks.

The pavilion was eventually completed on the day of the official opening, Tuesday, 26 December 1967. Eugene Davy, president of the IRFU, performed the honours and among those also present were Mayor of Limerick, G. E. (Ted) Russell; Chris Crowley, vice president, IRFU; Dr Reggie Sutton, president Munster Branch; Clem Casey, vice president, Munster Branch; F. J. Roche, president Shannon RFC; John O'Farrell and Gus O'Driscoll, hon. secretary and hon. treasurer, Shannon; Steve Coughlan TD.

To mark the occasion, an exhibition match took place between a Shannon selection and the Cuchulainns, which Shannon won 22–3.

The teams were:

Shannon Selected: A. Colbert, E. McNamara, B. O'Brien (all Shannon), B. Bresnihan (UCD), J. Tydings, J. O'Shea (both Young Munster), S. O'Connor (Shannon), T. Carroll (Garryowen), T. Barry (Old Crescent), J. Molloy (UCC), M. Molloy (UCG), W. Quane, J. Casey (both Young Munster), O. McLoughlin capt. (Shannon), D. Hickie (St Mary's College).

Cuchulainns: J. O'Mahony (Sundays Well), M. Manning, B. Begley (both Cork Constitution), J. Cummiskey (UCD), F. O'Driscoll, L. Hall (both UCC), P. O'Callaghan, T. Fitzgibbon (both Dolphin), K. Keyes (Sundays Well), T. Moore (Highfield), E. Kiely (UCC), L. Coughlan, J. Good, N. Murphy capt. (all Cork Con).

Donogh O'Malley (uncle of the aforementioned Desmond), a man who had the privilege of playing interprovincial rugby for Connacht, Munster and Leinster, was Minister for Education at the time. At the dinner that evening, he recalled training with Shannon on their grounds on the Mill Road in Corbally and winning a Munster Junior Cup medal with the club in 1939, the year he had also reached the final stages of the Bateman Cup with University College Galway (UCG). Donogh expressed the hope that Shannon's Brian O'Brien ('a nephew of a great Shannon man, Brendan O'Brien'), would trot out onto Lansdowne Road that season in an Irish jersey. The wish was duly granted when 'Briano' lined out against France, England and Scotland a few weeks later. And, almost needless to mention, the festivities duly concluded with a rousing rendering of the Shannon anthem, 'There is an Isle'.

Even greater things lay just around the corner for Shannon but first they had to deal with their resurgent near neighbours Bohemians, whose lone Munster Cup success had been achieved back in 1927. There were many difficult days for the club in the intervening years and it took the Herculean efforts of men like the Stokes brothers, Bill and J. W. ('Swig'), Ted Russell, Pat Power, the Treacy brothers, Donal Holland, Jim ('Tishy') Auchmuty and Dom Dineen to keep the ship afloat. Off the field, they were commendably active and in 1955 opened their new pavilion at Thomond Park, marking the occasion with a special fixture against Dublin side Old Wesley to mark the arrival of the first rugby club pavilion in Limerick.

The arrangement concerning visiting overseas teams coming to play Munster was that the Mardyke (and later Musgrave Park, now Irish Independent Park) in Cork and Thomond Park in Limerick would be the host venue in alternate years. So the 1954 All Blacks played Munster at the 'Dyke' and once again it was a desperately close and exciting affair before the tourists edged ahead 6–3. Thomond Park, however, also had its share of attractive fixtures, not least the visit of Auvergne (the forerunner of top-league French side Clermont Auvergne) to a packed Thomond Park to take on a Limerick selection. Tom Clifford led a side interesting for the inclusion of players from the two recently promoted clubs Old Crescent (Bobby Leonard, Jim Roche and Goff Spillane) and Shannon (Bobby Keane). Spillane, Tim McGrath and Roche were Limerick's try scorers and Roche kicked the remaining points as the home side pulled off a narrow and exciting win.

Irish rugby followers had looked on with envy as the Barbarians toured the four home countries and often further afield, playing an open, free-flowing style of football that appealed to those becoming a little tired of the safety-first tactics employed all too often in the competitive arena. To provide much of the same on a regular basis here in Ireland,

The Limerick selection that played Auvergne in 1955. Back row (l–r): W. W. Stokes, M. O'Connell (Young Munster), T. Nesdale, T. McGrath (both Garryowen), G. Spillane, B. Leonard (both Old Crescent), P. Tucker (Young Munster), S. O'Sullian referee; middle row (l–r): B. Keane (Shannon), D. Geary (Bohemians), G. Wood (Garryowen), T. Clifford capt. (Young Munster), K. Quilligan (Garryowen), J. Roche (Old Crescent), C. English (Bohemians); front row (l–r): M. English (Bohemians) and S. O'Dea (Garryowen). (Courtesy *Limerick Leader*)

the Wolfhounds were founded in the mid-1950s and, not surprisingly, one of their first ports of call was Thomond Park and a meeting with a Tom Clifford XV.

Thomond Park was once again thronged to watch many of the game's greats, several from across channel, display their skills. The biggest cheer of the day was reserved for Clifford who ran 20 yards for a try as he inspired his selection to a 19–16 win. The opposing out-halves that afternoon were rival Ireland and England internationals Mick English and Phil Horrocks-Taylor. Despite claims to the contrary, especially by Tony O'Reilly in his many brilliant after-dinner speeches, this was the game in which Horrocks-Taylor scored two tries on English.

Asked to explain afterwards how he had allowed this to happen, Micky replied: 'Horrocks went one way, Taylor the other and I was left with the bloody hyphen.' Tony O'Reilly claimed that it happened in an England v Ireland game at Twickenham but, in fact, Horrocks-Taylor and English never played against each other in an international fixture. Nevertheless, the story attained such fame that it was included in the *Oxford Dictionary of Humorous Quotations*.

An examination of the teams provides a clear indication of the quality of the players on duty:

Tom Clifford XV: P. Downes (Bohemians), D. McCormick (Dolphin), J. Roche (Old Crescent), C. Greally (Palmerston), M. Mortell (Bohemians), M. English and T. Cleary (Bohemians), V. Giltenane (Dolphin), D. Barry (Dolphin), T. Clifford capt. (Young Munster), M. Spillane and G. Spillane (Old Crescent), M. O'Connell (Young Munster), A. O'Riordan (Young Munster), T. McGrath (Garryowen).

Wolfhounds: T. O'Toole (Bective Rangers), A. J. F. O'Reilly capt. (Old Belvedere), R. W. Tucker (Clontarf), R. Lee (Liverpool), W. P. C. Davies (Harlequins), J. P. Horrocks-Taylor, A. A. Mulligan (both Cambridge University), G. Wood (Garryowen), W. O'Gorman (UCD), G. W. Hastings (Gloucester), J. B. Stevenson (Instonian), T. Reid (London Irish), H. S. O'Connor (Dublin University), D. O'Brien (Old Belvedere), A. O'Sullivan (Galwegians).

Referee: Paddy Frawley.

These games provided appropriate preparation for the visit of the Australians to Thomond Park on 21 January 1958, a game remembered more for the amazing conditions in which it was contested than the quality of the rugby, even if a three-all draw meant that an Irish province had avoided defeat by a major touring team for the first time. The entire country – the mid-west in particular – was covered in a blanket of snow in the preceding days and it took Herculean work by volunteers and a number of schoolboys gladly accepting the offer of a free morning to clear the pitch in time for the kick-off.

Injury denied Munster of a number of leading players so in the circumstances they did well to share the spoils, a Ray Hennessy penalty cancelling out a try by Alan Morton.

Munster: R. Hennessy (Constitution), S. Quinlan (Highfield), J. Walsh (UCC), F. Buckley (Highfield), D. McCormick (Dolphin), M. English (Bohemians), M. Mullins (UCC), G. Wood capt. (Garryowen), D. Geary (Bohemians), R. Dowley (Dolphin), T.

The Munster team that drew with Australia in Thomond Park, 1958. Back row (l–r): M. Keyes, Munster Branch president, M. O'Connell, M. Spillane, N. Murphy, T. Nesdale, D. Geary, D. McCormack, T. McGrath, R. Dowley, P. O'Kane, secretary North Munster subcommittee; middle row (l–r): J. Walsh, M. English, G. Wood capt., R. Hennessy, F. Buckley; front row (l–r): M. Mullins and S. Quinlan. (Courtesy *Limerick Leader*)

Nesdale (Garryowen), M. Spillane (Old Crescent), M. O'Connell (Young Munster), N. Murphy (Constitution), T. McGrath (Garryowen).

Australia: Curley, Morton, Potts, White, Fox, Harvey, Logan, Vaughan, Meadows, Davidson capt., Ryan, Shehadie, Yanz, Hughes, Gunther.

Where's The Cup?

Mick English of Bohemians was now at the height of his considerable powers, a point well made by the advent of the golden era of his club and his own elevation to the dizzy heights of a Lions tour and sixteen Irish caps. Born in O'Callaghan Strand within comfortable walking distance of Thomond Park, his footballing skills were honed at Rockwell College in County Tipperary where he was a member of the successful Munster Schools Junior Cup side in 1949 before starring on the team that captured the senior title twelve months later. As Bohemians did not possess an under-eighteen Juvenile Cup side at the time, he played under-age rugby with Shannon and it was not until his half-back partnership with Tom Cleary began to blossom in the mid-1950s that Bohs gradually came out of hibernation and began their march to the top of the Munster tree where they remained on and off for a decade or so.

Having waited forty-one years for their second Munster Cup success, one might have expected Bohs to clutch the coveted trophy firmly to their breasts after beating Highfield in the 1958 final at Thomond Park. And yet, on the very night of the game, they took their eye off it during a celebration party in the English homestead long enough for a group of 'gentlemen' to walk out the door with the famous trophy in their possession without any of its new 'owners' being aware of its departure. The realisation came too late: the cup was gone and on the following morning the inevitable hangovers were accompanied by many red and embarrassed faces. The *Limerick Leader* was less than impressed and warned: 'The practical joker responsible for this "coup" would be well advised to return the trophy without delay. Bohemians officials have a shrewd suspicion as to the whereabouts of the cup and its return is regarded as certain within a day or two.'

Bohs had won the cup but had no tangible proof of the achievement. Everybody had their own idea of the identity of the culprits but they remained tight-lipped until the trophy was returned to a garden seat in the English garden after seventy-two hours of considerable anxiety. To this day, nobody has accepted any responsibility for the foul deed.

The Bohemians team of the golden era was blessed with a half-back combination widely regarded as one of the finest to ever grace the club game in this country. Ironically, the brilliantly talented scrum half Tom Cleary was chosen as an Irish substitute on seventeen occasions at a time when replacements were not allowed during a game and he was never capped. Out-half Mick English may have pulled on the green jersey sixteen times but seven other number tens were also chosen between his first appearance in1958 and his last in 1964. It did not help either that Mick had to wait while the great Jack Kyle played out the final years of his illustrious career. English would eventually give way to Mike Gibson, unquestionably one of the finest footballers ever to play for Ireland.

Nevertheless, the treatment he received when clearly the best out-half available to the 'Big Five', as the Irish selectors were known, and still composed of two representatives each from Leinster and Ulster and one from Munster, angered his legions of supporters. Fellow Bohemians

Three great Bohemians supporters and ever-constants at Thomond Park (l–r): Tom O'Dowd, Bill Peacocke, Ted Russell. (Courtesy O'Dowd family)

Bohemians, Munster Senior Cup champions, 1959. Back row (l–r): Donal Holland, Jack Meaney, Billy Hurley, Maurice Walsh, Billy Slattery, Dom Dineen, Caleb Powell, Brendan O'Dowd, Johnny Ryan, J. W. Stokes; middle row (l–r): Mick English, Christy English, Basil Fitzgibbon, Dermot Geary capt., Paddy Moran, Paddy Downes, Paddy O'Callaghan; front row (l–r): Jimmy McGovern and Tom Cleary. (Courtesy *Limerick Leader*)

Brendan O'Dowd expressed his views forcibly when interviewed at the time by the *Limerick Leader*: 'Mick would get a cap and play well, the next week he'd be replaced by some Leinster player who wasn't half as good', O'Dowd said. 'Then they'd reluctantly play him again. They didn't care how good you were, if you were from Limerick, they didn't want to pick you.'

Because he loved life so much, Micky was invariably surrounded by fun and banter. Mai Purcell, a close friend and senior member of the *Limerick Leader* staff, frequently joined in the frivolity. When he was first capped for Ireland, she wrote him the following congratulatory note: 'Mikie – I should like to impress on you that I'm spending my whole week's wages, viz, £3.00, on the trip to Dublin just to see you play and I beseech you not to make an eejit of yourself on this occasion. I furthermore request that on this auspicious occasion, mindful of your duties and responsibilities not only to your club and the people of Limerick but to our country as a whole, that you keep your eye on the bloody ball. Good luck and God bless – Mai Purcell.'

The anger aroused at the cavalier manner in which Mick English's career was downplayed by a succession of Irish selection committees does not appear to have been matched by similar emotions where Tom

Cleary's treatment was concerned. He was a superb scrum half blessed with all the basic skills of a top-class number nine combined with an instinctive ability to do the right thing. A native of Carrick-on-Suir, he was articled in Limerick to the accountancy firm of W. H. O'Donnell and was immediately recognised not just as a gifted rugby and tennis player but also as a charming and courteous individual who quickly made close and lasting friendships.

Tom spent the latter years of his life in Mullingar. On his death, a suitcase containing many of his possessions was discovered and led to a much-acclaimed book, written by his niece Ursula Kane Cafferty and entitled *Suitcase Number Seven*. The name derives from the suitcase allocated to Cleary by the IRFU for the tour of South Africa in 1961.

Mick English in action for Ireland against France at Lansdowne Road. (Courtesy *The Sunday Press*)

It came as little surprise when the English/Cleary combination assisted by a range of other fine players like Paddy Downes, Mick's brother Christy, captain Paddy Moran, Dermot 'Gooser' Geary and Caleb Powell, a future president of the IRFU, inspired Bohemians to their first Munster Cup triumph in forty-one years at Thomond Park in

Tom Cleary (with the ball) clears his lines for Bohemians in their 1959 Munster Cup win over Shannon. (Courtesy Bohemian RFC)

1958. Ironically and not a little sadly, Dom Dineen, a Bohemians hero for more than a decade in some very difficult times for the club, had been forced to retire before the season began because of an eye injury. He compensated for the loss of the coveted medal by turning his attentions to coaching the side and duly got the best out of a talented group of players. Bohs defeated Highfield, a senior club for just six years, in a Thomond Park final dominated by gale-force winds. Highfield had the elements at their backs in the first half but were three points behind by the interval, so their goose was well and truly cooked. The point was well made by Brendan O'Dowd who recalled that 'Mick got the ball one yard from our line and kicked it into touch five yards from the Highfield line. He was absolutely incredible.'

Deeds of this nature had to be rewarded, however grudgingly, by the Irish selectors and one of Mick's greatest days came at Lansdowne Road in 1959 when he kicked a magnificent drop goal to help Ireland beat arguably the finest of all French sides up to that point by 9–5. As we have seen, it was a result that earned Mick and a whole host of other Irish players their places on the Lions tour of New Zealand. His number of appearances 'down under' was, however, reduced to two because

The crowd enjoys the presentation of the Munster Senior Cup to Bohemians after their victory over Shannon in the 1959 final. (Courtesy Brendan O'Dowd)

of a stomach-muscle injury and he returned early along with another Irish casualty, Niall Brophy. They travelled by luxury liner and by all accounts enjoyed every single minute of the voyage.

Because of the dominating manner in which English played in the 1958 Munster Cup triumph, there were a few veiled suggestions by envious rivals that Bohs were a one-man team. However, the begrudgers were silenced twelve months later when Mick, at the request of the Lions management, reluctantly agreed not to play any more domestic football once the squad was announced. Another talented footballer, Jimmy McGovern, took his place against Shannon in the final. It was a game that should never have been played. Thomond Park and Limerick had been battered for days by torrential rain and the pitch was totally waterlogged. It was one of the many pools that flooded the pitch that saved the day for Bohs. They were trailing by 6–3 late in the second half when the ball was booted pretty aimlessly over the Shannon line – until it got caught in a huge puddle, stopped suddenly and obligingly for the fast following-up Bohs wing Maurice Walsh who dived on it for a priceless equalising try.

As luck would have it, the following Saturday dawned warm and windless, just the way Bohs liked it. This time, Maurice Walsh scored two tries of a more conventional nature, Basil Fitzgibbon got another, McGovern kicked a drop goal and Bohs retained their cup in style. This time they kept a much closer eye on their prized possession.

Bohemians: P. Downes, P. Moran, C. English, B. Fitzgibbon, M. Walsh, M. English, J. McGovern, T. Cleary, P. O'Callaghan, D. Geary capt., W. Hurley, J. Meaney, B. O'Dowd, W. Slattery, C. Powell, J. Ryan.

5

'There is an Isle'

There is an isle, a bonnie isle,
Stands proudly from, stands proudly from the sea
And dearer far than all this world
Is that dear isle, is that dear isle to me.

It is not that alone it stands
Where all around is fresh and fair
But because it is my native land
And my home, my home is there
But because it is my native land
And my home, my home is there.

Thomond Park had witnessed many momentous occasions since its birth in 1934 but surely none to rival the excitement that greeted Shannon's first victory in the Munster Senior Cup in 1960. The *Murphys Story of Munster Rugby* put it as follows:

All the excitement, colour and passion generated over the years by the Munster Cup manifested themselves in the opening season of the 1960s. Shannon, after their near miss the previous year against Bohemians, came back twelve months later with courage and conviction and won possibly the most memorable championship of modern times. And when College were beaten at the end of an enthralling Thomond Park replay, the

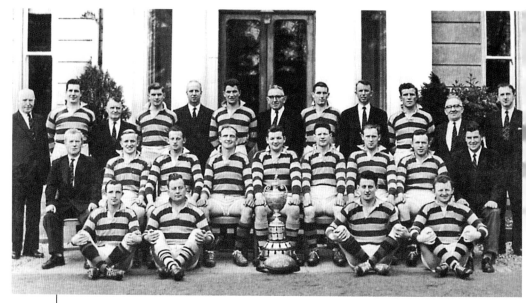

Shannon, Munster Senior Cup champions, 1960. Back row (l–r): J. O'Farrell hon. secretary, E. Clancy, P. Shanahan, M. Clancy, M. Bradshaw, T. Sheehan, S. McNamara president, J. Gallagher, F. Gallagher, P. O'Flynn, W. W. Gleeson team secretary, A. O'Driscoll; middle row (l–r): J. J. Cleary, J. McNamara, R. Keane, F. O'Flynn, M. N. Ryan capt., G. O'Halloran, D. Flannery, J. O'Donovan, J. O'Flaherty; front row (l–r): E. Ryan, S. O'Carroll, E. Keane and T. Sheppard. (Courtesy *Limerick Leader*)

'Parish' anthem, 'There is an Isle', was sung as never before and there and then became an important part of Irish rugby's music and literature.

It is a pleasure to look back again at the participants on that very special occasion. The contrast in big-name players could hardly have been more apparent ... the names of very few if any of the Shannon side would have registered with rugby fans outside of Munster. As against that, the great Tom Kiernan, the crash-tackling, sweet-passing Jerry Walsh and flying winger Paddy McGrath were just some of the outstanding talents in the College back division. Trouble for the students was that their forward pack wasn't as well endowed with the required level of seasoned campaigner and Shannon planned accordingly. They were a wily bunch alright ... few young, inexperienced forwards would have fancied eighty minutes against a front row of the Shannon captain Michael Noel Ryan, Donogh Flannery and Frankie O'Flynn.

The second-row pair, Jim O'Donovan and Paddy O'Flynn, were happy to hold their own in the line-out but placed greater significance on doing their stuff honestly in scrum, ruck, maul and anywhere they could help the overall cause. Eamonn Clancy at number eight was the most experienced of the lot, having lined out for Young Munster in the 1947 decider. On the flanks were a lightly built, blond-haired ball of fire in Jim McNamara, a tiger in the loose and a crash-tackler supreme, and John Gallagher, a strongly built, industrious and clever number six.

The forwards hunted as a pack but it would also be a mistake to think that this was an eight-man team. Far from it, indeed, and backs like Gerry O'Halloran, Tony Sheppard and Eamonn Ryan brought the first-up tackle to a fine art, the Keanes – Eamonn and Bobby – and Tony Sheehan had the pace and skill to turn every opportunity to their side's advantage while Sean O'Carroll at number nine was surely the shrewdest of all and adept at making the best possible use of the priceless possession gained by the men up front.

Ironically, Thomond Park staged the climax to the championship that year only because Shannon's first meeting with UCC had finished level at Musgrave Park the previous week. Shannon had reached the final by beating Young Munster and Garryowen and, even though they were rank outsiders, were followed to Cork by an immense band of supporters who belted out their songs, 'Roll Along, Shannon Forwards' and, of course, 'The Isle', and sported their black-and-blue rosettes, scarves and hats. Conditions favoured the fast and open style of the students, who led until close to the finish, with a Paddy McGrath try and a penalty and conversion by Tom Kiernan against an Eamonn Keane penalty. However, the Shannon pack was gaining the ascendancy and opened the way for those behind to create a try for Martin Clancy that Keane converted. The final whistle was greeted with delight by the Shannon hordes who carried off their men in triumph as if the trophy was already on its way to the parish.

The teams in the Thomond Park replay a week later were:

Shannon: G. O'Halloran, E. Ryan, M. Clancy, A. Sheppard, A. Sheehan, E. Keane, S. O'Carroll, M. N. Ryan capt., D. Flannery, F. O'Flynn, P. O'Flynn, J. O'Donovan, J. McNamara, E. Clancy, J. Gallagher.

UCC: T. J. Kiernan, P. McGrath, J. Hill, J. Walsh capt., J. Darcy, J. Harty, M. Mullins, J. Hyland, B. O'Gorman, T. Aherne, C. O'Hara, P. Riordan, M. Rekab, F. Golden, R. Lucey.

Referee: Comdt Tom Furlong.

Even standing room was at a premium for the second meeting of the sides. Thomond Park was about to play host to one of its most colourful occasions, which *Limerick's Rugby History* recorded as follows:

> Another lovely afternoon greeted the protagonists, yet there was nothing the likes of Tom Kiernan, Jerry Walsh and Pat McGrath could do about it as the Shannon pack took control. The College scrum was little more than a shambles as 'Michael Noel', Donogh and 'Frankie' won the first ten strikes of the match, had a lead of 16–4 by the interval and the set scrum count in Shannon's favour at the finish was an astonishing 23–8.
>
> The line-out saw Paddy O'Flynn and Jim O'Donovan, not to mention Michael Noel, who did great work at the front, also on top. All of this enabled Sean O'Carroll and Eamonn Keane to play it their way. There was no score in the first half but all hell broke loose when Keane put Shannon ahead with a fine penalty. Kiernan wasn't long in equalising, also with a penalty.
>
> Then came the score that set the bonfires blazing and the 'Parish' celebrating for weeks to come. Sean O'Carroll, cruelly taken from us not long afterwards in the prime of life, dropped a goal. Even then, College weren't beaten. A great midfield tackle by Tony Sheppard stopped a particularly likely looking move. Tom Kiernan opened up from everywhere and the talent that was to make him one of rugby's great full-backs and a Lions captain was fully evident.
>
> But 'Shep', his centre partner Martin Clancy and full-back Gerry O'Halloran defended as if their lives depended on it and the covering of Eamonn Ryan and Tony Sheehan was crucial. The pack maintained its stranglehold all the way with the back-row of Jim McNamara, Eamonn Clancy and John Gallagher tackling every College player with fanatical dedication.

At last the final whistle … and Thomond Park was promptly swept from view as thousands poured on to the pitch to carry off their heroes.

The name Noel Murphy has always been synonymous with Cork Constitution. Noel senior, winner of a Munster Cup medal with the club in 1933, was an outstanding Irish international around that period before going on to crown a distinguished administrative career with the presidency of the IRFU. Noel junior enjoyed an even more stellar career with club, province, country and the Lions but there was one occasion when things did not work out for him. Business brought him to Limerick for a twelve-month period in 1961 and he linked up with Garryowen and played a very significant part in getting them into the Munster Cup final.

As luck would have it, they were joined there by Cork Con, meaning that there must have been seriously contrasting mindsets in the Murphy household in the build-up to the game. Cork Con travelled to Limerick as outsiders but on the day they were much the better side with skipper

Denis O'Flynn scoring the all-important try for Cork Constitution in their Munster Cup final victory over Garryowen at Thomond Park in 1961. Also included are (l–r): Brian O'Farrell, Tony Colbert and Noel Murphy of Garryowen and Liam Coughlan and Dan Murphy of Constitution. (Courtesy *Cork Examiner*)

Bohemians, Munster Senior Cup champions 1962. Back row (l–r): S. McHale, K. Prendergast, W. Mulcahy, B. O'Dowd, D. Chambers, J. Ryan, J. Nagle; middle row (l–r): T. O'Brien, M. English, W. Slattery, C. English capt., P. Sheehan, M. McMahon; front row (l–r): S. Kenny and G. Sheehan. (Courtesy Ronnie Hurley)

Ray Hennessy, brothers Gary and Tony Horgan, Mick Keyes, Des Barry, Kieran Canniffe, Jos Cunningham, Jerry Murray and Liam Coughlan all contributing handsomely to a clear-cut victory.

Bohemians remained a major force in the early 1960s and they duly achieved their third Munster Cup success in five years in 1962. They had a nice blend of those who had picked up medals in 1958 and 1959 – Micky and Christy English, Tom Cleary, Brendan O'Dowd, Billy Slattery and Johnny Ryan – along with a host of talented newcomers, most notably the great Bill Mulcahy, a 35-times capped Ireland and Lions second-row forward and a native of Rathkeale, County Limerick; Sean McHale, an outstanding prop who would go on to represent his country on twelve occasions; Paddy O'Callaghan, a wily prop and a member of the successful Dolphin team in 1956; outstanding number eight Donal Chambers; and centre Kevin Prendergast, a champion athlete from Clonmel.

Bill Mulcahy first encountered rugby in his schooldays at St Munchin's, located at the time in Henry Street, Limerick, on the site of the current Garda barracks. He enjoyed his time there before moving to Dublin to study medicine at UCD. He was already a Lion and well-established Ireland second-row when on graduation he returned to Limerick in 1961 in time to join Bohemians and help them to Munster Cup glory. He was widely known as 'Wiggs', apparently because as a youngster he was constantly doodling a wigwam in his school copybook and his friends decided that should be his nickname. It was later abbreviated to Wiggs and that is how he has been known ever since.

He first captained Ireland against England at Twickenham in 1962. The 'Big Five' in their wisdom handed out new caps to nine players that day and Ireland were thrashed 16–0. But Bill, who in all skippered his country on ten occasions, was still at the helm two years later when that result was avenged to the tune of 18–5, a game highlighted by a brilliant try by Pat Casey after some great play involving Mike Gibson and Jerry Walsh, and two tries by Kevin Flynn. Mulcahy partnered Willie John McBride in the Lions second-row in all four Tests in South Africa in 1962 and earned this tribute from his colleague: 'Bill was excellent as a rucking, mauling and scrummaging type of player. He was not especially tall but was as tough as titanium.' Willie John may not have thought a whole lot about Mulcahy's line-out qualities but one magnificent shot of Mulcahy winning possession for Bohs in a Munster Cup game suggests

Bill Mulcahy wins a line-out for Bohemians against UCC in the 1962 Munster Senior Cup semi-final. (Courtesy *Limerick Leader*)

that he was no slouch when winning the ball in the air in an age when lifting was not allowed. And when Tony O'Reilly once asked him how he wanted the ball thrown to him at the line-out, Bill responded: 'Low and crooked.'

As captain of his country, Mulcahy adopted a democratic approach. He liked to recount how he asked for player input ahead of a game against France in 1962 and was proffered the following pearl of wisdom: 'I suggest we spend the first twenty minutes kicking the shit out of them and trying to upset as many of them as we can. Get them to fall out among themselves, that is the way to beat France.' With a rueful smile, Bill adds that France won the game in question by 24–5.

With Mulcahy an outstanding figure in his first and last Munster Cup campaign, Bohs played some fine rugby in disposing of Garryowen and UCC to reach the final and were hot favourites against first-time finalists Old Crescent, even though injury had deprived them of key men Tom Cleary and Paddy O'Callaghan. The latter's replacement, Hiram Wood, a brother of Gordon, was also unavailable so Marcus McMahon, hardly a year out of Glenstal, was pressed into service.

Crescent put up a brave battle but Bohs had too much power up front

Old Crescent scrum half Billy Leahy throws out a pass in the 1962 Munster Senior Cup final against winners Bohemians, watched by (l–r): Brendan O'Dowd (Bohs) and teammates Paddy Lane, Donal Ryan, Jim Foley and Stan Slattery. (Courtesy Brendan O'Dowd)

with Mulcahy at the peak of his considerable powers and Chambers, O'Dowd and McHale also very much to the fore. Seymour Kenny from Waterford stood in for Cleary at the base of the scrum and Mick English masterminded affairs in skilful fashion at out-half. His brother Christy was the victorious captain on an 8–3 scoreline.

There was to be one disappointment for Bohs that season. They qualified to meet UCC in the final of the Munster Senior League at Thomond Park and the game took place on 5 May with an evening kick-off to allow Mick English, Bill Mulcahy and Sean McHale time to return from the wedding of Tony O'Reilly in Dublin earlier in the day. The illustrious trio made a highly commendable effort but it was to no avail as the Cork students raised their game and won a cracking match, thanks to a drop goal by out-half Jim Harty. Bohs were left to rue their failure to accept a number of gilt-edged scoring opportunities. However, far more costly was the number of key members of the squad who departed club and city for Dublin and elsewhere during the summer of 1962, Mick English, Cleary, Mulcahy, McHale and Chambers among them. They have not won the Munster Cup since.

The 1962 Munster Cup final teams were:

Bohemians: G. Sheehan, P. Sheehan, C. English capt., K. Prendergast, T. O'Brien, M. English, S. Kenny, M. McMahon, J. Nagle, S. McHale, W. Mulcahy, B. O'Dowd, J. Ryan, D. Chambers, W. Slattery.

Old Crescent: F. O'Connell, D. Reddan, G. Clancy, J. Riordan, M. Manning, W. Foley, W. Leahy capt., J. Fitzgerald, P. Lane, S. Slattery, M. Spillane, J. Foley, J. O'Keeffe, D. Ryan, C. Downes.

Referee: Joe O'Donovan.

6

'Munster Midgets'

The Lansdowne club in Dublin has invariably been a happy home for Munster players moving to the capital and so it transpired for Mick English, Sean McHale and Donal Chambers. However, English was never going to be lost to the Munster provincial cause and he was to prove a central character on another famous Thomond Park day in December 1963 when the All Blacks came calling. There has rarely – if ever – been an ordinary New Zealand side and certainly the 1963/64 squad under the inspired leadership of a superb front-row forward Wilson Whineray deserved to be placed right up there with the greatest. They won all but two of their thirty-six matches, leading the country's most famous rugby journalist Terry McLean to title his book about the tour '*Willie Away – They May Have Been the Best.*'

The All Blacks arrived in Limerick on the back of a torrid encounter a few days previously against Ireland at Lansdowne Road. Inspired play by the likes of Tom Kiernan, Jerry Walsh and Mick English paved the way for a fine try by Johnny Fortune converted by Kiernan that put the home side 5–0 in front at half-time before a Kelvin Tremain try and a Don Clarke penalty squeezed the tourists home by 6–5. A very relieved bunch of New Zealanders made Limerick's Cruises Hotel their home for the next few days and endeared themselves to the locals through their willingness to mix and mingle and enjoy the customary warm welcome. However, their management had taken the close shave of Lansdowne Road on board and as the rain poured down on the eve of the game, turning the Thomond Park surface into something akin to a skating rink, they withdrew the top-heavy full back Don Clarke from their starting XV. They suspected that Clarke, who was there mainly for the accuracy and power of his goal kicking, would struggle to cope with the brilliant tactical kicking of Mick English.

Before battle was joined, however, the All Blacks took full and welcome advantage of the hospitality that the locals had laid on. Terry McLean certainly joined in when it came to the mediaeval banquet at Bunratty Castle.

'The All Blacks were wined and dined in most hilarious fashion', he wrote. 'Mead and mulled wine were drunk and pretty Irish girls in the softest of voices sang a delightful song about Jug of Punch and another delightful song about Cruskeen Lawn.'

McLean also caught up with Dermot G. O'Donovan, one of the great characters of Irish rugby and later to become president of the IRFU. The writer touched a chord with all those who knew the man

The Munster team that put up a great battle against the All Blacks at Thomond Park in December 1963 before losing a thriller 6–3. Back row (l–r): P. McGrath, B. O'Brien, P. Lane, M. Carey, H. Wall, N. Murphy, M. Spillane, J. Murray; front row (l–r): M. O'Callaghan, M. Lucey, M. English, T. Kiernan capt., N. Kavanagh, J. Walsh, D. Kiely. (Courtesy *Limerick Leader*)

when he noted that 'O'Donovan could always be relied upon for a story which never seemed to end but of which the detailing was wildly Irish and therefore madly amusing. Limerick, altogether, was a place to get the feel of Ireland, the crazy, mixed-up nature of the place.'

New Zealand is rugby's greatest nation for a reason and they had planned sagely enough to withstand a mighty Munster challenge. As Terry McLean put it, 'true to form, Mick English kicked superbly but Herewini was everywhere and fielded and kicked to the manner born. Had he not been there, the All Blacks would almost certainly have lost.'

Thomond Park, of course, was packed for the occasion and early on the 12,000 or so fans had little to cheer. The Kiwis' powerful pack kept the Munster men quiet and even though playing against the wind and rain, they led 6–0 at half-time with a penalty by Herewini and a try by Ian MacRae. It took some heroic defence up front by English, Tom Kiernan, Jerry Walsh, Brian O'Brien, Paddy McGrath, Mick Lucey and Noel Kavanagh to keep the New Zealanders at bay. However, the second half was a different matter. Under the dark, leaden skies, fifteen inspired men in red were led out by the irrepressible Mick O'Callaghan, a relatively lightweight prop who made little of his lack of poundage and went from one blood-soaked bandage to another, magnificently supported by his fellow forwards Mick Carey, Paddy Lane, Mick Spillane, Jerry Murray, Dave Kiely, Noel Murphy and Henry Wall.

O'Callaghan was a truly inspirational figure that day. Many others would have thrown in the towel, but he fearlessly entered the fray, receiving multiple cuts to his head, and on the day towered over all others. In spite of numerous outstanding performances for Presentation Brothers College (PBC), Sundays Well, Young Munster and Munster, he found it difficult to convince a succession of Irish selection committees that he was worthy of a place in the national team. They simply did not think he was big enough for the job.

An electrician by trade, he was working in the International Diamond Company in Shannon Airport when a workmate suggested a means of 'adding' to his natural weight prior to a final Irish trial. 'He produced two tiny bags which were used for the production of artificial diamonds,' O'Callaghan explained years later. 'They were an amazing weight for their size and he got me to put them into my jockstrap for the weigh-in just before the start and told me I would shoot up a stone. I tried it and got away with it. I weighed in at 14 st 8 lb and the next day I was on the Irish team. And that is the gospel truth.'

Terry McLean admitted it was 'shame-making to see these Munster midgets, who seemed to be three inches shorter and two stone lighter, boot the All Blacks around.' Henry Wall galloped over for a Munster try, English sent up a stream of Garryowens (a tactic popularised by the eponymous Limerick club and one frequently used today). On this occasion, English's kicks went so high they seemed to come down covered in ice on the bitterly cold December afternoon. McLean went on: 'the crowd were yelling blue murder and the players were charging about and knocking over everything that moved in case it was the ball.' Thanks largely to the brilliance and courage of stand-in full back Herewini, the All Blacks just about held on for their 6–3 victory but they would never forget Thomond Park.

All Blacks: M. Herewini, I. Smith, I. MacRae, W. Davis, B. Watt, E. Kirton, C. Laidlaw, J. Le Lievre, J. Major, I. Clarke, A. Stewart, R. Horsley, K. Tremain capt., K. Barry, B. Lochore.

Munster: T. J. Kiernan capt. (Constitution), M. Lucey, J. Walsh (both UCC), B. O'Brien (Shannon), P. McGrath (UCC), M. English (Lansdowne), N. Kavanagh (Dolphin), M. O'Callaghan (Sundays Well), P. Lane (Old Crescent), M. Carey (UCD), M. Spillane (Old Crescent), J. Murray, N. Murphy (both Constitution), D. Kiely (Lansdowne), H. Wall (Dolphin).

Referee: R. Williams (Ulster).

Thomond Park was now thirty years old and firmly established as the headquarters of rugby in north Munster. That is probably why it always looked the same from year to year, even when times were changing and a decent facelift was overdue. The front pitch was a picture of manicured perfection on the first day of every September but by November would have turned into a 50 x 10 yard rectangle of bare ground until the season's end. It was a muddy mess during the wet weather and a rock-hard, dusty stretch during the dry spells, usually in March and April.

Neither the players nor the spectators seemed to mind. It was Thomond Park, where it was an honour to represent school, club and province and a special place to come and support your favoured team. Most had a preferred spot from which to watch the action. Those seeking protection from the elements congregated in the stand or the west terrace, which was known as 'the stand side'. Directly opposite was the uncovered east terrace, 'the far side', 'the popular side' or 'the sixpenny side'. It was here that the wags indulged in the 'slagging' and witticisms for which they were renowned. Heaven help the visiting side that got ahead of itself. And on the day of a local 'derby' in the Munster Senior and Junior Cup, it was very much a case of every man for himself.

The Bohemians clubhouse incorporated into the Thomond Park stand was opened in December 1966. The *Limerick Leader* reported that:

> the pavilion built at a cost of £8,000 was a magnificent achievement and a great credit to everybody concerned, to the architect Mr Kevin O'Sullivan (a member of the Bohs side that played the first game at Thomond Park back in 1934), the building contractors Messrs Doyle and not least to the courageous club committee who decided to go ahead with the venture in the face of many daunting challenges. The premises were officially opened by the president of the IRFU Mr Dermot O'Donovan along with club president Alderman Ted Russell, TD. To mark the occasion, an exhibition game was won comfortably 35–18 by the Jerry Walsh XV against a Bohemians Past and Present side.

The *Leader* also reported that man of the match with four tries was Old Crescent winger Don Reddan (father of modern-day Ireland scrum half Eoin), while a teammate was Richard Heaslip, father of Ireland and Lions number eight Jamie. Pat Lawler, whose son, Mossie, was one of the Munster try scorers in the 'Miracle Match' against Gloucester in 2003, was full-back for Bohs. The teams included some of the country's finest players of the time.

Jerry Walsh XV: T. Kerins (St Mary's College), M. Lucey (Garryowen), J. Riordan (Old Crescent), P. McGrath (UCC), D. Reddan (Old Crescent), M. O'Mahony (Dolphin), T. Twomey (Lansdowne), M. O'Callaghan (Young Munster), T. Barry (Old Crescent), D. Gallivan (Old Crescent), E. Campbell (Old Wesley), M. Molloy (UCG), R. Heaslip (Shannon), A. J. O'Sullivan (Galwegians), J. Buckley (Sundays Well).

Bohemians Past and Present (Bohemians unless stated): P. Lawler, P. Sheehan, A. Duggan, P. Casey (both Lansdowne), K. Prendergast (St Mary's College), M. English (Lansdowne), F. Walsh, J. Hennessy, S. Kennedy, J. Nash, J. Finucane, C. Powell, R. Lawlor capt., B. O'Dowd, D. Chambers (Lansdowne).

Referee: Tony O'Sullivan.

7

History at Thomond

South Africa's visit to these shores in the spring of 1965 was of only five-match duration in Ireland and Scotland and it was at Thomond Park on 6 April that a major touring team was forced to bow the knee to an Irish side for the first time. It was not Munster, though, who enjoyed the privilege, rather it was a Combined Universities XV who lowered the Springbok colours. Thomond Park was a surprise venue given that at the time Limerick did not have a university nor was there a representative from the area on the Irish side. The IRFU decision, however, was a positive indication that, in their estimation, Thomond Park ranked second only to Lansdowne Road where support for the game was concerned and a proper atmosphere measured up to requirement. The home side was deprived of players of the calibre of Tom Kiernan, Paddy McGrath, Roger Young, Ray McLoughlin, Ken Kennedy and Bill Mulcahy at the request of the Irish selectors as the countries were due to meet a few days later at Lansdowne Road. This in turn afforded the opportunity for several up-and-coming players to show their worth and it helped, too, that Jerry Walsh, surely one of the finest centres produced by this country, was released to captain the team and lend his considerable experience to the cause.

Not surprisingly, the tourists' physically bigger and more experienced pack dominated possession but the universities (appropriately enough, perhaps, wearing red jerseys to avoid a clash of colours with the Boks' traditional green) performed with the zeal and determination that invariably marked Munster performances on such occasions and they pulled off a magnificent 12–10 victory. Mike Grimshaw from Queen's University and Eamonn McGuire, a terrier-like wing forward from UCG, went over for tries, UCD's John Murray drop-kicked a goal and another UCD man Tony Hickie kicked a penalty.

The history-making side was:

Combined Universities XV Tony Hickie (UCD), Mick Lucey (UCC), Jerry Walsh capt. (UCC), Mike Grimshaw (Queen's University), Billy Glynn (UCD), John Murray (UCD), Mike Whiteside (Queen's), Mick Carey (UCD), M. Argyle (Dublin University), Al Moroney (UCD), Mick Leahy (UCC), Ollie Waldron (UCC), Jimmy Davidson (Queen's), Henry Wall (UCD), Eamonn McGuire (UCG).

The following weekend, Ireland also defeated the Springboks for the first time, by 9–6 at Lansdowne Road, with Jerry Walsh the only man to figure on both successful sides.

The Bohemian v Old Crescent Munster Cup final of 1962 was the last to be staged at Thomond Park for seven years. Club rugby in Limerick played second fiddle to their Cork neighbours as UCC, Constitution and Highfield dominated until 1969 when Garryowen re-energised themselves and captured the trophy with an impressive final victory over Sundays Well. Their squad included a number of outstanding players, most notably international out-half John Moroney and his half-back partner, Liam Hall. 'Hally' toured Argentina with Ireland and was a number nine of the highest quality. For reasons best known to the 'Big Five' of the time, he never got to pull on the green jersey on the biggest days of all, very much in the same vein as another outstanding number nine, Tom Cleary, a decade or so earlier. Garryowen were captained by Army officer Ray ('Rusty') Keane who had an outstanding ally up front in former Rockwell schools star Frank Hogan.

Garryowen squad: B. Cobbe, P. McDonogh, T. Carroll, J. Rooney, J. Morrison F. Swords, J. Quinn, E. Tierney, D. Quaid, J. Moroney, L. Hall, M. O'Connor, P. O'Riordan, L. Harty, R. Keane capt., F. Hogan, A. Daly.

Nelson Mandela and his supporters were still incarcerated on Robben Island, South Africa, and worldwide disgust with that country's apartheid policy was at its height when the 1970 Springboks arrived on our shores. As a group they were surely the most unpopular touring team of all time. Some of the demonstrations went somewhat over the top, but it was understandable that the sporting representatives of the despicable regime should be made aware of the views of the majority of people in these islands. Their game against Ireland ended in an eight-all draw but is best remembered for the fact that the Lansdowne Road and Havelock Square terraces were devoid of spectators and the pitch itself was surrounded by barbed wire.

The 1970 Springboks bus leaves Limerick Railway Station surrounded by Gardaí, while protestors demonstrate against the apartheid regime in South Africa. (Courtesy *Limerick Leader*)

On the following day, the tourists made their way to Limerick by rail and were greeted, as usual, by Munster Branch representatives but also many hundreds of men and women protesting at the Springboks' presence in the city. The demonstrations remained peaceful with much praise for this going to Limerick politician Jim Kemmy who kept a lid on things while emphatically decrying what was happening in the Springboks' homeland. Kemmy's stance was opposed by another

An eerie scene at Thomond Park for the 1970 meeting of Munster and the Springboks. Present is a large contingent of Gardaí and their vehicles but no sign of supporters. (Courtesy *Limerick Leader*)

Labour party politician, Steve Coughlan, the mayor of the city at the time. Labour party supporter Fergus Finlay recalled the tempestuous few days in an *Irish Examiner* article in March 2015:

> While the protest was led by Jim Kemmy, the team was made welcome by another member of the Labour party, Stevie Coughlan. The row that ensued ultimately led to a split that saw both out of the Labour party. Along with a tiny group of friends from UCC, I was one of the little bank of protesters. We had been described a couple of days earlier in the *Limerick Leader* as 'dangerous thugs'. We were mocked, jeered and spat at by the crowd as they passed. There were a couple of priests in particular who seemed incensed by our presence and came right up to us to shout their anger in our faces. Thomond Park welcomed the ambassadors of apartheid and spat at their protestors.

Finlay wrote in the piece that the occasion turned him off rugby (only for the love affair to be rekindled eight years later when 'Thomond Park redeemed itself forever. Captained by the great Donal Canniffe, Munster did what no Irish team has done before or since. And I was there, not protesting this time, but cheering myself hoarse. And I've been in love with the game ever since.').

The sense of unease continued into the game itself and undoubtedly had an adverse affect on the home side. The Boks themselves were by now accustomed to a frosty reception and it also helped their cause that while another large mass of people – including a considerable number of good rugby folk – turned up at Thomond Park, they remained outside the ground and vented their feelings from there. There was an eerie atmosphere inside and what looked a very useful Munster side on paper was unable to lift its game and relied on three penalties by John Moroney for their points. The Springboks had tries by Myburgh, Grobler, Van de Venter and Nomis, a penalty by Visagie and two penalties and two conversions by their outstanding captain Dawie De Villiers, and they won 25–9. It was not the greatest day for either Thomond Park or Munster rugby.

South Africa: H. De Villiers capt., Grobler, Roux, Lawless, Nomis, Visagie, D. De Villiers, Myburgh, Barnard, Marais, de Wet, Carelse, Ellis, Jennings, Van de Venter.

Munster: A. Horgan (Constitution), J. Tydings (Young Munster), G. O'Reilly (Highfield), B. Bresnihan (London Irish), J. Moroney (Garryowen & London Irish), B. McGann capt. (Constitution), L. Hall (Garryowen), P. O'Callaghan (Dolphin), T. Barry (Old Crescent), O. Waldron (London Irish), S. Waldron (Constitution), E. Molloy (UCC), J. Buckley (Sundays), W. O'Mahony (UCC), T. Moore (Highfield).

Argentina were building a reputation around this time as a side worthy of attention from the traditional rugby nations and so there was a sense of expectation when they arrived in Ireland and Scotland in 1973 for a series of eight matches. However, they lost a lot of potential allies because of their overly vigorous approach on the field of play and their clash with Munster at Thomond Park on 31 November 1973 is remembered more for the free-for-alls than for any particular rugby skills. The Munster pack that day was comprised of men who had never turned the other cheek or ever would and the Pumas certainly met their match and then some. It was a pity that the game degenerated into little more than a brawl given that the visitors' Hugo Porta went on to fully merit a reputation as one of the game's finest out-halves. The affair ended in a twelve-all draw, four penalties for Munster by skipper Barry McGann against three penalties by Eduardo Morgan and a Hugo Porta drop goal.

Munster: R. Spring, P. Pratt, P. Parfrey, S. Dennison, P. Lavery, B. McGann capt., D. Canniffe, P. O'Callaghan, P. Whelan, G. McLoughlin, B. Foley, M. Keane, S. Deering, J. Buckley, T. Moore.

Argentina: A. Rodriguez Jurado, E. Morgan, R. Matarazzo, A. Travaglini, G. Perez Leiroz, H. Porta, A. Etchegaray, J. Carracedo, R. Sanz, H. Miguens capt., J. Virasoro, J. Fernandez, F. Insua, G. Casas, M. Carluccio.

Referee: Alan Sturgeon (Ireland).

Garryowen, Munster Senior Cup champions, 1974/75. Back row (l–r): Paddy Sullivan hon. secretary, Eugene O'Dwyer, Micky Martin, Shay Deering, Larry Moloney, Charlie O'Hurley, Mick Sheehan, Tommy O'Carroll, Pat Whelan, Pat Pratt, Clem McInerney, Rusty Keane, Frank Hogan, Pat O'Riordan coach; front row (l–r): Joe Mulqeen hon. treasurer, Johnny McDonnell, Tony Ward, Mervyn O'Connor, Des Quaid capt., Steve McDonogh president, Liam Hall, Mick McElligott, Eugene O'Shea, Seamus Dennison and Tom O'Brien team secretary. (Courtesy Garryowen FC)

St Mary's College, Centenary Club Championship winners, Thomond Park 1975. Back row (l–r): T. McCormack, T. Grace, M. Glynn, J. B. Sweeney, J. Donnellan, D. Hickey, T. Hickie, T. Feighery; front row (l–r): H. Murphy, L. Naughton, S. Lynch, F. Kennedy, J. Moloney capt., L. Grissing and E. Wigglesworth. (Courtesy St Mary's RFC)

On the club scene, Garryowen enjoyed success, winning the Munster Cup in 1971, 1974 and 1975 when most of the stars of 1969 were joined by others of international calibre: Larry Moloney, Seamus Dennison, Pat Whelan, Shay Deering and Tony Ward, all of whom would also play central roles for Munster against the game's major touring sides. Deering was a product of St Mary's College and UCD who came south on graduation as a veterinary surgeon and discovered that the Munster way of life and playing the game was right up his alley. He was hugely popular off the field while in the middle of the action he proved a fearless competitor who fulfilled every aspect of the wing-forward role to near perfection.

Ironically, he wore the light blue of Garryowen rather than the dark blue of Leinster champions St Mary's when the teams met in the final of the All-Ireland Club Centenary Championship at Thomond Park in 1975. It was a Bateman Cup-style event set up by Kevin Quilligan, himself a Garryowen man and president of the Munster Branch as part of the IRFU's centenary celebrations.

Both teams contained a large number of international and representative players. The game ended in a nine-all draw, the title going to St Mary's because they scored the only try, by Irish winger Tom Grace. Grace also converted and kicked a penalty, Garryowen replying with three penalties by Tony Ward, another product of St Mary's College. It was an extremely successful weekend (Garryowen defeated Galwegians and St Mary's eliminated Bangor in the semi-finals) with St Mary's earning the gratitude of the organisers for committing themselves to the occasion even though they had won the Leinster Senior Cup after a replay only a couple of nights previously. They included Lions Tom Grace, Denis Hickie, John Moloney and Sean Lynch in their ranks while the Garryowen side contained other big names like Larry Moloney, Seamus Dennison, Tony Ward and Shay Deering. They missed the experience of Pat Whelan and Liam Hall in the final, but nothing could detract from the outstanding achievement of St Mary's whose centenary history by Fred Cogley paid due tribute:

> The prospect of playing four cup matches in eight days to win the Centenary Cup was daunting in itself but in the Saturday semi-final against Bangor of Ulster, Marys turned in a magnificent display as if they had been resting all week! So it was they qualified for the Sunday final at Thomond Park facing the club's friendliest of rivals, Garryowen, in the final.
>
> The huge crowd marvelled at the quality of the play from both sides considering the amount of football they had played in such a short time. Garryowen got in front and three penalty goals saw them on target for victory as they led 9–3 going into the closing stages but for all their weariness, St Mary's never gave up and Tom Grace scored the vital try and his conversion saw the sides level at 9-all and into extra time again!
>
> That try turned out to be decisive with the Centenary Club Championship going to St Mary's and the proud captain-of-the-day Johnny Moloney who deputised for Terry Young whose Army superiors were unable to release him for this particular weekend. With the exception of Young, the same players figured in all the Leinster Cup and Centenary Cup matches which was a fair reflection of the tremendous spirit that existed among the players. The full side was: A. Hickie, T. Grace, F. Kennedy, L. Grissing, T. Young, H. Murphy, J. Moloney, T. Feighery, L. Naughton, S. Lynch, M. Glynn, J. B. Sweeney, E. Wigglesworth, D. Hickie, J. Donnellan. The only enforced change for the Centenary Championship saw Tom McCormack replace Terry Young on the left wing.

Shay Deering, who sadly died young after losing his battle with cancer, was also a member of the Munster side that drew with the 1973 All Blacks at Musgrave Park and which went down to the New Zealanders by 14–4 at Thomond Park the following year in a game to mark the centenary of the IRFU and again lost 15–13 to the Australians in Cork in 1976.

The 1975 All Blacks game was part of the IRFU celebrations and even though Thomond Park, as always, heaved with excitement and a packed crowd, the Kiwis emerged good winners. Their scrum half, the dynamic Syd Going, emerged man of the match; also very much to the fore was captain Andy Leslie, who would return to Limerick and Ireland many times, most notably as president of the New Zealand Rugby Union on the occasion of the official opening of the new Thomond Park stadium in 2008. He also served a stint here as coach of Garryowen. Wings Bryan Williams and Grant Batty scored All Blacks tries and Joey Karam kicked the points leaving Munster with a late consolation try by Terry Moore.

> **New Zealand:** J. Karam, B. Williams, Bruce Robertson, Morgan, G. Batty, Duncan Robertson, Syd Going, Tanner, Norton, Gardiner, MacDonald, Whiting, Kirkpatrick, Leslie capt., Stewart. Replacement: Stevens for Going.

> **Munster:** R. Spring (Constitution), P. Parfrey (UCC), L. Moloney (Garryowen), J. Coleman (Highfield), P. Lavery (London Irish), B. McGann capt. (Constitution), D. Canniffe (Constitution), O. Waldron (Clontarf), P. Whelan (Garryowen), P. O'Callaghan (Dolphin), J. Madigan (Bohemians), M. Keane (Lansdowne), C. Tucker (Shannon), S. Deering (Garryowen), T. Moore (Highfield).

For five of the Munster side, payback time was just four years away. Before that momentous occasion, however, several would also line out on opposing sides in the Munster Cup finals of 1977 and 1978 when underdogs Shannon turned the tables, not once but twice, on Garryowen in epic Thomond Park battles. The *Murphys Story of Munster Rugby* takes up the story:

> At club level, the struggle for the Munster Cup remained intense and in 1977 Thomond Park was bursting at the seams for the

Shannon, Munster Senior Cup champions, 1977. Back row (l–r): Mick McLoughlin, Noel Ryan, Gerry McLoughlin, Johnny Barry, Eddie Price, Colm Tucker, Denis O'Sullivan; front row (l–r): Paul O'Shea, Gerry Hayes, Michael Wilson, Terry Fitzgerald, Brendan Foley capt., Michael Houlihan, Sean Minihan, Johnny Ryan. (Courtesy *Limerick Leader*)

first final clash of Garryowen and Shannon. Garryowen went into the game on the back of a 19–0 semi-final win over holders UCC in Cork and a bonanza for fifteen-point man Tony Ward. Final day was wet and windy, the Garryowen pack was split apart by Brendan Foley and his merry men of Shannon who won a famous victory by two Terry Fitzgerald penalties to one by Tony Ward.

'There is an Isle' got some airing that night and for several others to follow but Tommy Creamer and his Shannon choir even took to paraphrasing the hit tune of the day from 'Don't Cry for me, Argentina' to 'Don't Cry for me, Garryowen'. Garryowen had to take it on the chin but when the sides duly qualified for final day once again twelve months later at Thomond Park, they were determined to have their revenge.

This time the pitch was firm, the sky was blue, the ball was dry – perfect for Garryowen, or so the pundits believed. Their backs, however, were a jittery lot and Eddie Price, Colm Tucker and Johnny Barry in the Shannon back-row had a field day. Price and Denis O'Sullivan scored a try each and Terry Fitzgerald kicked the remainder and Shannon were home by 16–10. Tony Ward got all Garryowen's points including a splendid try but it was not enough.

Shannon Munster Cup winners 1977/78: T. Fitzgerald, D. McKeogh, E. McNamara, D. O'Sullivan, G. Hayes, P. O'Shea, M. Wilson, G. O'Malley, P. O'Connor, S. Minihan, J. Ryan, G. McLoughlin, M. Houlihan, N. Ryan, B. Foley capt., M. McLoughlin, C. Tucker, E. Price, J. Barry, P. Herlihy, N. Noonan.

8

October 1978

The History of New Zealand Rugby Football by Arthur Swan records that the game was first played there in 1870. Swan explains that the country was populated at the time by immigrants of all classes from the British Isles seeking their fortune as businessmen, artisans, labourers, soldiers and so on. With the end of the Maori wars, the gold-diggers arrived from Australia and introduced Australian Rules. The labouring classes were all for soccer; what were known as 'remittance men' and public schoolboys preferred the Eton Wall game or the Rugby School game; and if you were from Cornwall (!) or Ireland, 'you agreed that Hurling was the game to break monotony as well as arms and legs.'

What roughly coincided with the game of rugby, as already established back in Britain and Ireland, gradually gained in popularity until tours to and from New South Wales took place and a British team played a number of matches in both New Zealand and Australia in 1888. The New Zealand Rugby Union was founded four years later and in 1893 a representative side dressed in a black jersey with a white fern leaf, black cap with silver monogram, white knickerbockers and black stockings toured Australia. In 1901, the white knickerbockers gave way to black shorts and this in turn led to the squad that toured Britain and Ireland in 1905 being called the 'All Blacks'.

'The Originals', as history records them, were captained by Dave Gallaher, a native of Ramelton, County Donegal, where he was born on 30 October 1873. He played twenty-six matches on the tour although he took a breather when Munster provided the opposition at the Markets

Field on 28 November 1905. Nevertheless, the All Blacks romped home by 33–0, a margin they frequently exceeded on tour. They lost only once and even then very controversially by 3–0 to Wales. Sergeant Gallaher died in action in Passchendaele on 30 October 1917.

Ever since, the All Blacks have regularly visited these islands although Ireland and Munster were not included on their rota until after the Second World War. There were some mighty matches between the Kiwis and Munster, most notably at the Mardyke in 1954 when the tourists edged home by 6–3 and again by the same margin at Thomond Park in 1963 while the teams also played a 3–3 draw at Musgrave Park in 1973. During that time, they resisted the best that Ireland, Ulster and Leinster (admittedly with fewer opportunities) could throw at them so this country was still waiting for any team to put one over on the All Blacks when Graham Mourie's men arrived in Limerick on 31 October 1978.

The All Blacks arrive at Shannon Airport in 1978. Included are: (from top) B. Ford, R. Kururangi, E. Dunn, A. McGregor, D. Bruce, B. Ashworth, D. Loveridge, S. Wilson, B. Robertson, W. Graham, J. Loveday, G. Knight, B. Johnstone, G. Seear, B. Williams, L. Ruthledge; (back row on tarmac): M. Taylor, C. Currie, J. Fleming, B. Bushe, B. McKechnie, J. Gleeson; (front row): A. Dalton, L. Jeffrey, E. Tobin, G. Mourie, S. Gavin Munster president, R. Thomas, S. McDonagh, K. Quilligan, T. Collery, P. Power, M. N. Ryan and S. Kiely. (Courtesy Thomond Park Museum)

Munster supporters had little to encourage them as the fateful day dawned. Whereas the New Zealanders had disposed of Cambridge University, Cardiff, West Wales and London Counties with comparative ease, Munster's preparations had been confined to a couple of games in London where their level of performance, to put it mildly, was a long way short of what would be required to enjoy even a degree of respectability against the All Blacks. They were hammered by Middlesex County and scraped a draw with London Irish.

Even before those two games, things had not been going according to plan. Tom Kiernan had coached Munster for three seasons in the mid-1970s before being appointed Branch president, a role he duly completed at the end of the 1977/78 season. However, when coach Des Barry resigned for personal reasons, Munster turned once again to Kiernan. Being the great Munster man that he was and remains, Tom was happy to oblige although one also suspected that as an extremely shrewd observer of the game he spotted something special in this group of players that had escaped the attention of most. He refused to be dismayed by what he saw in the games in London, instead regarding them as crucial in the build-up to the All Blacks encounter. He was, in fact, ahead of his time: he got hold of

video footage of the All Blacks games, something unheard of in those days, and was not averse to the idea of making changes in key positions. A major case in point was the introduction of London Irish loose head prop Les White of whom little was known in Munster rugby circles but who convinced the coaching team that he was the ideal man to fill a troublesome position.

Kiernan was confronted by many difficult issues. The team he envisaged taking the field against the tourists was composed of six players (Larry Moloney, Seamus Dennison,

Munster prop Les White during the match against the All Blacks. (*Irish Examiner*)

Gerry McLoughlin, Pat Whelan, Brendan Foley and Colm Tucker) based in Limerick, four (Greg Barrett, Jimmy Bowen, Moss Finn and Christy Cantillon) in Cork, four more (Donal Canniffe, Tony Ward, Moss Keane and Donal Spring) in Dublin and Les White who, according to Keane, 'hailed from somewhere in England, at that time nobody knew where'.

Always bearing in mind that the game then was amateur and these men worked for a living, for most people it would have been impossible to bring them all together on a regular basis for six weeks before the match. But the level of respect for Kiernan was so immense that the group would have walked over hot coals for him had he asked. So they turned up every Wednesday in Fermoy – a kind of halfway house for the players travelling from three different locations and over appreciable distances. Those sessions in a County Cork town not renowned for its rugby traditions and where the limited lighting had to be augmented by judiciously placed car headlamps helped to forge a wonderful team spirit. After all, men who had been slogging away at work only a short few hours previously would hardly make that kind of sacrifice unless they meant business.

Alone It Stands

The events in Fermoy became an integral part of John Breen's play *Alone It Stands*. Breen is a native of Limerick and a son of Myles Breen, one-time proprietor of the Limerick rugby pub on Shannon Street. Breen explained the rationale for the play to Len Dineen of Limerick 95FM:

> I first got the idea in 1998 when I was talking to Mike Finn who at the time was writing *Pigtown*. He asked me about the 1978 All Blacks game and we agreed it was a good story. I decided to write it myself. I began researching in the ILAC library in Dublin and that was where I first came across the reports of Dan Canniffe's death during the game and knew this was a story that had to be told. Everybody had a story, my brother Larry told me about Seamus Dennison's famous tackle, I rang some of the players, Tony Ward, Donal Canniffe, Seamus Dennison and I also interviewed Johnny Cole who was touch judge.

Programmes from various productions of *Alone It Stands*, the award-winning play that tells the story of the epoch-making encounter between Munster and the All Blacks in 1978. (Courtesy Mulqueen Collection)

I felt the story needed someone who had no interest in the game and so my twelve-year-old alter ego Spider was born. One of the first images I had in my head was of a woman in labour emerging from a ruck. Ironically, it is Mary who suffered most pain during the play. I finished it in a little cottage between Killaloe and Ballina. We rehearsed at the Island theatre company's headquarters near King John's Castle. We worked hard and played hard and became a winning team.

We opened in Waterpark Rugby Club in Waterford with three Kiwi prop forwards sitting in the front row. We got the first of many standing ovations that night. The rest is a bit of a blur … Andrews Lane Theatre, *Irish Times* Theatre Award, a Kevin Myers article in *The Irish Times* describing it as 'the cleverest, funniest play you are every likely to see.' Well, after that we were selling out in the Gaiety.

The world was their oyster and by a delightful piece of serendipity, Tony Ward was in the audience when it opened in the Sydney Opera House during the 2003 Rugby World Cup.

A multitude of different angles are interlinked in *Alone It Stands* to convey the drama of Thomond Park on 31 October 1978. There are stories of births, tragedies, bonfires and much else as the personal stories of various characters and what they got up to on the big day are hilariously depicted. Six actors ingeniously play 62 roles including the two teams, coaches, the ref, the crowd, the press, a pregnant woman, several children, a dog and even the ball itself.

From a rugby perspective, the Fermoy sessions were absolutely vital in Munster's preparation for the All Blacks game, creating a bond between the players and the coaches. Second-row forward and forthright Kerry man Moss Keane described this in his autobiography *Rucks, Mauls and Gaelic Football*.

> There were no floodlights in Fermoy so the selectors had to turn on the headlights of their cars instead. I'm sure Kiernan did this deliberately but he will never admit it. The thought of preparing to take on the greatest rugby team in the world by training under 'floodlights' from Cortinas and Ford Escorts gave us a real lift. It made for a lot of fun, too. Brendan Foley would pass remarks like 'Tommy, can you switch to dims? Mossy is having a gawk' or 'turn on the indicators, Mossy is about to turn' which had us laughing as we worked out. There was one area of the pitch that the lights did not reach which provided us with an escape from Tom's all-seeing eye. One night I headed for the dark of this black hole, totally knackered, and met full-back Larry Moloney lying down on the grass.
>
> 'Are you all right, Larry?', I asked.
>
> 'No Moss', he said, 'I'm going to die.'

Looking back, Kiernan recalled some other crucial moments: 'During the two days before the games in London, we trained at St Paul's School, Hammersmith, and there we set a standard of fitness for the team as a whole with special targets for the backs and forwards, the backs concentrating on sharpness and the forwards on endurance. After that we met on three Wednesdays in Fermoy and on the Sunday and Monday prior to the match in St Munchin's College, Limerick.'

Kiernan and a New Zealand 'spy', journalist Terry McLean, were quietly impressed with what they witnessed at St Munchin's. McLean

MUNSTER

v

NEW ZEALAND

THOMOND PARK,
LIMERICK
31st OCTOBER, 1978 – 3.00 p.m. PRICE 20

The programme sold out long before the kick-off. To mark the occasion, it was reprinted a few days later and is a prized possession in many Irish households. (Courtesy Mulqueen Collection)

observed that 'there's much more to Kiernan's team than what people are seeing.' He expanded: 'The session lasted no more than twenty minutes. The merits of the training were threefold: vigour, as to the forward effort, accuracy, as to the handling of the backs and most of all, speed, as to the support play of the forwards.'

Tom Kiernan was not easily pleased and always demanded the highest standards of those he played with and coached but even he was moved to comment that 'at the latter session, it was obvious to most onlookers that the Munster team was fitter and sharper than was the case for many years and that we would give the All Blacks a tough game. I was always of the belief that we had the skills.'

The Tackle

The morning of 31 October 1978 dawned wet and windy, prompting hope among the faithful that the conditions would suit Munster who could indulge in their traditional approach sometimes described rather vulgarly as 'boot, bite and bollock' and, who knows, with the fanatical Thomond Park crowd cheering them on, anything could happen. Ironically, though, the wind and rain gave way to a clear, blue sky and altogether perfect conditions in good time for the kick-off. Surely, now, that was Munster's last hope gone – but that did not deter more than 12,000 fans from making their way to Thomond Park and somehow finding a spot from which to view the action. The vantage points included hundreds seated on the 20-foot-high boundary wall, others perched on the towering trees immediately outside the ground and some even watched from the windows of houses at the Ballynanty end (since demolished).

The history-making Munster team of 1978. Back row (l–r): Sean Gavin Munster Branch president, Johnny Cole touch judge, Gerry McLoughlin, Les White, Moss Keane, Donal Spring, Colm Tucker, Pat Whelan, Brendan Foley, Corrie Thomas referee, Martin Walsh touch judge; front row (l–r): Tony Ward, Chris Cantillon, Moss Finn, Seamus Dennison, Donal Canniffe capt., Greg Barrett, Jimmy Bowen and Larry Moloney. (Courtesy *Limerick Leader*)

Andy Haden (far right) leads the All Blacks in the Haka. (Courtesy *Limerick Leader*)

The atmosphere was absolutely electric as the teams took the field, the All Blacks performed the haka and the Welsh referee Corris Thomas got proceedings under way.

The first few skirmishes saw the teams sizing each other up before an incident that was to be recorded in song and story occurred, described here – with just the slightest touch of hyperbole! – by Terry McLean in his book *Mourie's All Blacks*.

Seamus Dennison in action on that day of days. (Courtesy *Limerick Leader*)

In only the fifth minute, Seamus Dennison, him the fellow that bore the number 13 jersey in the centre, was knocked down in a tackle. He came from the Garryowen club which might explain his subsequent actions – to join that club, so it has been said, one must walk barefooted over broken glass, charge naked through searing fires, run the severest gauntlets and, as a final test of manhood, prepare with unfaltering gaze to make a catch of the highest ball ever kicked while aware that at least eight thundering members of your own team are about to knock you down, trample all over you and into the bargain hiss nasty words at you because you forgot to cry out 'Mark'.

Dennison was pretty badly hurt. Later, he was hurt again, more seriously. 'I think, Seamus', said the attending doctor, 'you would do well to rest by the sideline for two minutes.' 'Push off', said Seamus – they know that naughty word in Limerick, too. 'Seamus', said the doctor more earnestly, 'rest it for two minutes, that shoulder is quite damaged.' 'Push off', said Dennison, flatly, finally, forever. He was in pain. No question. But was he going to leave the field? Not bloody likely.

Moss Keane recalled the incident: 'It was the hardest tackle I have ever seen and lifted the whole team. That was the moment we knew we could win the game.'

Kiernan also acknowledged the importance of 'The Tackle': 'Tackling is as integral a part of rugby as is a majestic centre three-quarter break. The perfect timing and execution of a tackle gives me as much pleasure to watch as any other element of rugby. There were two noteworthy tackles during the match by Seamus Dennison. He was injured in the first and I thought he might have to come off. But he repeated the tackle some minutes later.'

Many years on, Stuart Wilson vividly recalled the Dennison tackles and spoke about them in remarkable detail and with commendable honesty: 'The move involved me coming in from the blindside wing and it had been working very well on tour. It was a workable move and it was paying off so we just kept rolling it out. Against Munster, the gap opened up brilliantly as it was supposed to except that there was this little guy called Seamus Dennison sitting there in front of me.'

Mark Donaldson briefly interrupted Wilson's train of thought to state that 'if you had a line-up parade and say, pick the rugby player to bring off that tackle, it just wouldn't be him but he almost singlehandedly set the whole trend for the day.'

Picking up the story again Wilson admitted that Dennison:

> just basically smacked the living daylights out of me. I dusted myself off and thought, I don't want to have to do that again. Ten minutes later, we called the same move again thinking we'd change it slightly but, no, it didn't work and I got hammered again. So two belts out of two moves and I said to the guys, that's it, I'm out of here for the rest of the afternoon and we'll just keep moving it wide.
>
> Things weren't working. The back line movements weren't going the way we expected. We were finding ourselves down in our own in-goal area instead of the other end where we expected to be. We didn't get a penalty shot, we couldn't even get a drop at goal, we had opportunities for tries but again their defensive strength was very good. They were playing with a huge amount of passion and their confidence was growing as each minute passed. We threw everything except the kitchen sink and the bus driver and the gear bags at them, but we couldn't get through. They went off at half time thinking, maybe we can roll these guys and I think that may have turned

the game for them. When they came out in the second half, nothing had changed. We thought that maybe we'd have a crack but it started just the same as the first. Wilson was right. The longer the game went on, so, too, did the self-belief of each and every Munster player reach stratospheric heights.

The game was eleven minutes old when the most famous try in the history of Munster rugby was scored. Tom Kiernan recalled: 'It came from a great piece of anticipation by Bowen who in the first place had to run around his man to get to Ward's kick ahead. He then beat two men and when finally tackled, managed to keep his balance and deliver the ball to Cantillon who went on to score. All of this was evidence of sharpness on Bowen's part.'

RTÉ came in for a lot of flak for their failure to cover the game live. They contracted out the coverage to two of their regular cameramen, Joe McCarthy and Pat Kavanagh, who did a two-camera shoot. 'We

Chris Cantillon scores Munster's try against the All Blacks in 1978. (Courtesy *Irish Examiner*)

Jimmy Bowen makes the all-important break that led to the Munster try against the All Blacks in 1978. (Courtesy *Irish Examiner*)

Pat Whelan celebrates the try. (Courtesy *Irish Examiner*)

were not allowed to film on the halfway line', says Joe. 'An official told us the crowd was too big, that we would have to set up on the 25.' Posterity has had to rely on this grainy footage, taken from a distance with inadequate technology, to understand the merits of a superb score. Nevertheless, it shows how well the move was planned and executed: Tony Ward's little kick from just outside his own 25, Jimmy Bowen's skill in gathering the ball, his magnificent weaving 50-yard sprint and perfect pass to the brilliantly supporting Chris Cantillon. The segment in question has been shown perhaps more than any other in the ensuing decades, most recently as the central element to a typically brilliant Guinness television commercial. As the wing forward finished off the move by touching down to the left of the All Blacks' posts at the Ballynanty end, a spectator can be seen to throw his coat high in the air, his neighbours to jump with joy and shout with total abandon, Pat Whelan to perform a jig of which Munster fan Michael Flatley might well be proud and for the 12,000-plus spectators to lose their reason. And when Tony Ward popped over the conversion to put Munster six points clear of their bewildered opponents, the Thomond Park crowd sensed that something very special was on the cards and responded accordingly. Chant after chant of 'M-U-N-S-T-E-R, M-U-N-S-T-E-R, M-U-N-S-T-E-R' rent the Limerick air, lifting the home side to hitherto unknown heights and shaking the visitors to their very core.

Very soon it would be 9–0. In the first five minutes, a towering Garryowen by skipper Canniffe had exposed the vulnerability of the New Zealand rearguard under the high ball. They were to be examined once or twice more but it was from a long range though badly struck penalty attempt by Ward – remarkably the only shot at goal all day – that full back Brian McKechnie knocked on some 15 yards from his line and close to where Cantillon had touched down a few minutes earlier. You could sense White, Whelan, McLoughlin & Co. in the front five of the Munster scrum smacking their lips as they settled for battle. A quick, straight put-in by Canniffe, a well-controlled heel, a smart pass by the scrum half to Ward and the inevitability of a drop goal. And that's exactly what happened.

It remained that way to half-time. In those days, there was no strident music or deafening public address announcements to prevent animated conversation. There was a considerable amount of that during the interval. People wondered aloud whether a miracle was about to unfold before their eyes. Nine points was a decent lead but it would hardly be enough against a team of the class of the All Blacks? The lads would surely tire the longer the game went on and the fitter, stronger tourists would take advantage. The doubts and qualms were understandable but incredibly they proved unfounded. Those nights in Fermoy were about to pay the richest dividend.

The All Blacks enjoyed the majority of forward possession but the harder they tried, the more they fell into the trap set by the wily Kiernan and so brilliantly carried out by each and every member of the Munster team. The tourists might have edged the line-out contest through Andy Haden and Frank Oliver but scrum half Mark Donaldson endured a miserable afternoon as the Munster forwards poured through and buried him in the Thomond Park turf. 'Their line-out was like a sieve', said Donal Spring.

And even when the ball reached the great Bryan Williams and Stuart Wilson on the wings, they were invariably on the back foot because of the pressure imposed on centres Bill Osborne (an early replacement for

Donal Spring later claimed the New Zealand line-out defence was like a sieve. In this shot, he links with Les White and Moss Keane to make the point graphically. (Courtesy *Limerick Leader*)

Brian Robertson), Lynn Jaffray and Eddie Dunn by Dennison, Greg Barrett, Larry Moloney, Moss Finn and Bowen. As the minutes passed and the All Blacks became more and more unsure as to what to try next, the Thomond Park hordes chanted 'M-U-N-S-T-E-R, M-U-N-S-T-E-R, M-U-N-S-T-E-R' to an ever-increasing crescendo until with, twelve minutes to go, the noise levels reached deafening proportions. And then ... a deep, probing kick by Ward put Wilson under further pressure. Eventually, he stumbled over the ball as it crossed the line and nervously conceded a 5-yard scrum. The Munster heel was disrupted but the ruck was won, Tucker gained possession and slipped a lovely little pass to Ward whose gifted feet and speed of thought enabled him in a twinkle to drop-kick a goal though surrounded by a swarm of black jerseys. So the game entered its final ten minutes with the All Blacks needing three scores to win and, of course, that was never going to happen.

Munster knew this; so, too, did the All Blacks. Stu Wilson admitted as much as he explained his part in Wardy's second drop goal:

> Tony Ward banged it down, it bounced a little bit, jigged here, jigged there, and I stumbled, fell over, and all of a sudden the heat was on me. They were good chasers. A kick is a kick – but if you have lots of good chasers on it, they make bad kicks look good. I looked up and realised – I'm not going to run out of here so I just dotted it down. I wasn't going to run that ball back out at them because five of those mad guys were coming down the track at me and I'm thinking, I'm being hit by these guys all day and I'm looking after my body, thank you. Of course it was a five-yard scrum and Ward banged over another drop goal. That was it, there was the game.

A high point for Munster arrived when they pushed the All Blacks off the ball at a scrum right in front of the stand and the melee ended up on the ground up against the perimeter wall. It looked like a bout of fisticuffs was about to break out but common sense prevailed. Why? Well, the story doing the rounds at the time was that Moss Keane turned to Andy Haden and said something like 'you've already lost the match, you don't want to lose the fight as well'. In his autobiography, however, Moss went no further than to comment: 'Maybe I did say that but it

The All Blacks' Andy Haden and Munster's Brendan Foley contest a first half line-out watched by the crowds on the wall at the Ballynanty end and in the neighbouring houses. (Courtesy *Limerick Leader*)

doesn't sound like me and I have no recollection of saying it. They were very sporting on the day. Still, we were the better team and it was a proud moment to have beaten such opponents and prouder again that we kept them from scoring.'

To be fair, Andy Haden was one of the greatest second-row forwards of that or any other era. He later claimed that he had won his line-out battle with the Kerry man and delighted in claiming that 'I had a little bit of success marking Moss. You know that when the opposition half-back calls the line-out – 22, 34, 22 – and Moss turns to him and says, "oh, f***, not me again."'

The final whistle duly sounded with Munster twelve points ahead but the heroes of the hour still had to get off the field and reach the safety of the dressing room without being torn apart by the overjoyed masses. Bodies were embraced, faces were kissed, backs were pummelled, the gauntlet was run. Even then, though, they were not allowed to rest on their laurels and the chants of 'M-U-N-S-T-E-R, M-U-N-S-T-E-R, M-U-N-S-T-E-R' echoed and echoed around the ground until the

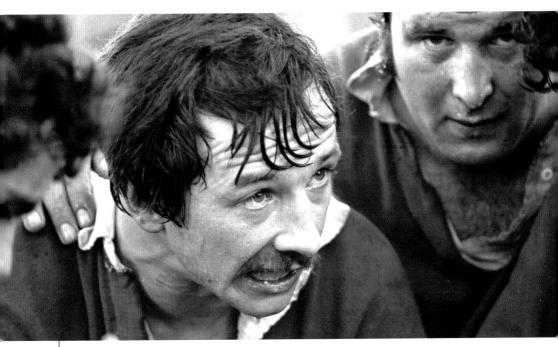

Captain Fantastic: the pressure of leading Munster to victory over the All Blacks shows on the face of skipper Donal Canniffe. (*Irish Examiner*)

players were left with little option but to come out again and salute their delirious supporters.

'It seemed as if no time had elapsed from the final whistle until we were engulfed from all sides', said Donal Canniffe. 'We barely had the opportunity to shake hands with our opposite numbers before the crowd invaded the pitch. We somehow made it back to the dressing room but there was such a din from the crowd in the stand overhead who were kicking their feet and from those outside who were still chanting MUNSTER-MUNSTER that I felt we should go back out. It was a wonderful thing for the crowd to be acknowledged by the team coming back out having played their part on such an historic occasion.'

Tony Ward recalls: 'It's the only time I've experienced it, maybe in GAA from time to time, seeing grown men cry. At the time, teams didn't do laps of honour or anything like that. We went into the dressing room with the crowd going berserk. They weren't leaving that ground without getting us back on the field again – and they did. I can still remember it. It would send shivers down your spine. Everything about the occasion just smacked of raw Limerick and Munster passion.'

Even the All Blacks seemed impressed with the sense of joy all about them. Andy Haden recalled 'the sea of red supporters all over the pitch after the game, you could hardly get off for the wave of celebration that was going on. It was there even before the finish when they knew the game was won.' Stuart Wilson described how 'they just swarmed the pitch. It's a little ground at Thomond Park. Normally the crowd would have rushed out to try and get an autograph from the All Blacks because nine times out of ten, the All Blacks would have won. That day, they basically bypassed us and went straight to hug their players. The game has become a talking point from one generation to the next. For those who saw the game, it was fantastic, for those who played in it, it was even better. The whole of Thomond Park glowed in the warmth that someone had done a job on the Blacks.'

The All Blacks manager Russ Thomas smiled affably as he looked on and proved himself a good loser, saying 'it was a great effort by Munster and a wonderful thing for Irish rugby. We made more mistakes today than we did in our four games combined up to now. We paid for them but we will learn from today.'

Almost as Thomas spoke, however, came the sad news that Donal Canniffe's father Dan, a retired Garda sergeant, had died suddenly in Cork while awaiting news of the game in Limerick. Devastated, Donal sped home to join his family.

Vice-captain Pat Whelan took over Donal's captaincy role at the official dinner in the Limerick Inn Hotel that night, an occasion on which the tourists further demonstrated their sense of sportsmanship and acceptance of a fair result by entering the function arm in arm singing 'Hi ho, Hi ho, it's off to work we go.'

'We obviously had been beaten by a team that was better than us on the day and were the first Irish team to beat the All Blacks and in the best traditions of Irish rugby, we thought we'd march in there singing that little ditty', explained Russell Thomas. 'I recall that it was very well received and I think the Irishmen felt that these guys can take their wins but they can take their losses as well.'

Controversially, the All Blacks coach, Jack Gleeson (usually a man capable of accepting the good with the bad and who passed away of cancer within twelve months of the tour), in an unguarded (although possibly misunderstood) moment on the following day, let slip his innermost thoughts on the game.

The great John B. Keane delighted in the Munster victory in his *Limerick Leader* column. (Courtesy *Limerick Leader*)

Hold the front page: the match made big news for *The Irish Press* and the *Cork Examiner*. (Courtesy *The Irish Press* and *Cork Examiner*)

'We were up against a team of kamikaze tacklers', he lamented. 'We set out on this tour to play fifteen-man rugby but if teams were to adopt the Munster approach and do all they could to stop the All Blacks from playing an attacking game, then the tour and the game would suffer.'

It was interpreted by the majority of observers as a rare piece of sour grapes from a group who had accepted the defeat in good spirit and it certainly did nothing to diminish Munster respect for the All Blacks and their proud rugby tradition. Tom Kiernan and Andy Haden, rugby standard bearers of which their respective countries were justifiably proud, saw things in a similar light. 'Jack's comment was made in the context of the game and meant as a compliment', Haden said. 'Indeed, it was probably a little suggestion to his own side that perhaps we should imitate their efforts and emulate them in that department.' Tom Kiernan concurred with this line of thought: 'I thought he was actually paying a compliment to the Munster spirit. Kamikaze pilots were very brave men. That's what I took out of that. I didn't think it was a criticism of Munster.'

And Stuart Wilson? 'It was meant purely as a compliment. We had been travelling through the UK and winning all our games. We were playing a nice, open style. But we had never met a team that could get up in our faces and tackle us off the field. Every time you got the ball, you didn't get one player tackling you, you got four. Kamikaze means people are willing to die for the cause and that was the way with every Munster man that day. Their strengths were that they were playing for Munster, that they had a home Thomond Park crowd and they took strength from the fact that they were playing one of the best teams in the world.'

As the tour went on and the Kiwis won one game after another, the more Munster people urged them on in the hope that they would be the only team to have lowered the colours of Graham Mourie's All Blacks. The New Zealanders had won every other match when they arrived in the Cardiff Arms Park shortly before Christmas for 18 December and traditional end-of-tour clash with the Barbarians. It was a thrilling game and it looked as if the All Blacks were about to founder at the final hurdle, that was until Eddie Dunn, one of those to suffer most at Thomond Park a few weeks earlier, sent over a drop goal in the dying minutes to see the tourists home by 18–16. The decibel levels of cheering in Munster very nearly drowned out those in Auckland and Otago.

You could rely on Terry McLean to be fair and sporting in his reaction to the Thomond Park defeat. Unlike Kiernan and Haden, he scorned Jack Gleeson's 'kamikaze' comment, stating:

> it was a stern, severe criticism which wanted in fairness on two grounds. It did not sufficiently praise the spirit of Munster or the presence within the one team of 15 men who each emerged from the match much larger than life-size. Secondly, it was disingenuous or, more accurately, naive. Gleeson thought it sinful that Ward had not once passed the ball. It was worse, he said, that Munster had made aggressive defence the only arm of their attack. Now, what on earth, it could be asked, was Kiernan to do with his team? He held a fine hand with top trumps in Spring, Cantillon, Foley and Whelan in the forwards and Canniffe, Ward, Dennison, Bowen and Moloney in the backs. Tommy Kiernan wasn't born yesterday. He played to the strength of his team and upon the suspected weaknesses of the All Blacks.

Tony Ward kicks the drop goal that put Munster's win over the All Blacks beyond doubt. (*Irish Examiner*)

You could hardly be fairer than that – even Graham Mourie himself in his 1983 autobiography was not far behind when observing: 'Munster were just too good. From the first time Stu Wilson was crashed to the ground as he entered the back line to the last time Mark Donaldson was thrown backwards as he ducked around the side of a maul. They were too good. We were unable to vary our play in the face of their inspired play. Unable to run the ball, we seemed incapable of kicking it effectively. Munster was a turning point of the tour.'

Referring to the sporting manner in which they accepted defeat, Tom Kiernan observed that 'the players congratulated us after the game and wished us the best, as did their manager Russ Thomas. I thought they were very gracious. And then Graham Mourie was a great captain and I think his example spread throughout the team.'

New Zealand Press Association correspondent Ron Palenski who co-authored Mourie's book and was in Thomond Park that day, wrote: 'Mourie's teams were not always winners and the All Blacks can hardly have had more comprehensive beatings than that by Munster in 1978. It was the manner of their loss or more fairly, Munster's win, which stuck in the mind. The tiny, intimate Thomond Park ground could not hold any more people – and all of them urged Munster on. It was eerie.'

One of the nicest tributes of all came from New Zealand photographer Peter Bush. He covered numerous All Black tours, was close friends with most of their players and a canny one when it came to finding the ideal position from which to snap his pictures. He was perched precariously on the pillars at the entrance to the pitch as the celebrations went on, which he described twenty years later in his book *Who Said It's Only a Game?*

> I climbed up on a gate at the end of the game to get this photo and in the middle of it all is Moss Keane, one of the great characters of Irish rugby, with an expression of absolute elation. The All Blacks lost 12–0 to a side that played with as much passion as I have ever seen on a rugby field. The great New Zealand prop Gary Knight said to me later: 'We could have played them for a fortnight and we still wouldn't have won.' I was doing a little radio piece after the game and got hold of Moss Keane and said 'Moss, I wonder if …' and he said, 'ho, ho, we beat you bastards'. With that, he flung his arms around me and dragged me with him into the shower. I finally managed to disentangle myself and killed the tape. I didn't mind really because it had been a wonderful day.

Such praise emanating from a great rugby nation like New Zealand came, of course, as sweet music to the ears of all Munster supporters. Closer to home, many of the tributes sounded close to self-praise. But there were those that struck a chord. Micky English was on the wrong end of a close affair against the All Blacks at Thomond Park in 1963 so one understood what he meant when commenting that 'it's been a long time waiting but I'm delighted that when the All Blacks were first beaten in Ireland, it had to be in Limerick and in Thomond Park. And I'm glad I was alive to see it.' Fighting back tears of emotion, Kevin Quilligan, president of the IRFU and a Limerick man, described it as 'a tremendous day for Irish rugby. It was an incredible performance to hold a touring team scoreless but Munster took them on in magnificent fashion and it was a fantastic occasion.'

It certainly was and the memories live on to this day. So, too, the celebrations continued. New programmes, autographed by the players, were printed, ties, car stickers and badges flooded the market, the Munster Branch held a banquet at which the heroes received specially created Munster caps, and every conceivable anniversary has been marked in every part of the province and far beyond as well. As Donal Spring put it: 'few teams have dined out so well and so often on one match as we have.' Moss Keane was being a little rueful when he suggested in his autobiography that 'perhaps it was too famous. I get embarrassed when people talk of how we humiliated the All Blacks at Thomond Park. We didn't. We beat them, that was all.'

Be that as it may, Big Moss (who passed away to nationwide sadness at the premature age of fifty-two on 5 October 2010) did not hide his enjoyment of and support for John Breen's play *Alone It Stands* which he first saw in the Dunamaise Theatre, Portlaoise. The part of Moss (6 foot 5 inches, 18 stone) was played at the time by Niamh McGrath whom he described as 'a petite girl of about five feet-feck-all bulked out with shoulder pads. She went about the stage tackling and mauling everyone in sight. She was brilliant.' On another occasion, they were all invited to a charity show in the Belltable Theatre in Limerick. Keane and his second-row partner and great mate Brendan Foley were seated alongside each other.

'At one point', says Moss, 'he leaned over and whispered, that small girl playing you, Karen Scully …'.

'What about her?'

'She jumps higher than you ever did.'

9

42-Year Gap Bridged

The victory over the All Blacks may have been fittingly celebrated but not to the extent that this Munster team could be prevented from completing a Grand Slam in the Interprovincial Championship over the following weeks. They defeated Leinster 12–3; Ulster 11–6 and Connacht by 19–3 at Thomond Park. With so much talent available and more coming on stream annually, it was hardly a surprise that the 1980 Australians came a cropper at Musgrave Park. Tony Ward along with Christy Cantillon and the Shannon trio of Gerry McLoughlin, Brendan Foley and Colm Tucker were the only survivors of the 1978 heroics. Wardy had another great game, this time contributing eleven points in a 15–6 victory over the Wallabies.

Garryowen reached their third successive Munster Cup final at Thomond Park in 1979, with a star-studded side containing five internationals – Larry Moloney, Seamus Dennison, Tony Ward, Pat Whelan and Mick Sherry – lining out hot favourites against Young Munster. The story goes that in a desperate attempt to prove the bookmakers wrong, a black-and-amber bedecked fan walking to Thomond Park well in advance of kick-off time called into St Munchin's Church and knelt in front of a statue of the Blessed Virgin. Ruefully noting that it was dressed in light blue and white, he blessed himself, looked up and implored: 'Even though you are wearing their ******* colours, just this once could you help us to win the cup. After all, it's been forty-one years since we have done so.'

Alas, his prayers were in vain. Even though the conditions for that

1979 decider were perfect and the customary huge Thomond Park throng was in attendance, skipper Pat Whelan adopted a safety-first policy and once Ward put Garryowen ahead with a penalty, he closed up shop and that was how a poor game ended.

However, that campaign reawakened the kind of passion and spirit for which Young Munster were renowned. Twelve months later they were back in a Thomond Park final, with the opposition this time provided by Bohemians. Known as the 'wasps' for their black-and-amber jerseys, their fourth cup triumph was long overdue and the fear was that if they could not pull it off under the shrewd coaching team of Tony Grant and former Ireland prop forward Mick O'Callaghan, they might never do so. The fact that twelve of the side had come through the club's under-age ranks made success even more of an imperative. Forty-two years had elapsed since they had won the first Thomond Park cup final in 1938 which in turn meant that one of Irish rugby's greatest players and characters, Tom Clifford, did not have a medal in his locker. Into the same category fell legends of the club like Willie Allen, Pax O'Kane and Martin O'Connell, to mention but a few.

The Munster team that defeated Romania at Thomond Park in 1980. Back row (l–r): Rory Moroney, Gerry McLoughlin, Moss Keane, John Daly, Donal Spring, Brendan Foley, Anthony O'Leary, Brendan O'Connor, Michael Wallace Munster Branch president; front row (l–r): Declan Aherne, Gerry Casey, Tony Ward, Pat Whelan capt., Peter Rolls, Jimmy Bowen and Colm Murphy. (Courtesy *Limerick Leader*)

Bohemians had also suffered a number of very frustrating years since the golden era of 1958–62. The cream of those teams was scattered far and wide and the club was in the doldrums for quite a while. However, a youth policy began to pay a rich dividend towards the late 1970s and the arrival of a number of outstanding recruits from St Munchin's College led by two Teds – Mulcahy and Sheehan – Steve Hennessy, Peter Rolls and Michael Murphy plus the steel provided by tough, experienced forwards like John Madigan, Pat O'Donnell and Ken Rennison meant that they were worthy cup finalists in 1980.

The clash of Young Munster and Bohemians was a fourth successive all-Limerick decider and also a novel pairing resulting in yet another capacity Thomond Park crowd on a fine April afternoon. It was a terrific game which Munsters edged by 9–7 and even then they prevailed only because a late conversion attempt by Bohs' Steve Hennessy sailed inches to the wrong side of their posts. Mick Bromell, a product of Thomond RFC and a wing who wore the red of Munster on several occasions, put Bohs into the lead with a drop goal before Gerry Casey levelled matters with a Young Munster penalty before half-time. The vital score came five minutes after the break from Young Munster's number eight Mick Sheehan who crashed over for a try that Casey converted. Even though playing into the fresh breeze, Bohs had the better of matters from there to the finish and duly got to within striking distance with a try by out-half Mick Wixted. Young Munsters were able to breathe easily again when Hennessy's conversion for a draw just missed. Shortly afterwards they were belting out a particularly joyous rendering of 'Beautiful, beautiful Munsters' under the baton of an exuberant Willie Allen:

Beautiful, beautiful Munsters
Star of my soul fade away.
I sigh when I think of Young Munster
With whom I played many a game.

Now there was Bohs in red, UCC,
Garryowen are the boys in blue,
With Sundays Well, 'twould be hard to tell,
What the Dolphin boys would do,
and Cons all white made a right good fight,
In the final well they showed,

But they all gave it up, for the Bateman Cup
Was won by the Yellow Road.

It was a memorable occasion for the players themselves and also some outstanding officials who had remained loyal through all the lean years. Joe Kennedy, one of Limerick rugby's greatest gentlemen, gave many years of invaluable service to the game as honorary secretary of the North Munster Branch and was ever present when any team in black and amber took to the field. One of the key men throughout the campaign was out-half Gerry Casey, whose father, Clem, wore his fingers to the bone year after year as Young Munsters went from one cup disappointment to another. His elation when the barren spell was broken after forty-two years and that his son had played a major role in the success was palpable. Clem was later elected Mayor of Limerick and president of the Munster Branch. There, too, was Pat Cross, short of stature but stout of heart and whose crash tackling in midfield had been crucial. Pat was a son of Micky Cross, another outstanding Young Munster man.

Young Munster, Munster Cup winners 1979/80. Back row (l–r): D. McCarthy, G. McNamara, Brian O'Connor, M. Sheehan, J. McNamara, Brendan O'Connor, J. Murphy, G. Casey; front row (l–r): F. Brosnahan, M. Moore, P. McGrath, R. Daly capt., P. Cross, E. Costelloe, E. Madden. (Courtesy *Limerick Leader*)

It was a busy weekend for prop forward John Murphy: he was back in Thomond Park twenty-four hours later to help Thomond defeat UCC by 15–9 in the final of the Munster Junior Cup. Declan Kidney, who was to coach Ireland to the Six Nations Grand Slam in 2009 and Munster to two Heineken European Cup titles, did all the scoring for College that day with two drop goals and a penalty.

The 1980 senior final teams were:

Young Munster: G. McNamara, M. Moore, F. Brosnahan, P. Cross, D. McCarthy, G. Casey, E. Costelloe, Brendan O'Connor, P. Mullane, J. Murphy, Brian O'Connor, R. Daly capt., J. McNamara, M. Sheehan, E. Madden.

Bohemians: S. Hennessy, B. Barron, J. O'Grady, P. Rolls, M. Bromell, M. Wixted, M. Pierse, T. Hensman, P. O'Donnell, T. Mulcahy capt., J. Madigan, K. Rennison, D. Muirhead, M. Murphy, T. Sheehan.

Referee: Michael Reddan.

Young Munster battled their way into the final again in 1982 when their Limerick rivals Shannon provided the opposition. Thomond Park coped well with the huge attendance on a sunny April afternoon. Just as Bohemians had missed a last-minute conversion to draw the 1980 final against Munsters, now Young Munster's hopes were dashed when Gerry Casey just failed to add the points to a late Francis Brosnahan try that would have earned them a share of the spoils.

Terry Fitzgerald, an outstanding full back who had starred in the club's triumphs in 1977 and 1978, led Shannon to victory. Players of the calibre of Gerry McLoughlin, Brendan Foley and Colm Tucker assumed superstar status and were joined up front by the outstanding Connacht and Ireland second-row Mick Moylett and powerful number eight Niall O'Donovan (a son of Jim of the famous 1960 team). The eight/nine partnership of O'Donovan and Oliver (Sonny) Kiely played a huge part in Shannon's success that day, just as it would on countless occasions in the future. O'Donovan went on to become a major influence on a succession of Munster teams in the professional era. Fitzgerald kicked all of Shannon's nine points, Young Munsters staying in touch with a Gerry Casey penalty.

A spectacular Michael Bradley try for Cork Constitution foiled Shannon's hopes of a repeat in the 1983 final and it was Young Munster's turn to savour once again the glory when they qualified to take on Waterpark in the 1984 decider. While it was Young Munster's third final appearance in five years, it was a complete novelty for the Waterford club who had qualified thanks to wins over Highfield and Bohemians. They brought a large and colourful contingent of supporters from the south-east to Thomond Park and it looked for quite a time that they might upset pre-match calculations. A single point separated the sides until the closing minutes when Gerry Casey kicked a Young Munster penalty and flanker Kieran Considine clinched the issue with a try to make the final score 17–9. Derek McCarthy also scored a first-half try for Munsters with Casey sending over a couple of penalties and a drop goal. Waterpark had a Carl Phelan try and penalty and conversion by Brendan Moran. This certainly was a golden era for the Young Munster club as they went on to defeat Thomond in a Munster Junior Cup final replay thus becoming the first Limerick club to complete the senior/junior double in the same year.

The 1984 Munster Senior Cup final teams were:

Young Munster: G. McNamara, M. Moore, P. Cross, F. Brosnahan capt., D. McCarthy, G. Casey, J. Moloney, J. Fitzgerald, P. McGrath, J. Murphy, R. Daly, P. Meehan, K. Considine, M. Sheehan, G. Clohessy.

Waterpark: G. Walsh, T. Eiffe, J. O'Neill, C. Phelan, E. Jackman, B. Moran capt., A. Walsh, B. Murphy, R. Walsh, G. Walsh, M. McNamara, L. Whelan, B. O'Connor, P. Sheehan, C. Anderson. Replacement: M. Purcell for G. Walsh.

Referee: Stan Fuller.

The 1984 Australians were the next touring side to visit Thomond Park to play Munster and for once the venue was found wanting: a pea souper of a fog enveloped the ground and reduced visibility to little more than 30 yards. It never relented for a minute and while there was every credit due to the two teams for their honest commitment throughout the eighty minutes, that was small consolation for a huge crowd that saw little or nothing of the action.

This was arguably the finest Wallabies squad to visit Thomond Park. They won their four Tests against England, Ireland, Scotland and Wales with their outstanding out-half Mark Ella scoring a try in each one. Munster fielded a useful side captained by the outstanding Donal Lenihan in the second-row and included future Irish coach Eddie O'Sullivan on the right wing. Fog or not, they were never going to put a halt to the march of this Australian side who emerged worthy winners by 31–19. Scrum half Nick Farr-Jones was on the threshold of a fine career, the highlight of which would be victory in the 1991 World Cup when he was one of their three try scorers. The others were touched down by Simon Poidevin and Ian Williams.

In fairness to Munster, they would have been a lot closer at the finish had it not been for the remarkably accurate goal-kicking of Aussie full back Roger Gould who was able, in spite of the fog, to pick out the goalposts well enough to put over five penalties and two conversions. Tony Ward maintained his enviable record of invariably coming up trumps on the biggest days by almost matching Gould with five penalties and a conversion while the Munster tries came from Cork Constitution full back John Barry, and Michael Kiernan whose drop goal later that season would earn for Ireland a dramatic victory over England and a second Triple Crown in four years. Skipper Lenihan was an integral part of those two signal achievements.

The 1984 teams at Thomond Park were:

Australia: R. Gould, I. Williams, M. Hawker, A. Slack capt., R. Hanley, M. Ella, N. Farr-Jones, E. Rodriguez, M. Lawton, G. Burrow, S. Williams, S. A. G. Cutler, D. Cody, S. Tuynman, S. Poidevin.

Munster: J. Barry (Cork Constitution), E. O'Sullivan (Garryowen), M. Kiernan (Lansdowne), J. O'Neill (Waterpark), D. Aherne, A. Ward (both St Mary's College), M. Bradley (Cork Con.), T. Hennessy (London Irish), P. Derham (Cork Con.), T. Mulcahy (Bohemians), D. Lenihan capt. (Cork Con.), M. Moylett (Shannon), P. O'Hara (Sundays Well), P. Collins (Highfield), W. Sexton (Garryowen).

Although the importance of the Munster Senior Cup diminished considerably with the advent of the All-Ireland League in 1990 followed by the arrival of professionalism in 1995, and there were indications as the 1980s moved on that change was on the way, however, until such time as it was implemented, the Munster Cup remained the main target for every club in the province

Accordingly, Shannon's pride at completing the 1986–88 hat-trick of titles was understandable. The year 1986 was the centenary of the great old competition and Shannon's achievement in going through the season unbeaten – played 28, won 27, drew 1 – was hugely impressive, although with players of the experience of Terry Fitzgerald, Sonny Kiely, Gerry McLoughlin, Mick Moylett, skipper Ger McMahon, Niall O'Donovan and Mick Fitzgibbon, it was not too much of a surprise. Oddly enough, though, they were so much better than Garryowen in the cup final that they probably took more satisfaction from a 21–6 defeat of a particularly strong Cork Constitution side in the final of the Senior League.

However, the cup is the cup and Shannon justified their favouritism in a one-sided decider. A typical Sonny Kiely try on the stroke of half-time relieved any worries caused by an early John Duggan penalty for Garryowen; a second try by the scrum half along with two penalties by Fitzgerald and a drop goal by John Pearse saw them home safely. Eddie O'Sullivan, usually a wing, was pressed into out-half service by Garryowen and included a drop goal in a useful all-round display. It mattered little … it was time once again for the 'Isle' to ring out over Thomond Park and the surrounding countryside. The centenary Munster Cup final teams were:

Shannon: T. Fitzgerald, N. O'Shea, S. Minihan, J. Willis, M. Ryan, J. Pearse, O. Kiely, T. Healy, N. Glynn (acting captain in place of injured G. McMahon), G. McLoughlin, M. Moylett, T. Heffernan, R. Irwin, N. O'Donovan, M. Fitzgibbon.

Garryowen: J. Duggan capt., D. Moore, K. O'Connor, G. Griffin, M. Long, E. O'Sullivan, G. Fitzgerald, J. Cleary, M. Fitzgerald, B. O'Kane, R. Sheehan, P. O'Leary, M. Sherry, D. Leonard, W. Sexton. Replacement: M. Dawson for Duggan.

Referee: Ronnie McDowell.

Shannon were not going to rest on their laurels. In 1987 they travelled to Musgrave Park for the final and defeated Highfield 16–9 with the irrepressible Kiely again scoring two tries. They now had their sights firmly set on the hat-trick last achieved by UCC in 1935/37. The 1988 campaign was moving along sweetly until an unlikely hurdle in the shape of Old Crescent presented itself. The first meeting ended in a nine-all draw and the sides were still level at the end of normal time in the replay. Thomond Park could hardly believe it when Crescent edged into a two-point lead in the dying minutes of extra time but Shannon were not to be denied: Kiely to Pearse, drop goal from 40 yards.

The three-in-a-row was still far from being a done deal. The Shannon v Cork Constitution semi-final at Thomond Park resulted in another draw, the replay in a Musgrave Park quagmire in a 6–3 Shannon victory before it was back to Thomond Park for another decider against Garryowen. It was a keenly contested affair with the decisive difference a Shannon try by Mick Galwey to augment two penalties and a drop goal by Johnny Pearse against three Nicky Barry penalties for Garryowen.

10

1980s

Fire – and a Badly Needed New Stand

Ever since the first Munster Cup final was contested at Thomond Park in 1938, the old wooden stand had accommodated 1,000 spectators on innumerable occasions and played a very significant part in creating the kind of special atmosphere for which the venue has always been renowned. Nevertheless, there were those who believed it had outlived its usefulness and when it was badly damaged by fire in 1988 the sense of regret among Thomond Park regulars was not all that noticeable. Indeed, there was a body of opinion that believed a member of Bohemians leaving his clubhouse late one night would have served the cause better had he 'neglected' to notice the smoke billowing from under the seats. In any case, the fire brigade was quickly on the scene and managed to limit the damage to about 30 per cent of the structure. As it transpired, a fire in the stand at Bradford City Football Club a short time previously led to new health and safety regulations in the UK and Ireland and the Limerick structure was duly condemned.

Funding a replacement was always going to be as expensive as it was essential. Thomond Park without a stand was unimaginable. The North Munster Branch led by honorary treasurer Michael Wallace and chairman Charlie Quaid launched a drive that included members of the committee actually going door to door to sell tickets for a raffle. The response was highly favourable and took off when super-salesman Pat Webb joined the team, the result being that sufficient money was raised for the erection of a new stand. It was built by the Lynch company from Ennis with Elliott McGuire as architects and Michael Punch & Partners as engineers. It was opened by A. R. (Ronnie) Dawson, president of the IRFU, on 10 March 1990.

The occasion was marked by a game between the USA Eagles and an Irish under-25 selection which the home side won 17–10. Bohemians also acquired a new pavilion as the original had been damaged in the fire and this in turn was opened the following September by IRFU president Tony Browne, followed by a match between Bohs and the Wolfhounds.

While the Munster Cup still remained the event that meant most to rugby followers in the province, it became more and more apparent that the game was facing irrevocable change. The Munster Senior League had played second fiddle to the cup but now assumed new significance with qualification for several clubs for the impending All-Ireland League dependant on their finishing positions in that competition. However, that was far from the minds of Shannon when they travelled to Cork in search of a cup four-in-a-row in 1989. The final opposition was provided

(L–r): A. R. (Ronnie) Dawson, president of the IRFU, and Munster Branch president Charlie Quaid officially open the rebuilt Thomond Park stand. Looking on is Christy (Tasty) McCarthy, one of the great characters of Munster rugby for many years. (Courtesy Charlie Quaid)

by a Constitution side packed with international and interprovincial players and the expectations of a great game were high. Shannon were leading 12–10 with time almost up when they strayed offside close to their own posts and Kenny Murphy held his nerve to land the penalty that earned Constitution their twenty-second Munster Cup.

It was back to Thomond Park for the 1990 final. UCC had played five cup games in as many weeks immediately before, including three semi-final meetings with Dolphin before taking on Young Munster; UCC were no match for the fired-up Greenfields club in the decider. These were great days for the Young Munster. They had opened the superb new pavilion at Tom Clifford Park the previous October and they would not be denied. Gerry Casey was again their scorer-in-chief with a try, conversion and two penalties on the way to a 19–0 victory. Ger Copeley with a try and a Mike Benson drop goal completed the scoring. Casey (who lined out on the wing and contributed fifty-six points over four cup games), Ger McNamara, Francis Brosnahan and Pat Cross were the survivors from the successful side ten years earlier.

'Beautiful, beautiful Munsters' was sung for days afterwards but it was another great rugby anthem that rang out in 1991 and 1992. On the first of those two fateful years, Young Munsters were red-hot favourites as they lined out against Shannon at Thomond Park. They did so on the back of a series of fine performances culminating in their promotion to Division One of the All Ireland League. By now, though, winning Munster Cups had become second nature to Shannon and they were waiting in the long grass when the teams took to the field in front of the usual capacity cup final attendance. Young Billy O'Shea had captained Crescent College to the Munster Schools Cup the previous season and he completely turned the game in Shannon's favour early on with a couple of penalties and a try that he converted himself. Jim Galvin added a penalty and even if Mike Benson landed a drop goal and two penalties, there was no way back for Young Munsters. Cue 'There is an Isle'.

If the Shannon fans sang the great anthem with their customary relish in 1991, they belted it out with even greater gusto twelve months later when they more or less perpetrated daylight robbery against Munsters. The black-and-amber boys looked the better side for much of the game and led 7–3 into the dying minutes when Shannon initiated a last desperate attack into the Ballynanty end on the stand side of the pitch. It was Jim Galvin, in the game as a replacement for a short few minutes, who levelled the scores by just beating the cover to dive over in the corner for a try. And as the usual total hush fell over the ground – another great tribute to both the traditions of Thomond Park and the Young Munster faithful – John Pearse landed a magnificent conversion from the edge of touch to leave Shannon winners by 9–7. It was their ninth Munster Cup – their eighth in fifteen years. Far from being satisfied, however, Shannon now set their sights on conquering all before them at national level.

The All-Ireland League

Plans were under way through the mid- to late 1980s for the introduction of an All-Ireland Club League. The IRFU came up with several ideas as to how best it could be organised and who the participants should be. After a considerable degree of controversy and disagreement, it was decided that there would be a Division One of nine clubs, with ten in Division Two and those left outside to battle for places in subsequent years through the provincial leagues.

Positions in the Munster Senior Leagues of 1987/88, 1988/89 and 1989/90 were the determining factor in Munster and the top three admitted to the AIL were Shannon (31 points), Cork Constitution (28) and Garryowen (26). This trio, along with Lansdowne, Wanderers, St Mary's College, Ballymena, Instonians and Malone, made it to Division One. Sundays Well with twenty-five points were admitted to Division Two and were joined by Greystones, Old Wesley, Terenure College, Bangor, Church of Ireland Young Men's Society (CIYMS), North of Ireland Football Club (NIFC) and Corinthians. Interestingly, not very long afterwards, Bangor, CIYMS and NIFC no longer enjoyed senior status.

The AIL duly got under way – without a title sponsor – on 6 October 1990, and the first fixture at Thomond Park resulted in an 18–9 victory for Shannon over Malone. Significantly, the great Mick Galwey scored two tries that day in the first of numerous outstanding performances he would turn in for Shannon in the competition for years to follow. The bookmakers had installed Wanderers and Ballymena, the champions of Leinster and Ulster respectively, as tournament favourites but even they had underestimated the strength of Munster rugby and the burning desire of the clubs to put their Ulster and Leinster rivals in their place. Garryowen and Young Munster defeated Wanderers and Terenure on the opening day and set the tone for many years of Munster AIL domination.

As luck would have it, the draw in the inaugural year meant that Garryowen and Cork Constitution would meet in the final series of matches. The Dooradoyle ground did remarkably well to accommodate 9,000 spectators, an indication of how the new competition had captured the public imagination. The Michael Bradley skippered Constitution came out on top by 9–3 when their supremacy at the set scrum earned them a crucial second-half penalty try.

Meanwhile, Young Munster were earning promotion from Division Two, meaning that Limerick now had three teams in the top division and fans were relishing the prospect of so many local derbies. This was serious business, a fact appreciated by the Insurance Corporation of Ireland who came on board as sponsor. Healthy gate receipts and handsome sponsorship deals meant that coaches and players were being paid meaningful sums of money, with Garryowen setting down a marker when they brought Murray Kidd from New Zealand to Dooradoyle as head coach. Out of luck in 1991, they left little to chance the following season and emerged worthy champions under the captaincy of the many-times-capped Philip Danaher and with Kiwi second-row Brent Anderson emerging as the player of the season.

The Limerick derby that caught public attention that season featured Shannon and Garryowen in the fourth round at which point they were both favourably placed. Although Thomond Park should have been unable to cater for 15,000 spectators, that is the figure widely accepted as the number that witnessed the battle of Limerick's big two. Michael O'Flaherty in his excellent book on Limerick rugby, *The Home of the Spirit*, described developments.

> Unbeaten table toppers Shannon faced Garryowen who were just one point behind. A record 15,000 crowd filled every vantage point in this famous old ground for one of the greatest club games ever staged at a local venue. With the league at the halfway stage, it was realistic to believe the eventual winners would be front runners for title success. Shannon may have been pre-match favourites particularly when Nicky Barry injured an ankle in training and was forced to watch the proceedings from

the stand. Garryowen problems were compounded when left wing Gary Quilligan was stretchered off after four minutes and flanker Paul Hogan was forced to retire after half an hour.

However, Garryowen overcame these setbacks to turn in a magnificent display and emerge with a totally deserved 20–9 victory. While it was a superb team effort, two players – Brent Anderson and Keith Wood – featured prominently throughout the eighty minutes of play. Shannon, playing with the wind in the first half, fell behind to a Kenny Smith penalty before Mick Galwey forced his way over for a try that Billy O'Shea converted. After 25 minutes, Wood got in for a try that Smith converted but an O'Shea penalty regained the lead for Shannon at the interval. Garryowen controlled the second half and went in front with a Dan Larkin drop goal and tries by Ger Manning and Richard Wallace and a conversion by Smith. At the finish, Garryowen were deserving winners and they also took over league leadership with three series remaining.

The Garryowen team that defeated Shannon in the 1991/92 All-Ireland League game at Thomond Park. Back row (l–r): D. Henshaw, D. O'Sullivan, P. Hogan, K. Wood, L. Lannan, R. Costelloe, B. Cronin, B. Anderson, D. Costelloe; front row (l–r): G. Quilligan, D. Larkin, P. Danaher, I. Barry, K. Smith, R. Wallace. (Courtesy *Limerick Leader*)

Shannon: Pat Murray capt., Billy O'Shea, Niall O'Shea, Bobby Roche, David Sheahan, Jim Galvin, Oliver Kiely, Mark Allen, Paddy Kenny, Mick Fitzgerald (Pat McLoughlin), Mick Moylett, Paddy O'Grady, Kieran Maher, Mick Galwey, Mick Fitzgibbon.

Garryowen: Kenny Smith, Richard Wallace, Philip Danaher capt., David Costelloe, Gary Quilligan (Ger Manning), Dan Larkin, Ian Barry, Liam Lannen, Keith Wood, David Henshaw, Richard Costello, Brent Anderson, Paul Hogan (Mark O'Donoghue), Dara O'Sullivan, Ben Cronin.

Keith Wood

Garryowen went on to win the AIL with a game to spare. Their three-quarter line contained two internationals, skipper Philip Danaher and Richard Wallace, a serial try scorer at the time, while up front Keith Wood, David Costello, Paul Hogan and Ben Cronin all wore the green and Anderson was capped by the All Blacks. Although only just out of his teens, Wood was already a formidable performer. He picked up a second AIL medal with Garryowen in 1994 before heading off to London and Harlequins. In time, Woody would go on to captain Ireland on thirty-six occasions, make two Lions tours and earn a reputation as one of rugby's greatest hookers. His fearless, thundering open-field bursts that decimated defences and led to a record fifteen international tries for a hooker in his fifty-eight appearances for Ireland will be warmly remembered by rugby fans wherever the game is played. He figured in five Test matches for the Lions and was one of the outstanding figures in the side that won the series against South Africa in 1997.

Keith was the inaugural winner of the IRB World Player of the Year award in 2001 and retired after captaining the Irish team in the 2003 Rugby World Cup in Australia. Blessed with a warm, throaty laugh and a mischievous sense of humour and nicknamed Uncle Fester because of his similarity to the character in the Addams Family, he likes to boast about figuring in the Clare hurling team that competed in the inaugural Nenagh Co-Op tournament in 1988. Even those closest to Woody have only a very hazy memory either of his involvement or of

Keith Wood emerges with the ball and celebrates his last-minute try against Saracens in the Heineken Cup in 2000. Alan Quinlan shares his delight. (Courtesy Sportsfile)

the event itself. Nevertheless, there is no doubting his commitment to his native place, Killaloe, County Clare, or to his Alma Mater, St Munchin's College, Limerick, where his son Alexander is enrolled as a student.

The 1991/92 season brought success for Old Crescent as they won the Munster Senior League, their first senior trophy. That put them into a Round Robin for AIL Division Two qualification which they duly attained with the help of two Bill Hanley tries and another by Tim Coughlan in a 14–7 victory over NIFC in Belfast. The Old Crescent team that day was:

P. Boland, K. Barrett, J. Hogan capt., T. Coughlan, W. Hanley, A. Keane, D. Reddan, R. Duggan, D. Murphy, N. Maher, R. McGravie, M. Crowe, Tom Brown, Terry Browne, G. Dineen.

Although most of the unforgettable drama concerning Young Munster's AIL triumph in 1993 took place on the final day at Lansdowne Road when they defeated St Mary's College 17–14, on the way they had to travel across Limerick to tackle Shannon at Thomond Park. In front of yet another packed house, they returned to Clifford Park winners by 15–6 thanks to four penalties and a drop goal by out-half Aidan O'Halloran. While O'Halloran would continue to rack up the points, outstanding forwards like captain Ger and Peter Clohessy, John 'Pako' Fitzgerald, dynamic flanker Ger Earls, crafty number nine Derek Tobin and Francis Brosnahan in the centre, maintained control on the big days to pull off a very famous triumph.

Garryowen remained a considerable force. They defeated Young Munster in another all-Limerick Munster Cup final in 1993 at Thomond Park by four Kenny Smith penalties to a try by Derek Tobin and captured their second All-Ireland League the following year. Demonstrating their intent, they appointed Andy Leslie, who had captained the All Blacks to victory over Munster at Thomond Park in 1974, as coach and clinched the title by beating their chief rivals Blackrock College in the decisive match at Dooradoyle. The AIL was extended to four divisions in 1993/94 with eleven clubs rather than nine participating in Division One and Bohemians competing for the first time.

11

1990s

Bohemians opened their new clubhouse at Thomond Park on 31 August 1990, marking the occasion with a game between the President's XV and the Wolfhounds. President that year was John O'Sullivan, whose father, Kevin, had been a member of the first Bohs team to play at Thomond Park back in 1934 and in 1990 John also had the satisfaction of seeing the completion of the dressing rooms at the club grounds in Annacotty. The teams on that occasion were:

President's XV: C. Haly (UCC), R. Wallace, P. Danaher, D. Larkin (all Garryowen), J. Galvin (Old Crescent), N. Barry (Garryowen), M. Bradley (Cork Constitution), P. Clohessy (Young Munster), T. Kingston (Dolphin), J. Fitzgerald (Young Munster), D. Lenihan capt. (Cork Con.), F. Kearney, K. O'Connell (both Sundays Well), P. Collins (Highfield), P. O'Hara (Sundays Well). *Replacements*: G. Doyle (St Mary's College), J. Moloney (Young Munster), E. O'Sullivan (Old Crescent), M. Benson (Young Munster, L. Lannon (Dolphin), F. Hogan (Garryowen).

Wolfhounds: K. Murphy (Cork Constitution), D. O'Brien (Clontarf), M. Ring (Cardiff), M. Kiernan (Dolphin), E. Holland (Glamorgan Wanderers), L. Cusworth (Leicester), B. McGoey (Wanderers), T. Merry (Clontarf), S. Smith (Ballymena), D. Bourke (Monkstown), V. Ryan (Lansdowne), R. Theron (Natal), I. Counihan (Monkstown), F. Lawlor (Bective Rangers), S. Legg (Wanderers). *Replacements*: M. Goldsworth (Wanderers), J. Clarke

(Dolphin), A. Twomey, W. Burns (both Lansdowne), T. Lenehan, D. Ryan (both Bohemians), R. Costello (Garryowen).

Referee: Stan Fuller.

Seven-a-side rugby, or Rugby Sevens, has begun to come into its own, being recognised as an Olympic sport for the first time in 2016 in Rio, but it has not caught on to any great extent in Ireland. Determined efforts have been made from time to time at Thomond Park, with the Aer Lingus International Sevens Championship being staged there in 1992 and again in 1993, while the Limerick World Club Sevens lit up the early part of the 2013/14 season. The 1992 championship was the brainchild of Tom Collins, at the time tax manager for Craig Gardner/ Price Waterhouse. At a Shannon Development seminar in 1990, he suggested an International Sevens for Limerick. David Deighan of SFADCO and senior Munster Branch officials Brendan O'Dowd and Michael Wallace were in full agreement, sponsors led by Aer Lingus supported by Beamish & Crawford, Shannon Development, Limerick Ryan Hotel, Limerick Inn Hotel, Jurys Hotel and The Great Southern Hotel, Shannon, came on board and the competition for the Tom Clifford Trophy duly took place at Thomond Park on 2 May 1992.

Youth teams from all four provinces participated. Leinster included in their ranks Limerick man Richard Heaslip (Curragh), father of Ireland and Lions number eight Jamie, and Trevor Brennan (Barnhall) of Toulouse and Ireland fame. Of the senior sides, Philippe Bernat-Salles for France, Alain Rolland (Ireland), Maurice Mortell (Bective Rangers), Brian Spillane and Eddie Halvey (Munster) and David Pickering (Wales/ England, represented by Penguin RFC) were among the better-known players who revelled in the Thomond Park atmosphere and provided great entertainment for the crowd.

There was quite a buzz among players and public alike after the 1992 series with many of the overseas teams happy to make a return visit. Wellington were there from New Zealand with Martin Leslie (a son of former All Blacks captain Andy Leslie) in their line-up while Alain Rolland captained an Irish squad that included international winger Richard Wallace. The Penguins again represented England with flying wing Audley Lumsden their star participant. Once more, the event proved a success but the advent of the professional game proved its undoing and the Aer Lingus Sevens was not held again.

International Sevens returned to a very different Thomond Park in August 2014 when a youthful Munster squad expertly coached by Colm McMahon did well to win all of its three group games only to go down 12–10 to Fijian side Daveta in the quarter-finals. This was especially hard luck on McMahon's squad given that they had defeated the eventual champions 36–12 in the preliminary rounds. Daveta beat Vancouver Bears in the final and among the other competing sides were San Francisco, Moscow, Auckland, Western Province and Blue Bulls of South Africa, Waratahs from Australia, Saracens, New York and Stade Français. The Munster squad was Gerhard van den Heever, Shane Buckley, Luke O'Dea, Stephen Fitzgerald, Tomas Quinlan, Darren Sweetnam, Ronan O'Mahony, Cian Bohane, Ryan Murphy, Jamie Glynn and Ned Hodson.

Shannon's Four-in-a-Row

It was with a certain degree of envy that Shannon looked on as their Limerick neighbours carried the AIL trophy around the various hostelries with which Young Munster and Garryowen were most associated and they had nothing similar to show off to their loyal and enthusiastic supporters. However, they were far from idle, putting strategies in place on and off the field that would yield undreamt of riches from 1994 through to 1998.

Shannon's achievements speak for themselves: prior to the 2015/16 season, they had won nine All-Ireland League titles, five more than their nearest challengers Cork Constitution and six more than third-placed Garryowen, and the Munster Senior Cup nineteen times, all but one of which had been won since 1977. Too frequently they were accused of sticking rigidly to a nine-man game and, while that may have been the case to some extent prior to the advent of the AIL, they realised that a more expansive approach would be needed and they adapted superbly.

All these successes were accomplished in the 'old' Thomond Park, which evokes happy memories of great days for the game not just in Limerick but throughout the country. True, the impending professional game would change club rugby throughout Ireland forever but until that happened, those who deeply loved the club game remained enthralled.

Few were surprised that a Shannon team of considerable all-round strength should have succeeded Garryowen as champions in 1994/95. They went through the series unbeaten, the strength of a pack – which included an all-international second-row of Mick Galwey and Brian Rigney, Ireland back-row men Mick Fitzgibbon, Anthony Foley and Eddie Halvey – augmented by a fine back division which featured captain Pat Murray in imperious form at full back and a reliable place kicker in Andrew Thompson. Combine those factors with the magnificent spirit that permeated the club on and off the pitch and you were left with an irrepressible force. They had the trophy in safe keeping before ever Instonians travelled to Thomond Park for the final game, which resulted in a home win by 16–13.

As Frank O'Flynn and his black-and-blue bedecked choir belted out 'The Isle', not even coach Niall O'Donovan, fellow selector Brian O'Brien and all of those at the heart of the Shannon cause realised that even greater things lay in wait in the succeeding years. Not even a three-month break between October and January could throw them off course in 1995/96. O'Donovan had a powerful squad at his disposal but as one match after another was won in convincing fashion, changes had to be kept to a minimum. As a result, only eighteen were chosen to start, with another five used as substitutes.

They defeated St Mary's College on the opening day of the campaign at Thomond Park with the following team:

P. Murray capt., B. O'Shea, A. Thompson, C. McDermott, D. Gallagher, J. Galvin, G. Russell, J. Hickey, P. Kenny, T. Walsh, B. Rigney, M. Galwey (K. Maher), E. Halvey, M. Fitzgibbon, A. Foley.

Thomond Park remained a happy hunting ground. Lansdowne were demolished by thirty-nine unanswered points, Old Wesley provided a few heart-stopping moments before going down by 12–6. The long break seemed to frustrate most clubs but Shannon sensibly accepted the situation as they found it and in early January 1995 again held the opposition, this time Young Munster, scoreless while they themselves ran up twenty points of their own. The key game after that was against Blackrock College at Stradbrook where Billy O'Shea grabbed the only try in desperate conditions. There was no stopping Shannon, all the more so when Anthony Foley (son of the great Brendan who was on the 1978 Munster team that defeated the mighty All Blacks) declined the customary rest, having been chosen a week earlier for his first Irish cap – yet another demonstration of the indomitable spirit in the Shannon club. They went on to squeeze through tricky away matches at Cork Constitution and Dungannon before wrapping it all up against Instonians.

A performance that might have gone unnoticed was produced by Bohemians who topped Division Four of the league, losing only once: away to Dungannon by a single point. Niall Lawler proved an outstanding captain and 1985 Triple Crown hero Brian Spillane was still there to lend his experience and expertise.

As the 1990s proceeded, it was not always clear where rugby was heading. The AIL had taken over as the premier competition, relegating the interprovincial championship to a bad second place although it could not be foreseen how things would change, and change utterly, in a short few years with the advent of the European Cup which got under way for Munster at Thomond Park on 1 November 1995.

That event would take another few years to find its feet, during which time Shannon confirmed yet again what a powerful force they were in the All-Ireland League. In their wisdom, the IRFU decreed that there would be no relegation from Division One and that there would be a five-month interval between the first and second series of games. The climax was as extraordinary as it was dramatic. Shannon, again captained by Pat Murray with Niall O'Donovan as coach and Brian O'Brien as chairman of selectors, had completed their programme and were involved in a Munster Cup match against UCC in Cork at much the same time as Garryowen needed only a draw from their clash with Young Munster at Dooradoyle to be crowned champions. The final score? Garryowen 12, Young Munster 37. On hearing the news at Musgrave Park, a shocked but delighted Niall O'Donovan said: 'If I could have chosen a team to play against Garryowen like this, it would have been Young Munster. There is great pride in the club and while they were not in the running for the league, I knew they would never give anything away too easily, especially in a Limerick derby.' Having joined in the rendering of 'The Isle' and 'Beautiful, beautiful Munsters' with the other Shannon players and fans, skipper Murray pointed out that 'it just shows the competitive nature of Limerick rugby when anything can happen.'

Needless to say, Munsters followers informed their Shannon counterparts at every opportunity how they had won the league for them. A league by its very nature is, of course, all about accumulating more points than any of the other teams: Shannon achieved that and there really was nothing more to say. As always, their games at Thomond Park were absolutely crucial and they used its advantages superbly for crucial wins towards the end of the campaign against Constitution 19–10, Ballymena 25–12, and Old Belvedere 8–0.

Shannon captured the Munster Senior and Junior Cups for good measure in the season of 1995/96 so they were in perfect fettle as they went in search of the hat-trick the following season. Now there were fourteen teams in Division One including Old Crescent who were also enjoying successes in the AIL. These included a 53–7 trouncing of NIFC as they earned promotion after leading the way in Division Two – and then picked up a cool £5,000 on being named IRFU team of the year.

Nor were Richmond to be left out of the equation. They won all of their eleven games in the Munster Junior League to gain admission to Division Four of the AIL for 1996/97. It all painted a very healthy picture of the game in Limerick, a view that was to be further enhanced as Shannon duly completed the hat-trick. Niall O'Donovan and Brian O'Brien continued as coach and chairman of selectors respectively with Conor McDermott taking over from Pat Murray as captain. On the playing side of things, Eddie Halvey was available again after a stint in London with Saracens while John Hayes returned from New Zealand and Alan Quinlan was about to establish himself as an outstanding operator in the back row. Ronan O'Gara was also on the way to becoming a legend of the Irish game when he lined out against Shannon at Thomond Park early in the campaign but even he could not prevent Cork Constitution going down 24–11 to the Shannon juggernaut.

There was the odd setback subsequently but they invariably delivered at Thomond Park – if only by a single point, 17–16, against Garryowen who found themselves fourteen points behind on a couple of occasions. If that was nerve wracking, the 51–15 thrashing of Old Belvedere reflected the squad in a more positive light and included tries for Alan Quinlan, Eddie Halvey and John Hayes and a couple for scrum half Gavin Russell. A final round of matches remained to be played when the hat-trick was clinched with a 28–15 defeat of Old Crescent.

The Thomond Park crowd was more than a little taken aback when John Forde and Fergus Walsh ran in a couple of Crescent tries and there was one subsequently for David Bowles. True to form, however, Shannon refused to panic and Andrew Thompson's ever-accurate boot complemented tries by Alan McGrath, Thompson, Noel Healy and McGrath again to see Shannon home with plenty to spare. A week later, Shannon won their thirteenth match in fourteen league outings, by 38–16 against Instonians at Shane Park.

By this stage, the professional game was taking a very strong hold and clubs could not always be sure which players would be available to them. Furthermore, Allied Irish Bank came on board as the new sponsors of the AIL and a 'top four' system was established to decide the champion side. It did not matter to Shannon. They had a 'four' of a different kind in mind – achieving what no other club even envisaged doing by winning the AIL for a fourth successive year – and duly reached the objective. Pat Murray retired and took over the coaching role from Niall O'Donovan who simply moved a little sideways to assume the role of Director of Rugby. The big guns – Galwey, Quinlan, Foley and Halvey – were joined by New Zealander Rhys Ellison, Leinster's Mark McDermott, John Lacey and others.

There was never any doubt that Shannon would continue to roll along. They began 1997/98 with a solid Thomond Park win over Dungannon before moving across town to Rosbrien where they put fifty points on Old Crescent without reply in the first league game contested under floodlights. Clontarf were next to feel the might of Shannon, demolished 31–6 at Thomond Park. Having edged out Cork Constitution by a point at Temple Hill, they slipped up against Lansdowne in Dublin; a penalty try proved crucial in a single-point defeat of Garryowen at Dooradoyle. By now, it did not seem to matter where they played: Thomond Park, Shannon 30, Dolphin 3: Anglesea Road, Old Belvedere 20, Shannon 70.

Young Munster pushed them to 16–10 in front of a Thomond Park crowd estimated at 13,000, but Shannon did enough to prevail. It was a magnificent rugby match memorable for a marvellous individual try for Shannon by Jason Hayes and ensured a home semi-final against St Mary's College. Shannon, of course, had all their big-name players on parade but Mary's were not short in that department either. In their ranks they included many-times-capped back-row forwards Trevor

AIL 1998 Shannon RFC, All-Ireland League champions 1998. Back row (l–r): Jason Hayes, Mark McDermot, John Hayes, Kevin Keane, Mick Galwey, Alan Quinlan, John Lacey, Marcus Horan, Eddie Halvey; front row (l–r): Frankie McNamara, Anthony Foley capt., Jason Finn mascot, Jim Galvin, Andrew Thompson, Paul McMahon, Rhys Ellison. (Courtesy Andrew McNamara)

Brennan and Victor Costello, and also Emmett Byrne; flying wing Denis Hickie was a man to keep a close eye on. Understandably, it was the kind of game much beloved of Thomond Park fans and they turned up in their thousands. Shannon had the wind in the first half and yet turned over 18–16 behind. Urged on by their wildly excited supporters, they answered just about everything Mary's could throw at them and in the end, an Anthony Foley try and seven penalties and a conversion by the admirably cool Andrew Thompson saw them home by 28–21.

So it was all down to the one-time kindred spirits: Shannon and Garryowen left to do battle for the national championship at Lansdowne Road on 25 April 1998. The final was the talk of Limerick and many were of the belief that Garryowen had the ability to prevent the four-in-a-row. They might have, too, had they not lost key man David Wallace, the Ireland and Lions flanker, to injury after a half hour. In the end, it was the boot of Andrew Thompson that held sway. He knocked over four penalties and a drop goal against three penalties by Killian Keane. Cue Frankie Flynn and 'There Is an Isle' yet again.

Shannon: Jason Hayes, J. Lacey, P. McMahon, R. Ellison, A. Thompson, J. Galvin, F. McNamara, M. Horan, M. McDermott, John Hayes, M. Galwey, K. Keane (C. McMahon), A. Quinlan, E. Halvey, A. Foley capt.

Garryowen: D. Crotty, J. Clarke, K. Keane capt., J. Brooks, K. O'Riordan, B. Everitt, S. McIvor (T. Tierney), P. Spain, P. Humphreys, G. Walsh, S. Leahy (C. Varley), V. Humphreys, P. Hogan, A. Bermingham, D. Wallace (D. O'Sullivan).

Referee: Dave McHugh.

Two much-loved voices of Limerick rugby, commentators Tommy Creamer and Len Dineen do their thing. (Courtesy *Irish Examiner*)

In spite of the significance now placed in the AIL, the Munster Cup remained a coveted prize and Thomond Park housed some great finals even as the league and then the European Cup came on stream. Garryowen claimed the title for the second time in three years at the expense of their luckless opponents Young Munster, who seemed to have no trouble at all in reaching the final without quite being able to finish off the job. Having gone down to Sundays Well at Musgrave Park in 1994, they lost 23–3 to Garryowen in 1995. It was a pretty one-sided affair with Philip Danaher, Michael Coughlan and Paul Hogan running in Garryowen tries.

> **Garryowen:** D. Larkin, A. White (B. Everitt), P. Danaher, K. Smith, Derek Costelloe, K. Keane, S. McIvor, P. Spain, P. Cunningham, M. Hannon, M. Coughlan, S. Leahy, P. Hogan capt., D. O'Sullivan, B. Cronin.

> **Young Munster:** G. McNamara, N. McNamara, N. O'Meara, capt., P. Clohessy, G. Fitzgerald, M. O'Halloran, D. Clohessy, A. Herlihy, D. Edwards.

The all-conquering Shannon machine drove to a 15–13 triumph over Constitution in the 1996 decider at Musgrave Park. In 1997, Garryowen met Young Munster on final day. This was a much closer affair with tries by Jack Clarke and Kieran Ronan and a conversion by Kenny Smith for Garryowen against two penalties by Michael Benson putting Garryowen six points ahead going into the final ten minutes. Young Munsters camped on the opposition line from there to the finish and on at least four occasions they were held out by inches from snatching the try that would have won the day. But Garryowen resisted their best efforts and scraped home.

Young Munster were contesting their seventh Munster Cup decider in eight years when they lined out against Shannon at Thomond Park in May 1998. They were out of luck once again, going down by the narrowest of margins 19–18, to the Anthony Foley-skippered Shannon.

Half-Time At Thomond Park

by Tom Kiernan, Ireland and Lions captain and coach of the Munster team
that defeated the All Blacks at Thomond Park on 31 October 1978.

Thomond Park was only twelve years old when I first attended a game there. It was in 1946 when Presentation Brothers College Cork played Rockwell in the final of the Schools Senior Cup. The Pres centre Flor O'Leary dropped a goal (then four points) to win the cup for Pres.

Some years later, in the late 1950s, I was to play for Pres in Thomond Park against Glenstal in the Junior Cup final and Crescent College in the Senior Cup, both of which we won. Thomond Park seemed like a home from home to me but I was to have a rude awakening.

When playing for UCC in 1960, we reached the Munster Senior Cup final versus Shannon in Cork. We were a young team with an exciting three-quarter line and, as Shannon were relatively new to senior ranks, we were installed as favourites. They kicked a goal to equalise in the last few minutes and so we headed to Thomond Park for the replay.

Thomond Park was packed with Shannon supporters that day and they outnumbered those from Cork by 10–1. And they also played superbly on the day. They demolished our set scrum and the final result of six points to three flattered us students. The Shannon team and its mentors treated us royally after the game. We were taken to 'Angela's' where the likes of Eamon Clancy, Michael Noel Ryan, Frankie Flynn, Gerry O'Halloran and others looked after us well.

I had played for Munster against the All Blacks in Thomond in 1963 when we lost 6–3 and again in Musgrave Park in 1973 when a last-minute penalty by Trevor Morris ensured the New Zealanders a draw. It was my last playing season and thus one of my ambitions as a player – to beat New Zealand – was gone forever. In 1974, as Munster coach against New Zealand in a match to celebrate the Irish Rugby Union's centenary and we lost 14–4, I handed over the coaching reins to Des Barry who for personal reasons handed the job back after one season.

Munster were to play the All Blacks again in 1978 so I was asked to coach the side for the one year. This was to be my last chance against the All Blacks and I decided the one thing we wouldn't lack was fitness

– so often the reason it was so difficult to beat the tourists. The Munster Branch allowed us to go on a trip to England for two games and allowed us train in Fermoy months before the game.

Then arrived 31 October 1978. Thomond Park was full to capacity with probably the most knowledgeable rugby crowd you could find anywhere and they gave full vent to their feelings, circumstances which were perfect from a Munster point of view. They did not get any bigger than Munster versus a touring team – especially the All Blacks in Thomond Park. The game itself was tough but clean and we witnessed probably the best display I have seen from a Munster side.

A converted try by Christy Cantillon and two drop goals and a conversion by Tony Ward gave us a most unexpected win. Thomond Park had established itself as a fortress for Munster. The ground has seen many great days since 1978, especially in the Heineken Cup and Pro 12. It has recently been developed and now has a capacity of over 26,000. Sure to say that 31 October 1978 will never be forgotten or surpassed.

Tom Kiernan, surrounded by highly excited Munster supporters, as Munster take control against the All Blacks, Thomond Park, 31 October 1978. (*Irish Examiner*)

12

The Game Goes Open

On 16 May 1995, the day before the Irish party left for South Africa and the third Rugby World Cup, the IRFU issued the following statement: 'The IRFU will oppose the payment of players to play the game and payments to others such as coaches, referees, touch judges and members of committees for taking part in the game because the game is a leisure activity played on a voluntary basis.'

It was not the best-timed or most perceptive release to emerge from Lansdowne Road. It was hardly going to placate the players who for several years past had been openly protesting at what they considered to be their 'second citizen' treatment by the Union. And, of course, whether the IRFU liked it or not, the game would be 'open' – in other words, professional – within a short few months and they would have no choice but to go along with everyone else.

Post-apartheid South Africa won the 1995 World Cup and everybody was happy on that score. In truth, though, something revolutionary was happening in the game. On 26 August, the International Rugby Board at a meeting in Paris declared the game open, removing all restrictions on payments to players and those connected with the game. This was, they claimed, the only way to end the hypocrisy of sham amateurism. This was only partially true because quite clearly the 'big three' in the southern hemisphere had jumped into bed with Rupert Murdoch and his television stations along with other well-heeled sponsors. Those in the northern hemisphere could do what they wished: New Zealand, South Africa and Australia were going professional.

It would be unfair to say the IRFU did not see this coming. There had been fair warning for a couple of months or more prior to that fateful meeting in Paris, But they had not anticipated the extent and speed of the change and struggled to cope. The legal fraternity gained a number of new clients as some tricky issues had to be dealt with.

The inaugural European Cup, the brainchild of Ireland's Tom Kiernan, Vernon Pugh of Wales and Marcel Martin of France, who reacted quickly and wisely, was launched as others struggled to adjust. That first European Championship accommodated three Irish teams: Munster, Leinster and Ulster. Each home-based player received a match fee of around £300 to £600 with another rate for those internationals who had decided to represent clubs in the UK. By the beginning of the 1996/97 season, only three of a starting team humbled by Samoa at Lansdowne Road were still playing their rugby in Ireland.

It was in this kind of atmosphere that the three Irish provinces prepared for their first appearances in Europe. Players had to be signed, coaches appointed, deals agreed. Not all of this happened. People were paid, however, and so that made the game professional. Apart from the extra few bob in their pockets, life for the elite players continued very much as before. They were bankers, company reps and directors, students and so on, and in some cases remained so. If anything, loyalty to their clubs in the AIL outweighed the feelings they held for their province. The twelve teams chosen to launch the new tournament in addition to the Irish trio were Toulouse, Castres and Bègles-Bordeaux from France; Cardiff, Swansea and Pontypridd from Wales; Benetton Treviso and Milan from Italy; and Farul Constanta of Romania. Even back then, England's elite were in a sulk and did not enter. Each team would meet the others in their group only once, with the pool winners going through to the semi-finals.

And so on the Wednesday afternoon of 1 November 1995, Thomond Park was the stage for another mould-breaking rugby game: Munster's clash with Swansea in the first round of the European Cup. If anything, the Welsh were marginally better prepared for this new scenario but even so Munster just edged them out by 17–13 in front of a decent attendance of around 7,000. Free-scoring winger Richard Wallace touched down for Munster in the first half and Kenny Smith converted and landed a penalty to push them 10–6 ahead at the interval. However, an Alan Harris try converted by Aled Williams had Swansea

Pat Murray touches down for a try against Swansea in Munster's first European Cup game at Thomond Park in 1995. (*Irish Examiner*)

13–10 in front but with only two minutes remaining the outstanding Pat Murray outpaced the Welsh cover after a nice break by Paul Burke for a great try and Smith's conversion left Munster 17–13 ahead at the final whistle. Thus began a trend that was to serve Munster so well on innumerable occasions in the future, that of snatching victory from the jaws of defeat in the dying minutes of a game.

Munster: P. Murray capt., R. Wallace, S. McCahill, D. Larkin, K. Smith, P. Burke, D. O'Mahoney, J. Fitzgerald, T. Kingston, P. Clohessy, M. Galwey, G. Fulcher, E. Halvey, D. Corkery, A. Foley.

Swansea: G. Thomas, A. Harris (L. Davies), R. Boobyer, D. Weatherley, S. Davies, A. Williams, R. Jones, C. Loader, G. Jenkins, C. Anthony, S. Moore, A. Moore, A. Reynolds, R. Appleyard, S. Davies capt.

A week later, Munster lost the first of many fractious encounters in France. The game against Castres actually took place in Mazamet and they went down to a late converted try. Swansea won the pool and the eventual winners in the inaugural year were Toulouse, the aristocrats of the game in France.

The 1996/97 season was slightly less dysfunctional as administrators, players and fans began to realise that the professional game was here to stay. The number of teams increased to twenty with England and

Scotland involved. Having disposed of the formality presented by Milan in their first European outing by 23–3 at Musgrave Park, the Jerry Holland-coached, Colm Tucker-managed Munster took on three games of decidedly mixed results. They were walloped 48–18 by Cardiff at Cardiff Arms Park and with a mere three days to recover, faced up to the visit of star-studded Wasps with no little trepidation. Astonishingly, it was to be another game redolent of the spirit of Munster and Thomond Park as they took the visitors apart on a 49–22 scoreline. Wasps included the great England number eight Lawrence Dallaglio and a host of other internationals in their ranks, including the almost-unstoppable Samoan Inga Tuigamala and the free-scoring Canadian Gareth Rees but as the rain poured down, the wind freshened and the huge crowd cheered and sang, they never had a chance.

Captain Mick Galwey revelled in the atmosphere and was one of Munster's seven try scorers as Wasps were made to look very poor indeed. Killian Keane, originally from Skerries, County Dublin, but a 'naturalised' Munster man, underlined Jerry Holland's instructions from the outset. The first time you get the ball, he was told, kick it as high in the air as you possibly can. Let the rain, the wind and the crowd do the rest. Keane duly obliged. As soon as the opportunity arose, he launched a Garryowen so far into the clouds that the ball was almost covered in ice as it landed in the general direction of Wasps full back Jon Ufton. As the crowd bayed and Galwey and company charged like madmen in pursuit, it was hardly surprising that Ufton failed to gather and Anthony Foley, with the help of the seven other Munster forwards, swooped and crashed over for a try. Essentially, that was the end of the game as a contest. Galwey, Keane, Ben Cronin, Richard Wallace and Dominic Crotty touched down further tries. And then for a team and group of supporters born to love and admire outstanding forward play came the icing on the cake, a penalty try awarded when the Wasps scrum collapsed once too often for the referee's liking.

There was to be a sting in the tail, however. Wasps somehow thrashed Toulouse 77–17 the following week which meant that Munster would only qualify from the pool should they also manage to defeat the French side. However, just as Thomond Park was Munster's fortress, so too did Toulouse regard anything but victory at Stade des Sept Deniers as an ignominy not to be suffered. The message was delivered loud and clear: Toulouse 60, Munster 17.

The Munster camp took the hiding with typically good humour. In a self-deprecating manner, Mick Galwey used to recount how he begged his teammates as things went from bad to worse to 'keep the score under 50'. A short few minutes later, he implored 'don't let them get to 60'.

Declan Kidney Takes Over

During an ill-fated Irish development tour of New Zealand in 1977, the IRFU announced that Andy Leslie, a former All Blacks captain and Garryowen coach, had been appointed Munster's new Director of Rugby. This came as news to Leslie, one of the game's gentlemen. He was still thinking over the offer and, after due deliberation, turned it down. Earlier that year, Munster had had an agreement with former Wales and Lions wing John Bevan who, however, had second thoughts and decided to stay at home.

Declan Kidney at a Munster press conference in May 2008. (Courtesy *Irish Examiner*)

Now it was time for the IRFU to look at suitable candidates at home. Declan Kidney had a distinguished record as a schools player at Presentation Brothers, Cork – Pres – and later at UCC and Dolphin but he really caught the eye when turning his attention to coaching the Senior and Junior Cup teams at his Alma Mater, where he was also a member of the teaching staff. Pres won all around them and while there were those who hardly believed this entitled Kidney to such a prestigious post, the Union to their credit followed their instincts. Kidney and Shannon's formidable Niall O'Donovan as assistant proved an inspired choice even if at that time they were very much on trial.

The 1997/78 Heineken Cup still catered for twenty teams with five pools of four. Each team would meet the others twice, on a home-and-away basis, which was good news, of course, for Thomond Park and its legion of supporters. Nevertheless, the 1997/78 campaign proved a poor one for Munster, the positive being Thomond Park wins over Bourgoin and Harlequins but they also shipped more than forty points away to 'Quins and Cardiff and another thirty-seven to the Welsh side at Musgrave Park.

Accordingly, the Kidney/O'Donovan ticket was only just keeping its head above water. Kidney stressed that they were building things from scratch, even to the extent, he quipped 'of going out ourselves and buying paper clips and rubber bands for the office'.

Although the English clubs boycotted the European Championship once again in 1998/99, things were heading in a positive direction. At long last, it looked as if the IRFU was getting its head around the challenge presented by professional rugby and appointed Declan

Coach Declan Kidney and manager Brian O'Brien lead the players in a rousing rendition of 'Stand Up and Fight' in the Thomond Park dressing room after beating Saracens 31–30 in a Heineken Cup clash in 2000. (Courtesy *Irish Examiner*)

Kidney and Niall O'Donovan on a full-time basis in good time for the 1998/99 season. On top of that, the provinces were able to sign twenty-one players on full-time contracts and several others as part-timers. Not everybody realised it then, perhaps, but very special players were also coming through the ranks: Ronan O'Gara made his Heineken Cup debut against Padova at Musgrave Park and others at his side that day included John Kelly, Anthony Horgan and David Wallace. Peter Stringer and John Hayes would also make their first appearances later that campaign. All had been cutting their teeth with their clubs in the highly competitive All-Ireland League and so were sufficiently battle-hardened to tackle the best that Europe could throw at them. They duly reached the quarter-finals in 1999 only to lose 23–9 to Colomiers who in turn went down in the final to Ulster. However, Munster's surge to the top of the European tree could not be delayed any longer.

The 1999/2000 season will be remembered for so many reasons that it is difficult to know where to start: almost at once, it seemed, the likes of Kelly, Jason Holland, Mike Mullins, Horgan, Jeremy Staunton, O'Gara, Stringer, Hayes, Alan Quinlan and Wallace arrived on the scene. Keith Wood was lured back from Harlequins for the season and the tremendous second-row Australian John Langford was brought on board. Still there to lend a helping hand and an experienced ear were Killian Keane, Dominic Crotty, Peter Clohessy, Mick Galwey, Anthony Foley and Eddie Halvey. Kidney and O'Donovan could never have imagined they would have such an array of talent at their disposal.

Expectations were high. The season got off to a particularly bright start, not exactly on the field of play, but in a Belfast pub after they had defeated the then European Cup champions, Ulster, in the city for the first time in nineteen years. The new team manager Brian O'Brien, he the wily one of countless great days for Shannon, Munster and Ireland, was asked to contribute to the sing-song. He lashed out 'Stand Up and Fight' from the Broadway musical *Carmen Jones* (which is Bizet's opera *Carmen* updated to a Second World War era and given an African-American setting). There and then, it became the rallying song of Munster rugby teams and that is why it is sung on every big match day at Thomond Park.

Munster teams have rarely, if ever, enjoyed what might be described as a 'handy' draw in Europe and 1999/2000 was no different, their pool populated by the mega-rich Saracens from England, the previous year's beaten finalists Colomiers and the tigerish Welsh club Pontypridd. 'Ponty' were first up at Thomond Park where a powerful second-half performance by the home team saw them off by 32–10. There then followed the never-to-be-forgotten 34–33 win over Saracens at Vicarage Road and the first success on French soil against Colomiers by 31–15. When that was followed up in the return at Musgrave Park on a 25–3 scoreline, Munster had won four out of four.

Kidney, however, pointed out a few home truths, especially where defeat by Saracens at Thomond Park eight days into the new millennium might leave them. This game captured the imagination like no other up to this stage of the European Cup. Saracens were owned by Nigel Wray, a wealthy businessman who has stuck with them ever since without ever quite reaping the rewards he must have expected for his considerable investment. His cosmopolitan squad that year contained the brilliant French out-half Thierry Lacroix, the formidable Argentinian prop Roberto Grau and South Africa's 1995 World Cup winning captain Francois Pienaar, not to mention two Munster-born players, Paul Wallace and Darragh O'Mahony, and a whole host of highly rated English and Scottish internationals, including Danny Grewcock, Richard Hill and Scott Murray.

The businessman in Wray would have been delighted with the size of the crowd and the atmosphere that evening had they been experienced at Vicarage Road rather than at Thomond Park. The ground looked overcrowded before the kick-off and in truth many of the throng, estimated to have been around 19,000, saw very little of the action. It is safe to assume that the Bohs and Shannon pavilions did a roaring trade. The Munster Branch and the fire department subsequently came together and agreed on an attendance limit of 13,500 for all future Heineken Cup matches.

The outcome was remarkably similar to the first meeting of the sides. Saracens cruised into a 17–8 lead after tries by Cork man Darragh O'Mahony and Mark Mapletoft with one for Munster by Mick Galwey. True to form, Munster engineered a try by Jason Holland with Ronan O'Gara's boot also keeping the scoreboard ticking over. Mapletoft, however, got over for his second try with time almost up and when Lacroix converted, Sarries were six points ahead. In his autobiography, Mick Galwey graphically and grippingly described what happened next:

After that try we tried to put it together behind the posts. Let's give it a lash and go down and get a try. We were awarded a penalty. We kicked to touch. Woody threw it in, Langford caught it, was driven and Woody got over the line. It all sounds simple but it's a very hard thing to do against such fantastic opposition. Then there was the famous kick by Ronan. It was an awful situation for him to be in after winning it for us in the same circumstances just a few weeks previously. But he did it again and to his eternal credit. There were still a few minutes to go and they had a drop goal chance again but this time Langford blocked it down.

Then the final whistle and one of the hardest things I had to do was to get from the far side of the pitch to the dressing room. The crowd just went mad, out of their head. It was MUNSTER, MUNSTER, MUNSTER, nothing else seemed to matter. Of all the games we played that season, the hardest were against Saracens. It was a privilege to be part of those games. They were great to play in, absolutely memorable.

ROG converts off the post and wins the day once again! (Courtesy Sportsfile)

Munster: D. Crotty, J. Kelly, J. Holland, M. Mullins, A. Horgan, R. O'Gara, P. Stringer, P. Clohessy, K. Wood, J. Hayes, J. Langford, M. Galwey capt., A. Quinlan, D. Wallace, A. Foley.

Saracens: M. Mapletoft, R. Constable, J. Thomson (B. Johnston), K. Sorrell, D. O'Mahony, T. Lacroix, N. Walshe, D. Flatman, G. Chuter, J. White (P. Wallace), S. Murray, D. Grewcock, F. Pienaar capt., R. Hill, T. Diprose.

The two Saracens games were highly significant for the Wallace family with brothers David and Paul on opposite sides. Munster's David saw it like this:

> There must have been 30,000 in Thomond Park that day. It was unbelievable and there will never be a game like it – the ball hit the post and went over. We were training there the following week and we challenged Ronan to do it again – and didn't he do it, in off the post again! Paul came on for Sarries in both games and he did not like losing, especially to the younger brother. There was huge belief in the team. Woody had come back to us and he copped a lot of us on in terms of not accepting certain things at training.

Paul of the Saracens allowed: 'To be honest, it was a bit embarrassing not to have started the two matches. We seemed to be walking away with the first but from nowhere Munster came back. It just showed the fight Munster had in them. Then we went over to Thomond Park and again we seemed to have it under control until there was that last-minute try by Woody converted by Ronan. It was an amazing day. David didn't give me such a hard time but a few of the others didn't spare us. A core of players from those games went on to do great things for Munster and indeed Ireland.'

Munster had now guaranteed a home quarter-final so there was little to play for in the final qualifier against Pontypridd at Sardis Road. They lost by two points. There was a twelve-week gap between that game and the quarter-final visit of Stade Français to Thomond Park for the quarter-final, an occasion that aroused unprecedented interest. Tickets were at a premium and thousands of supporters were disappointed. Kidney made two changes from the Saracens game with Killian Keane starting in the centre as Jason Holland was not available because of a family bereavement back in his native New Zealand, and preferring Eddie Halvey to Alan Quinlan at number six. This was a controversial call by the coach given that Quinlan had been forming a highly successful back-row combination with David Wallace and Anthony Foley whereas Halvey was not professionally contracted with Munster at the time.

Just like Saracens, Stade Français were bankrolled by a multi-millionaire, Max Guazzini, and were well known and indeed liked for the colour they brought to the game on and off the pitch. They had emerged from a tough group also involving Leinster, Leicester and Glasgow and included in their squad a number of high-profile French players, including wing Christophe Dominici, prop Sylvain Marconnet and back-row Marc Lievremont, and most significantly ace goal kicker and captain Diego Dominguez, the Argentinian who had established himself as Italy's free-scoring out-half.

Thomond Park was heaving and once again the atmosphere was electric. It became apparent from an early stage that Kidney knew exactly what he was doing when deciding to go with Eddie Halvey. This remarkably gifted footballer was there to augment the line-out presence of John Langford and Mick Galwey. The game was only a few minutes old when he pinched a couple of Stade throws and set an attack-minded Munster team on the move. Winger Anthony Horgan and full back Dominic Crotty ran in two early tries of the highest quality and Ronan O'Gara converted and added five penalties. The French were completely outplayed by 27–10. The crowd were beside themselves with joy and serenaded the visitors with several renderings of 'Au revoir, Au revoir, Au revoir' while for the first time adopting 'The Fields of Athenry' as their favoured Thomond Park chorus. Back in the dressing room after the final whistle, Brian O'Brien led the players in 'Stand Up and Fight'.

What followed next were two Heineken Cup games that will never be forgotten by Munster supporters, the marvellous 31–25 defeat of Toulouse in the semi-final in Bordeaux followed by the 9–8 final loss to Northampton Saints at Twickenham. Tears were shed that afternoon by thousands of Munster fans and most of the players but the sporting manner in which the defeat was accepted further embellished the deep regard in which they were held throughout the rugby world.

13

Pizza For Life

Thomond Park was still a very long way from the splendid stadium we know today when the International Board decided it would be suitable for the 1999 World Cup clash of Australia, the eventual champions, and the USA. That call spoke volumes for the ground's sense of atmosphere and tradition which in IRB minds compensated for its decidedly mediocre facilities and tawdry appearance. There was never any doubt as to the outcome of the game – 55–19 for the Wallabies – it was a notable occasion in that American centre Juan Grobler touched down for the only try the champions conceded in the entire event.

Jack Clark and Eddie O'Sullivan were the coaches of an American side that contained players of the calibre of Luke Gross, Tom Billups and skipper Dan Lyle, all of whom made their mark in the European arena. In addition to Grobler's try, they also had three penalties by Kevin Dalzell and a drop goal by David Niu. However, for the most part it was one-way traffic with the Wallabies running in tries by Scott Staniforth, 2; Stephen Larkham, Michael Foley, Matt Burke (who also kicked a penalty and four conversions), Tiaan Strauss, Chris Latham and future Leinster scrum half Chris Whitaker. Joe Roff also landed a conversion. For Jim Williams, a man who a short few years later would earn a reputation as one of the true greats of Munster rugby, it was a first look at a ground that would come to mean so much to him. The teams in the only World Cup match to take place at Thomond Park (14 October 1999) were:

Australia: Chris Latham, Scott Staniforth, Jason Little capt., Nathan Grey, Matt Burke, Stephen Larkham, Chris Whitaker, Dan Crowley, Michael Foley, Rod Moore, Mark Connors, Tom Bowman, Owen Finnegan, Tiaan Srauss, Jim Williams. *Replacements:* Joe Roff, Rod Kefer, Matt Cockbain, David Giffin, George Gregan, Richard Harry, Jeremy Paul.

USA: Karl Shuman, Vaea Anitoni, Juan Grobler, Mark Scharrenberg, Brian Hightower, David Niu, Kevin Dalzell capt., Joe Clayton, Tom Billups, George Sucher, Luke Gross, Alec Parker, David Hodges, Tasi Mo'unga, Rob Lumkong. *Replacements:* Tomas Takau, Tini Saulala, Jesse Coulson, Shaun Paga, Marc L'Huiller, Kirk Khasigan, Eric Reed.

Referee: A. J. Watson (South Africa).

For much of Thomond Park's first seventy-four years, one needed to visit either the Shannon or Bohemian clubhouses to find sustenance. A pint of the black stuff was the most popular item on the 'menu' with little thought for the cuppa or even a sandwich and it remained very much that way until everything changed with the opening of the new stadium in 2008.

Order a pizza in the old days and people wondered where exactly you had come from! However, when the offer of such a delectable piece of nutrition was dangled in front of the Munster squad in the build-up to the Heineken Cup quarter-final against Biarritz at Thomond Park on January 2001, one particularly distinguished player had no hesitation in putting his hand up.

Anthony Foley, widely known as 'Axel' after the character Axel Foley played by Eddie Murphy in the film *Beverley Hill Cop*, is a big man who had always looked forward to mealtime, whether at school in St Munchin's or back home in Killaloe with parents Brendan (he of the legendary Munster team of 1978) and Sheila and siblings Rosie (the Channel swimmer and rugby international) and Orla. So when his good friend Brian McGoey of Domino's Pizza came up with the incentive of free pies for life for the first Munster player to score a hat-trick of tries in a Heineken Cup game, Axel's thought process went into overdrive.

With good reason, many wondered whether Munster could lift themselves to a similarly high peak given the bitter disappointment of Twickenham and the 2000 Heineken Cup final when they lost to Northampton Saints. Mick Galwey wrote about how 'we were listening to people in the street and reading the newspapers. They were wondering if Munster would ever get back, if we'd ever be the same again, if we'd ever have the same hunger again.' The others were just as uncertain. However, the pep was back in their step early in the 2000/01 season after a training camp in Scotland followed by a Grand Slam in the Interprovincial Championship. Australian John Langford had originally stated that he was here for only one season but he enjoyed the scene so much that he succumbed to overtures to give it one more shot.

Thomond Park was full and buzzing once more when Gary Teichman, a former Springboks captain, led Newport out for their first appearance in the Heineken Cup. Aware of the Welsh side's inexperience, Munster hit them hard and early with tries by Galwey and Frankie Sheahan and when required later to defend their line, did so with commitment and authority. A week later, they came from behind to win in Castres which meant another mad scramble for tickets for the Thomond Park visit of Bath, a powerhouse of English rugby. Anthony Horgan scored two tries in a comfortable 31–9 victory only for Bath to gain their revenge by 18–5 at the Recreation Ground the following week. Munster had scored the game's only try through David Wallace and as the excitement died down, the Bath captain John Hall joined all those who had nothing but praise for the Thomond Park crowd: 'The atmosphere last week when a kick at goal was being taken was something special, everything is quiet, and it's the way rugby should be played. It's not just me, the young players in our dressing room are saying the same thing. The Munster fans are really fantastic.'

When the Heineken Cup resumed after Christmas, Munster came from 15–0 down in Newport to win a marvellous match, inspired by an almost unbelievable contribution of 29 points (1 try, 4 penalties, 3 conversions, 2 drop goals) by Ronan O'Gara, to claim the precious points. They then clinched the all-important home quarter-final by beating Castres at Musgrave Park.

Crack French side Biarritz were on their way to Thomond Park for the quarter-final clash with Munster on 28 January 2001. The sense of expectation had gone through the roof with people prepared to wait in line overnight in Limerick and Cork to lay their hands on the precious tickets. Queues that began at the Munster Branch office inside Thomond

Lengthy queues for tickets before a big European Cup fixture at Thomond Park in 2001. (*Irish Examiner*)

Park extended out onto the Cratloe Road, continued by the Mayorstone Garda Station and almost as far as the Limerick Institute of Technology. The story goes that when a hard-pressed Garda phoned a colleague and asked for some moral support he was told: 'No chance, I'm in the queue myself and I'm not leaving.'

This scene was being re-enacted much too often for the liking of many good rugby people and there were dark murmurings that the tickets were finding their way into the hands of the corporate sector.

Seven more years passed before the problem was resolved and to the credit of all members of the 'Red Army' as the legions of fans bedecked in Munster jerseys are known, their loyalty remained constant.

Those who stuck it out were certainly well rewarded. As a team, Munster were good that day against Biarritz. Very good. And yet the throngs walking back through Thomondgate to the city after many happy renditions of 'Stand Up and Fight' and 'The Fields of Athenry' were talking about only one man: Anthony Foley had been a law unto himself for the eighty minutes and not even a Biarritz pack, including such truly outstanding players as Serge Betsen, Olivier Roumat, Christophe Milheres and a whole host of other French internationals, could contain him. It was also a glory day for Munster who shrugged off the concession of two early tries to the Scot Stuart Legg to dominate the proceedings and eventually the scoreboard. The first of Foley's tries came early enough to quell the crowd's anxieties and Munster led 17–15 at the interval. He bagged his lifetime of pizzas in the sixty-fifth minute although complacency – not a vice usually

Anthony 'Axel' Foley scores one of his three 'pizza' tries against Biarritz in 2001. (Courtesy *Irish Examiner*)

associated with Munster teams – set in and Biarritz salvaged their reputation if not their place in the semi-final.

Foley claimed in his autobiography that he 'didn't do the dog' on the pizzas, that he was 'cutting down on the fast food' but he was still enjoying his friend McGoey's misgivings about that generous offer: 'Brian was afraid I'd eat them out of business. He must have been suspicious when he saw me hanging out wide and slipping in at the corner. Two more opportunities came along in the second half and what could I do but take them?'

The foot-and-mouth crisis then hit Europe and put competitive rugby on hold. Munster atoned for the lack of action by taking on a Rest of Ireland selection at Thomond Park which was again packed by the Red Army deprived of their Heineken Cup fix for eight weeks. Mick Galwey's side won 24–22. Now it was time for many thousands to make their way to Lille in France, where Ireland had lost rather ignominiously to Argentina in the previous season's World Cup. The manner of Munster's 16–15 defeat will live forever in the minds of the fans who, with every justification, still wonder to this day how touch judge Steve

Lander disallowed a perfectly fair try by Munster wing John O'Neill.

As interest in the Heineken Cup grew with each passing year and the big French and English clubs accumulated the wealth that would enable them to sign a whole host of big-name players from the southern hemisphere, the fear grew in Munster that they would not be able to keep in step. Heart-breaking defeat in two successive years was bad enough. Contemplating a bleak future made it worse. It did not help that John Langford had returned home although that did not mean the end of the Aussie influence in Munster.

Declan Kidney signed Jim Williams, the outstanding Wallabies back-row, as the kind of forward from 'down under' perfectly suited to the Munster psyche, on and off the pitch, and also reckoned that Paul O'Connell, Donncha O'Callaghan and Mick O'Driscoll, although not long out of their teens, would make ideal second-row replacements for Langford. The marvellous half-back partnership of Ronan O'Gara and Peter Stringer was now fully established at Ireland level. So too were props John Hayes and Peter Clohessy. Mick Galwey stood down as captain to be replaced by Jim Williams, not quite a traumatic development as might have been expected given that the Kerry man was approaching the end of his magnificent career. However, it was a different matter when Kidney was replaced by Alan Gaffney, an extremely likeable Australian who, however, had previously worked with Leinster. That left him with a lot to prove to the Munster fans.

For once, the group draw for the Heineken Cup qualifying stages was reasonably favourable: Castres, Harlequins and Bridgend. Munster and Castres crossed swords once again at Thomond Park. The doubts about this Munster team were not alleviated by an unimpressive 28–23 victory with a Jason Holland try proving crucial. Keith Wood was by now back with Harlequins but even he could not prevent a 24–8 defeat when Munster triumphed at The Stoop in Twickenham. Then followed two handy enough wins over the Welsh side Bridgend. Thomond Park was buzzing again and the crowd sang and joked as Harlequins (minus Woody) were thrashed 51–17. Ronan O'Gara was running up big scores as if for fun: 6 penalties, 1 conversion, 1 drop goal (23) against Castres; 1 try, 2 penalties, 1 conversion, 1 drop goal (16) v Harlequins; 2 penalties (6) v Bridgend away; 3 penalties, 3 cons (15) v Bridgend home; 5 penalties, 3 conversions (21) v Harlequins home; 2 penalties, 1 conversion (8) v Castres away.

Could he and the team do it all over again when taking on Stade Français at Stade Jean-Bouin in Paris on 26 January 2002? Of course they could, somehow clinging on to a two-point lead while playing into a gale-force wind for the entire second half. Then it was on to the lovely town of Béziers in the south of France for another smashing performance and a 25–17 semi-final defeat of their old friends Castres. Finally, it was the Millennium Stadium in Cardiff for another agonising final defeat, this time by Leicester in a game notorious for the 'Hand of Back', when Leicester flanker Neil Back illegally slapped the ball from Stringer's hands as he was putting it into a scrum in front of the English side's posts in the dying minutes, causing a turnover that enabled Leicester to retain a narrow advantage to the final whistle.

The redevelopment of Thomond Park was still several years off but that did not deter the IRFU from again recognising its potential to stage lower-grade international fixtures. So in June 2002, Romania turned up to test their mettle only to leave Limerick in the knowledge that they still had a lot to learn. Much to the delight of the 8,000 local fans, one of their great heroes, John Hayes, scored the first try in a comprehensive win for a near full-strength Irish side. There were tries apiece for Keith Gleeson, Girvan Dempsey, Brian O'Driscoll and Rob Henderson with a penalty try thrown in for good measure. Ronan O'Gara tacked on three conversions and a penalty.

Ireland: Girvan Dempsey, John Kelly, Brian O'Driscoll, Kevin Maggs, Denis Hickie, Ronan O'Gara, Peter Stringer, Reggie Corrigan, Shane Byrne, John Hayes, Gary Longwell, Malcolm O'Kelly, Simon Easterby, Keith Gleeson, Anthony Foley capt. *Replacements*: Paul Shields, Paul Wallace, Leo Cullen, Victor Costello, Guy Easterby, David Humphreys, Rob Henderson.

A little more than a year later, on 30 August 2003, Thomond Park was the stage for another international fixture, this time the World Cup warm-up game between Ireland and Italy. The Irish were fancying their chances of a successful campaign in Australia (which, alas, did not come to pass) while the Italians were still finding their international feet. It is doubtful whether Irish coach Eddie O'Sullivan learned a whole lot as his side romped home by 61–6. Perhaps it caused a few people to get ahead of themselves given that the Italians included great forwards like Sergio Parisse, Mauro Bergamasco and Martin

Castrogiovanni. But Ireland were so dominant everywhere that Denis Hickie on the left wing ran in four tries and there was one each for Shane Byrne, Girvan Dempsey, David Humphreys and John Kelly. Humphreys converted six of the eight tries and also landed three penalties.

Ireland: G. Dempsey, J. Kelly, B. O'Driscoll, R. Henderson, D. Hickie, D. Humphreys, G. Easterby, M. Horan, S. Byrne, R. Corrigan, G. Longwell, L. Cullen, E. Miller, V. Costello, S. Easterby. *Replacements*: P. Shields, J. Fitzpatrick, D. O'Callaghan, K. Dawson, B. O'Meara, G. Murphy, J. Bell.

Italy: G. Peens, N. Mazzucato, C. Stoica, M. Barbini, D. Sacca, F. Mazzario, A. Troncon, A. Lo Cicero, F. Ongaro, M. Castrogiovanni, C. Bezzi, M. Giachere, A. de Rossi, M. Bergamasco, S. Parisse. *Replacements*: C. Festuccia, R. Martinez-Frugoni, A. Persico, M. Phillips, M. Mazzantini, R. Pez, A. Masi.

Referee: S. Landers (England).

14

A New Millennium

The Miracle Match

Thomond Park has been associated with countless remarkable occasions over the years. Everyone will have their own idea of the one that means most although it is inevitable that the Heineken Cup 'Miracle Match' between Munster and Gloucester on 18 January 2003 will feature very close to the top of every list.

If Thomond Park was regarded as an amazing stadium before that day, it now officially achieved legendary status. What does it say about a place, people wondered, where any rugby team could go out on the field needing to score four tries and win by twenty-seven points against the reigning English champions and do precisely that, even if their new coach Alan Gaffney and the players themselves seemed as uncertain about what was happening as just about everyone else?

If ever the word 'surreal' fitted the bill, this was surely it. Early on the morning of the game, Limerick was buzzing with reports that a copy of the Gloucester game plan had been discovered in a taxi and that it had been given to Gaffney and his players. It happened all right and we shall never know if it made any difference to the result. Even Gloucester insiders doubt that it played any part in the outcome. Come kick-off time and Thomond Park, as usual on these days, was packed even if deep down the fans believed that it was an impossible ask and that, very simply, the chance of a Europe victory was over for another year. Earlier defeats to Gloucester and Perpignan by relatively wide margins had apparently seen to that.

Munster's Jeremy Staunton on a Thomond Park day of days, the 2003 'Miracle Match', Munster v Gloucester. (*Irish Examiner*)

Donncha O'Callaghan claims line-out possession against Gloucester in 2003. (*Irish Examiner*)

To give a vivid picture of how Munster actually achieved the miracle is well nigh impossible for even the most detached of observers. We all know *now* what Munster needed to do. But even Ronan O'Gara, the man who clocked up the thirty-second and thirty-third points that turned the impossible into actuality admitted years later in his life story that he was not aware of the importance of the conversion.

'I wasn't clued into that', he wrote. 'We had discussed the numbers at the start of the week but it didn't really come up after that. We didn't want it to be a distraction. There was such pandemonium after the fourth try that I thought we were home and dry. I treated it like any other kick. That conversion mattered to me and my standards. I can't claim nerves of steel on that one because I was oblivious to the wider consequences.'

O'Gara also admitted that one of his towering Garryowens, which helped to unsettle the Gloucester full back Henry Paul, was something of a miskick, but its flight path totally flummoxed the former Rugby League star. The Munster chasers led by skipper Jim Williams, Alan Quinlan, Donncha O'Callaghan, Mike Mullins and the rest were on him like a pack of hounds and he was a beaten man for the rest of the day. John Kelly slipped over for the first try in the right corner, Mossie Lawler for the second on the other side of the pitch just before half time.

Kelly struck for a second time and late on, Mick O'Driscoll, for reasons he has never adequately explained, found himself all alone in the right-hand corner at the Ballynanty end. O'Gara's precise cross kick landed a few yards in front of the second-row, bounced favourably and Micko did the rest. Now all it needed was for ROG to land the conversion. Not for the first or last time, he made it look easy. A few minutes later, the final whistle sounded and the players were deliriously mobbed by 12,000 fans who themselves were only just beginning to understand the implications of what had happened: Munster were through to the quarter-finals. The players re-emerged from the dressing room just as the heroes of 1978 had done before them. Thomond Park and Munster had come good again!

The teams that day were:

Munster: J. Staunton, J. Kelly, M. Mullins, J. Holland, M. Lawler, R. O'Gara, P. Stringer, M. Horan, F. Sheahan, J. Hayes, M. O'Driscoll, D. O'Callaghan, J. Williams capt., A. Quinlan, A. Foley.

Gloucester: H. Paul (T. Beim), J. Simpson-Daniel, T. Fanalua, R. Todd, T. Delport, L. Mercier, A. Gomersall, R. Roncero, O. Ozam, P. Vickery capt., R. Fidler (A. Eustace), R. Cornwall, J. Boer, P. Buxton (A. Hazell), J. Paramore (C. Collins).

Munster's four tries v Gloucester in 2003, touched down by John Kelly (2), Mossy Lawler and Mick O'Driscoll. (*Evening Echo*)

The plaudits for the Munster performance, Thomond Park and the Red Army came in thick and fast with one of the most glowing from Nigel Melville, head coach of Gloucester who in spite of his own understandable disappointment couldn't contain himself as he wrote in *The Guardian*:

> Only by being in Limerick on a big match day can you understand why the place is such a fortress – 20 European wins out of 20. I played there myself and in the past two years I've taken Gloucester there in the Heineken Cup. On each occasion we arrived having beaten Munster at Kingsholm; on each occasion we climbed back on the plane at Shannon as losers. Thomond Park is in another league altogether. Teams know they are in for something special as soon as they land at Shannon and drive into town. Limerick is rugby. Everyone knows who you are and why you're there. The banter is knowledgeable and entertaining.
>
> Then on the day of the match the build-up really starts. Our hotel was a five-minute walk from the ground but the coach had two motorcycle outriders, whose blaring sirens sped us through red lights and pre-match traffic until, even with nearly two hours to go, we were temporarily halted by a wall of fans outside the main gate.
>
> Once you are through the huge double gates you get your first glimpse of Thomond Park itself. To flatter the stadium would be to call it unprepossessing. It is a sort of mini Lansdowne Road without the frills. There's lots of concrete, lots of tin, loads of history and space for 12,000 which, come kick-off, looks and sounds like many more.
>
> I don't know whether these things are choreographed for maximum effect but, when we re-emerged, the noise was stunning. An old boy was banging out 'The Fields of Athenry' – probably the third time it had been sung in 60 minutes – and the best was yet to come. Stand Up and Fight owes a lot to Bizet and Carmen but an awful lot more to the choir of 10,000 (it must have been more) who particularly relished a chorus that includes the lines:

'Stand toe to toe,
'Trade blow for blow'

and ends

'Stand up and fight like hell'.

Which is exactly what Munster did for the next 80 minutes. Initially the preferred method of attack was the Garryowen: a steepling kick which falls on defenders through a crescendo of aaahs from the crowd. By way of contrast, the silence afforded to a kick at goal was total but just as unnerving. Munster would have beaten anyone in Europe.

Rupert Bates of the *Daily Telegraph* quite obviously enjoyed every minute:

Never has 'The Fields of Athenry' been sung with such fervour. Men and women of Munster hugged, wept and cheered and landlords across Europe planned their early retirement parties knowing Munster and their supporters would be marching on to fill bars across a continent. Gloucester, magnificent all season as Zurich Premiership leaders, will be as sick as it is possible to be. They were simply blown out of the Heineken Cup by a force of rugby nature.

Phil Vickery, the Gloucester captain, as a former Redruth man, knows all about Hell Fire Corner, but Thomond Park is where Hades holds its dinner parties. By comparison, Gloucester's Kingsholm is the Garden of Eden.

The mathematics were finally cracked but it would surely be a technicality. The Irishmen may be one of the most driven teams in all sport at their Limerick home, but to stuff Gloucester, a team fashioned in Munster's image, was not thought possible. Yet the mantra all week in the home camp had been: 'With Munster everything is possible.' Only Thomond Park can do this.

The Guardian's Rob Kitson enthused:

Not many sporting days rate once-in-a-lifetime status but Munster's performance on Saturday belongs among the greatest rugby tales in history. Think Red Rum hunting down Crisp at Aintree or Ian Botham taking Australia apart at Headingley in 1981, set it in the wild west of Ireland in front of a delirious crowd and it is hard to imagine anything better.

For all Munster's past epic triumphs, this was unquestionably their most amazing hour. Not even their most faithful fans gave them a prayer of beating England's leading club by four clear tries and 27 points, the near-impossible margin they needed to qualify for the knock-out stages. Somehow, in circumstances part cavalry charge, part mathematical teaser and, ultimately, pure comic fiction, they managed it.

Alan Quinlan, Peter Stringer and Frankie Sheahan celebrate the incredible 2003 victory over Gloucester. (*Irish Examiner*)

The scoreboard at the end of the 'Miracle Match' – but it tells only part of the story. (*Irish Examiner*)

Ian Randall was in Thomond Park that day representing BBC Radio Gloucestershire and thereby viewing affairs, so to speak, through cherry-and-white spectacles. Like all good journalists, though, he was able to see all sides of the story:

> Little did I know just how much the 16th man – the crowd – would inspire the Munster team. Surveying the ground empty, it was a spartan venue with three sides open to the elements. The transformation when full was astonishing. Andy Deacon confessed after the match that he'd never heard anything like it in his career. Moreover, this apparently ageing team – built around the likes of skipper Jim Williams in the back row, and Peter Stringer and Ronan O'Gara at half back – never panicked.

Forward, then, to an 'away' quarter-final at another of rugby's famed fortresses, Welford Road, the home of the powerful Leicester club. In spite of their heroics in the 'Miracle Match', Munster were again rated outsiders against a powerful side led by England World Cup-winning Martin Johnson and also containing players of the stature of Neil Back, Martin Corry, Darren Garforth and Austin Healey, all England internationals, and seasoned Ireland caps Geordan Murphy and Tom Tierney. Tierney figured on many successful Munster teams and later became coach of the Ireland Ladies team. The Stringer/O'Gara half-back partnership has rarely been seen to better effect, each scoring a try and ROG kicking the rest in a 20–7 triumph. Alas, yet another bad draw meant a visit to the south of France where they went down 13–12 to Toulouse in Toulouse. Hardly a disgrace for sure, but by now Munster had reached a level of eminence that meant reaching the semi-final in Europe was no longer enough.

Downgrading of the Club Game

It is timely here to pause and contemplate the way in which the club game and especially the Munster Senior Cup and, to a slightly lesser degree, the All-Ireland League were being systematically downgraded. As soon as the AIL arrived on the scene in 1990, the clubs agreed among themselves that it was the only game in town and more or less to forget about the Munster Cup, the competition that had carried the game since 1884. Once the European Cup began in the mid-1990s, the agenda changed as the clubs were put in their place and told to hand over their best players to Munster or Leinster or whoever and accept second-class citizenship. Many good rugby people tried to stand up and fight against the new order but they never really had a chance. The players who had been 'hardened' and trained in the teak-tough school that was the Cup and the League were no longer available to the clubs that had developed them physically and mentally. Several of the fine back-room men who battled gamely but in vain against the trend gradually drifted away in sadness, frustration and disillusionment. Nowadays, those who turn up in depressingly small numbers for club matches at Thomond Park and Musgrave Park, Dooradoyle and Temple Hill, Tom Clifford Park and the Mardyke, Eaton Park and Castle Avenue, Glenina and Templeville Road are all too often looked upon disparagingly as diehards.

They battle on, however, and their reward comes in producing a string of talented youngsters whom they nurture from their pre-teen days until they are ready for a competitive but relatively low-standard AIL. Then the frustration starts all over again. Those who show a spark of promise are offered academy contracts, which understandably they accept, and the clubs who created them can go whistle in the wind. Just think about it: drawn Munster Cup matches today, including the final, are decided in favour of the team that scores the first try!

Garryowen captain Paul Neville holds the Munster Senior Cup aloft after one of the club's four major trophy wins in 2006. (*Irish Examiner*)

The total domination of the AIL by Munster clubs was ended in 2000 by Dublin's St Mary's College. Shannon recaptured the title in 2002 before once again ruling the roost from 2004 to 2006 until being replaced by Garryowen in 2007, a year in which the influence of Munster's Killian Keane and several other knowledgeable coaches helped the Dooradoyle club to capture the Bateman Cup also and the Munster Senior and Junior Cups.

In 2001, Thomond housed another AIL final, and it was decided in a manner that graphically reflected how far down the pecking order the competition had fallen. Concerned that Shannon and Clontarf might finish on level terms with the need for a replay, the IRFU decided that, as in drawn Munster Cup matches, the team scoring the first try would be declared champions. As if to underline the irony of the situation, the sides drew a superb match, nineteen points each, but because David O'Donovan touched down for the first of his two tries in the twenty-third minute, Shannon were declared All-Ireland champions. Even though their performance on the day probably merited the accolade, this way of deciding the country's champion club demeaned the competition just at it did the Munster Cup. The fact that the final was voted 'a great advert for club rugby' did absolutely nothing to assuage Clontarf's feeling of being very hard done by. And who could blame them?

The 2009 Shannon team to win the AIL title at Thomond Park were:

David O'Donovan, Richie Mullane, Fionn McLoughlin, John Clogan, Stephen Kelly (Marcus O'Driscoll), Tadhg Bennett, Frankie McNamara, Killian O'Neill (Les Hogan), Mike Essex, Kevin Griffin, Padraic O'Brien (Emmett O'Callaghan), Fergal Walsh, Donnacha Ryan, Eoghan Grace, David Quinlan capt.

Cork Constitution kept the league trophy in Munster in 2010 but it had not been back by 2015 and with so many young men in their twenties leaving their native place to seek employment in jobs-rich Dublin, the trend in favour of Leinster clubs did not look like ending any time soon.

If anything, the demise of the Munster Cup has been even more devastating. Sadly, it looked as if the greatest of all cup competitions was being regarded as something of a nuisance for much of the early years of the new century. The Munster Branch was an easy target and deserved some of the opprobrium that came their way but the clubs were not without blame either. Not surprisingly, public interest dwindled away to such an extent that the attendance at Thomond Park finals was a lot closer to 1,000 (or even fewer) rather than the 10,000-plus that were part and parcel of such occasions just a short few years previously.

Undaunted, Shannon pursued the title with creditable zeal and won it every year from 2000 to 2006. A few more of the usual suspects, Garryowen, Shannon again, Cork Constitution and Young Munster, followed in their footsteps but the Munster Cup desperately needed a new name on the trophy when the 2010/11 campaign got under way. Few, however, would have predicted before a ball was kicked in anger that Bruff would be the side to fit that particular bill.

Bruff RFC was founded in 1969/70 by Nicholas Cooke and Willie Conway and were immediately competitive, initially in underage rugby from which they graduated to capturing the Munster Junior Cup in 1998, 1999 and 2004 and the AIL under-twenty title in 2001 before

Cork Constitution, Munster Senior Cup champions, 2013/14. (Courtesy Cork Constitution RFC)

gaining senior status by winning the AIL Provincial Round Robin series in 2003/04. They moved up to Division One B for the 2010/11 season and had their sights set on the Munster Cup. Although handed the worst possible draw, they were up to the challenge, beating none other than mighty Cork Constitution and Shannon on the way to the Thomond Park decider and a meeting with Garryowen. Bruff were skippered by their excellent hooker Cathal O'Regan and coached by Peter Malone, who had won the cup with Garryowen in 2007 along with other major honours before returning 'home'.

Malone, who has worked with the Munster academy for several years, marshalled his willing forces to considerable effect. This was the first final to be staged in the 'new' Thomond Park and while the attendance was but a fraction of what it used to be in the halcyon days of the championship, the enthusiasm of the Bruff supporters bedecked with flags, club jerseys, jackets, ties, scarves, etc., made for a very special atmosphere. Nor did O'Regan, Malone, the Cahills or indeed any member of the Bruff squad let them down. Thirteen of their team were bred back in their own native habitat and the spirit engendered by such a sense of community meant that they were going to fight every inch of the way. They did all of that – and more. Tries by Malone and

Bruff RFC, Munster Senior Cup and Bateman Cup champions, 2011/12. Back row (l–r): Brendan Bourke, Paddy Cleary, Gearoid Ryan, Peter Malone, Brian Morrissey, Maurice O'Connell, David Horan, Alfie Laffan, Alan Bourke, John Moore, Paul O'Brien, Ger Collins, Gary Leonard, Martin O'Rourke, Michael Leahy; front row (l–r): Tom O'Callaghan, Mossy O'Donnell, Brendan Deady, Eoin Cahill, Tony Cahill, Cathal O'Regan capt., Andrew Cashman, Eoghan Maher, Brian Cahill, John Shine, Mike Carroll and John Carroll. (Courtesy Ger Malone, Bruff RFC)

Alan Bourke and thirteen points from the boot of Brian Cahill did the trick. Garryowen, of course, were no pushover. Conor Murray, set to be the Munster and Ireland scrum half and a Lion in not much more than twelve months, scored a try and they had cut their arrears to four points with plenty of time remaining. But a magnificent Bruff defence held out under fierce pressure for a sweet and deserved victory. For the Cahill family – dad Mick who had coached most of the squad from their youngest days and brothers Brian with his thirteen points, Eoin, and Tony who was voted man of the match – it was a day they will never forget

And if that was not enough, they then went on to win the All-Ireland Bateman Cup, beating Dungannon 24–18 in the final. The successful Munster Cup final Bruff team was:

B. Deady, A. Cashman, B. Cahill, E. Cahill (G. Leonard), P. O'Brien, T. Cahill, E. Maher, D. Horan (G. Collins), C. O'Regan capt. (M. O'Donnell), G. Ryan, A. Laffan (M. Carroll), M. O'Connell, A. Bourke, J. Shine, P. Malone. *Also*: T. O'Callaghan, T. Carroll, J. Malone, D. Murnane, G. Collins.

15

Chasing The Holy Grail

Victory in the Heineken Cup remained Munster's chief target in the early years of the new millennium and they were intent on strengthening their squad whenever the right man became available and the financial realities were observed. The arrival of Jim Williams in 2000/01 had made a big difference to the forward pack and in 2003/04 Christian Cullen, a full back who already enjoyed legendary status in New Zealand, came on board. These were signings of clear intent – Munster would not settle for second best. Cullen was only twenty-eight years old at the time, a superstar whether playing full back, centre or wing, the record All Blacks try scorer with forty-six tries (subsequently beaten by another Munster player, Doug Howlett, before he arrived on these shores). The acquisition of such a totemic figure demonstrated that Munster possessed the resources and the ambition to attract rugby's finest and it certainly looked like the final piece of the jigsaw had slotted into place. The general belief was that Cullen's acquisition would inject the necessary penetration into a back line that struggled to turn quality possession into line breaks and try-scoring opportunities. At the time, Cullen was the real deal although, ironically, had it not been for a difference of opinion with the All Blacks coach of the time, former Garryowen player John Mitchell, Cullen would have earned more than fifty-eight All Blacks caps.

Sadly, a shoulder injury that troubled him from the time he set foot on Irish soil meant that Cullen was never the same player; it drastically reduced his number of appearances in the Munster jersey and his impact on the team's level of performance and achievements. Jeremy Staunton and Shaun Payne (who had joined from Swansea and duly became one of the province's most valuable 'imports' before being appointed manager on his retirement) filled the full-back position with considerable distinction through the pool rounds of the 2003/04 Heineken campaign. Bourgoin were beaten home and away and, in similar fashion to the previous season, Munster overturned defeat by Gloucester at Kingsholm with a clear cut 35–14 win at Thomond Park.

No need for a miracle this time and once again all hell broke loose as the battle for tickets for the quarter-final against Stade Français got under way. Once more, Thomond Park was unable to cater for the demand. Even so, the atmosphere remained as electric as ever. The scoreboard said 37–32 in Munster's favour at the finish but the margin actually flattered the French. Christian Cullen made his first European Cup appearance and tries by Payne, playing on the wing, Rob Henderson, Mike Mullins and Marcus Horan were augmented by three penalties and four conversions from O'Gara: in all, enough to counter the best efforts of a star-studded Stade line-up that also touched down for four tries. It was a cracking game of football that really whetted the appetite of the

The indomitable Paul O'Connell scores against Treviso in 2003. (*Irish Examiner*)

The class of Christian Cullen (left) and Shaun Payne (right) is in evidence as they combine to score a Munster try against Stade Français in 2004. (*Irish Examiner*)

fans who, for once, could look forward to a 'home' semi-final, albeit at Lansdowne Road, against London Wasps.

Cullen had come through the Stade game without any further injuries and retained his place for the semi-final. But it was not to be Munster's day. David Wallace cried off on the morning of the game, the targeted Ronan O'Gara hobbled off after twenty minutes and eventually Wasps were winners on a 37–32 scoreline, thanks to a last-minute try credited to the gargantuan Trevor Leota. It was hugely controversial, however, with Wasps captain Lawrence Dallaglio agreeing that Leota was probably short of the line. The great England back-rower also deemed it one of the best club matches ever played but that was little consolation to Munster – they seemed as far away as ever from the Promised Land.

Christian Cullen played all the group matches in 2004/05 and, as ever, Munster qualified for the quarter-finals. Harlequins, Castres and Neath-Swansea (with Cullen contributing an important try to the delight of the Thomond Park faithful) all received the same treatment on home territory but defeat away to the French side cost the coveted home quarter-final.

One of the gentlemen of the professional game, Munster's outstanding Australian coach Alan Gaffney. (*Irish Examiner*)

Without Cullen, they lost tamely enough to Biarritz in San Sebastian. It was Alan Gaffney's last match as Munster coach, leaving with these prescient words: 'I am positive that Munster will be a force for years to come. They will win the Heineken Cup and win it soon.'

Gaffney's three-year stint had come about essentially through Declan Kidney's appointment as assistant Ireland coach to Eddie O'Sullivan in 2002. Declan never looked altogether happy in the role and by summer 2004 he had departed Dublin for the less salubrious surrounds of Rodney Parade and the Newport Gwent Dragons. Quickly realising how much he missed his native heath, Kidney accepted the offer of the position as head coach at Leinster, even though he was still pining for a return to Cork and Munster. The opportunity duly came his way in 2005 and he took it with open arms. He would have been happy, too, when the players chose Anthony Foley as captain. They knew each other well, initially from schools rugby times, Kidney as coach at Pres, Foley as a budding star at St Munchin's and from there through the early days with Munster when Mick Galwey and Jim Williams held the position. Both did the job superbly but now it was the turn of 'Axel' Foley, the man Keith Wood described as 'the smartest rugby player I have played with or against'. There were other positive developments – such as the emergence of two fine three-quarters, centre Barry Murphy from University of Limerick/ Bohemians and Ian Dowling, a native of Kilkenny and a product of the Shannon nursery. Perhaps even more significantly, Denis Leamy, a tough Tipperary man and an outstanding number eight during his Rockwell days, was ready to challenge for a place in the highly competitive back row. He was just the kind of home-grown talent ideal to serve the Munster cause. Much the same could be said of hooker Jerry Flannery who was to prove such an outstanding successor to Keith Wood and Frankie Sheahan. Thomond Park was preparing itself for several more big days.

However, the campaign got off to a less-than-auspicious start as Munster departed Edgeley Park, Sale, on the back of a 27–13 thumping by Jason Robinson's Sale Sharks.

Reliable old Castres were next on the list at Thomond Park. If you needed a result or a bonus point, Castres were the team to play as they rarely, if ever, tried their utmost in Europe and this was no different. Nevertheless, it was a nervous place that day for no one ever knew beforehand what kind of resistance the French club might offer. The fans needn't have worried: Munster prevailed 42–16 in a game that provided a useful introduction to this new level of rugby for several younger prospects like Barry Murphy, Jeremy Manning, Tomas O'Leary, Denis Fogarty, Trevor Hogan, Stephen Keogh and Federico Pucciariello, with the majority gaining some game time off the bench. Pucciariello, a highly popular recruit from Argentina, was used largely as a replacement in his three years with Munster and did so superbly well, most famously in Gloucester in 2008 when he came in at a particularly parlous stage of a Heineken Cup quarter-final and shored up a gaping hole in the Munster scrum. On and off the field, his teammates and the fans were mad about this portly character whose stated ambition was one day to be President of Argentina.

Even though Munster went on to wallop Newport Gwent Dragons home and away and hapless Castres by 46–9 at Stade Pierre-Antoine, the early pointless loss to Sale meant that they desperately needed a bonus point for the return game at Thomond Park on 21 January 2006 if they were to enjoy the advantage of a home quarter-final. To say the place was rocking that night would be an understatement. The crowd went berserk when the great French forward Sebastian Chabal was all but driven over the Ballynanty wall by Paul O'Connell, Donncha O'Callaghan and the rest of the Munster pack.

A moment Munster supporters will never forget: Paul O'Connell and Donncha O'Callaghan propel the powerful Frenchman Sebastian Chabal back 30 metres during the game against Sale Sharks, Thomond Park, 17 October 2006. (*Irish Examiner*)

All of the essential four Munster bonus-point tries were magnificently engineered and executed. Nevertheless, the tackle on the powerfully built Chabal has become part of Munster and Thomond Park folklore. It started when O'Gara launched a restart high into the dark Limerick sky. Chabal called and claimed. O'Connell hit him as he did so and O'Callaghan, Leamy and Foley joined in to drive the Frenchman back a good 30 metres at frightening speed – although in the mists of time it may have been forgotten that the bearded Frenchman, quite admirably, retained possession and got the ball away. Even then, Sale out-half Charlie Hodgson, understandably unnerved by what he had just witnessed, sliced his kick into touch, Munster won the line-out, the pack mauled over the line and a beaming Foley emerged triumphantly with the ball. Memories, memories indeed! They don't come any better than this.

There was little sign of the vital fourth try for much of the proceedings. French referee Joel Jutge was a little busier than he would have wished as he waved three yellow cards in what was a decidedly fractious encounter. The great Puma forward Ignacio Fernandez Lobbe was a victim; so, too, was Marcus Horan, but there was also plenty of rugby, like terrific tries for skipper Foley and winger Dowling. Good as these scores were, they didn't quite match that produced by Barry Murphy as he sped onto a loose ball just inside the Sale half and took off for the distant line like a bat out of hell. His triumphant dive was greeted with a deafening roar from the massed terraces and stand.

All the time, Ronan O'Gara kept the scoreboard ticking over and Sale could manage only three penalties by Hodgson. While they didn't score again, the English side defended manfully throughout the second half, leaving the home fans to chew their fingernails in anxiety until, with two minutes of stoppage time on the clock, David Wallace displayed remarkable stamina and speed to reach a ruck close to the Sale line, sweep up the ball and power his way home. The din was deafening. Munster were winners by 31–9 and once again the knockout stages of the Heineken were beckoning.

Thomond Park had come up trumps again but the knowing ones shook their heads and acknowledged that a ground restricted to crowds of around 13,000 had outlived its usefulness. Wallace's late try against Sale had earned Munster a 'home' quarter-final but the rules stipulated that the host venue had to be able to accommodate more than 20,000 spectators. That immediately ruled Thomond Park out of the equation, leaving Lansdowne Road – which itself wasn't exactly a thing of beauty at the time – as the only option. Consequently, there was a conspicuous lack of

(L–r): Paul O'Connell (aloft), Peter Stringer and Denis Leamy taking a line-out during Munster's 2006 victory over Leinster at Thomond Park. (*Irish Examiner*)

Penalty try for Munster v Leinster, 2006. (*Irish Examiner*)

atmosphere for the quarter-final clash with Perpignan who proved difficult opposition and were not easily overcome. After that, it was on to Lansdowne Road for the 'home' semi-final against Leinster which was memorably won by Munster 30–6. The Holy Grail of a Heineken Cup final win was finally secured thanks to a 23–19 victory over Biarritz in Cardiff's Millennium Stadium.

~

It can be safely stated that at least 95 per cent of the British journalists who came to Thomond Park during these exceptionally exciting years really enjoyed the experience. But sour notes were sounded on a few occasions, most notably by Paul Ackford, a former England and Lions forward and a policeman in his amateur days. Ackford wrote for the *Sunday Telegraph* and in keeping with one other member of the cross-channel rugby writing fraternity, appeared afflicted by the belief that there was something unsavoury about most things Irish. The following piece by Ackford in the *Telegraph* in the build-up to the Leinster v Munster game in 2006 is a case in point.

> Before we get to the match itself, let's disabuse ourselves a little of the legend that is Munster. Yes, they have strung together a 24-match unbeaten sequence of European games at Limerick's

Thomond Park over 10 years. Yes, this is their sixth European semi-final in seven seasons. Yes, they play in front of some of the most loyally partisan and wonderful supporters in the whole of the rugby world.

And, yes, the word 'some' qualified that last sentence considerably.

Thomond Park is the only stadium I've been to where the press is subjected to synchronised thieving after the match. Regular as clockwork, as soon as laptop lids are flipped up or mobile phones reached for to file copy after the final whistle, a team of dirty, dishevelled children approach the media area. One diverts attention while his mates reach for binoculars, cases, pens – anything that looks unattended. That is also the reality of the great Munster experience and it is not particularly pleasant.

Nor did Ackford stop there. Alan Quinlan, who enjoyed a particularly warm relationship with the Thomond Park faithful, also felt the wrath of the man's laptop a few years later after a game against Northampton:

Alan Quinlan was what Munster were all about. The flanker, who missed the Lions tour because of a 12-week ban handed out for eye gouging in last year's Heineken Cup semi-final, was Munster's enforcer, their bully boy. In one brief passage of mischief-making Quinlan picked a fight with Reihana before throwing his scrum-cap away. Then he moved on to a pushing match with Courtney Lawes and finally charged into a couple of mauls and tried to knock Roger Wilson's head off. All this, by the way, without attracting as much as much as a finger wagging from the officials. In many ways, Quinlan's behaviour was a disgrace.

Then came the punchline: 'But that is what players mean when they talk about the Thomond Park factor.'

These kinds of comments hurt for a while but most regarded them as simply a dose of sour grapes. Nobody ever pretended the old Thomond Park was perfect and there may have been a few regrettable incidents but the vast majority of visitors actually expressed a desire to return some time in the future.

16

'Just a Field'

Munster and Ireland rugby fans have considerable admiration for Nigel Owens, the world-class Welsh referee, which, of course, is not to say they have always agreed with his decisions, some of a crucial nature. However, no one was complaining when he penalised Leicester's Leinster man Shane Jennings an extra 10 metres for backchat in the last minute of a Heineken Cup season opener at Welford Road in 2007. With the Tigers leading 19–18, the rain bucketing down, the pitch as slippery as an ice rink, the ball saturated and as heavy as a lump of lead, the partisan home crowd jeering and whistling and the ball teed as far out as the halfway line, there seemed no way even Ronan O'Gara could launch the projectile that far and with the requisite accuracy. Somehow, this legend of the Munster game did precisely that, the ball skimming over the crossbar by a matter of inches. Leicester 19, Munster 21 and another big Munster European challenge was under way. The Tigers, though, would have their revenge, by becoming the first team to beat Munster at Thomond Park in a Heineken Cup match.

Munster's French opposition in 2006/07 came from Bourgoin who numbered former Munster scrum half Mike Prendergast in their ranks while Leicester and Cardiff were also expected to provide formidable opposition. Bourgoin proved more troublesome at Thomond Park than might have been anticipated, probably because of the presence of 'Prendy', not the kind to allow them to surrender tamely in front of his friends and family. Nevertheless, they eventually conceded six tries and when Munster followed up with wins over Cardiff both at home and away, their place in yet another quarter-final looked assured before the Christmas break.

They made certain by eking out a three-point victory over Bourgoin in Geneva. However, that still left them needing to beat Leicester in the final match to guarantee a home quarter-final. Paul O'Connell, who had taken over the captaincy from Anthony Foley, tried all he knew to lift the team, and Thomond Park as always acted as a sixteenth man, but it still was not enough. Ulster's Ian Humphreys had a fine game at out-half for the visitors who battled resolutely, very much in the Munster way, and got home deservedly by 13–6. Suffering a first Heineken Cup defeat there after twenty-five successive victories since 1995 was a bitter pill to swallow, all the more so because this was the last Heineken Cup game at the old stadium. Thomond Park was a quiet place that night.

'We are hurting and everyone in the dressing room is very down', reported Declan Kidney, shortly after the final whistle.

The visitors had played against the wind and rain in the first half and still led 8–6 at the interval. Humphreys used the elements cleverly after that and the only try of the second half came from Tigers wing Ollie Smith. Even Paul O'Connell did not escape criticism for his leadership as he opted for an attacking scrum after the award of a close-range penalty instead of taking a guaranteed three points with his side 8–6 behind. Leicester fielded four Irishmen that night: Humphreys, Geordan Murphy, Leo Cullen and Shane Jennings.

Robert Kitson painted an accurate description of the drama that unfolded on this historic and dramatic evening in his *Guardian* report:

> Until Saturday night there were three certainties in Irish life: death, taxes and Munster winning at home in the Heineken Cup. For 12 seasons every visiting side had fallen victim here, reduced to their component parts by a seemingly irresistible force of nature. Leicester's ram-raid in their Pool Four contest was the rugby equivalent of watching the Walls of Jericho come tumbling down.
>
> All records get broken eventually, all great teams get dragged back into the pack. The magnitude of the Tigers' groundbreaking effort, though, should not be underestimated as Munster were hardly complacent. The bulldozers are about to flatten much of Thomond Park as part of a planned redevelopment and

this was supposed to be a raucous farewell to the rackety old place. Little did the locals imagine that their champion squad would be knocked over as well ... It may or may not have been a good idea to describe Thomond Park as 'just a field', as the Tigers' head coach Pat Howard did beforehand, but the basic psychology worked for Leicester.

An elated Martin Corry, the Tigers captain, described it as 'an incredibly special feeling. We went out there and performed. Every player stood up to the challenge, our mentality had been right throughout the week. It is a fantastic place to come and play rugby'. True to form, Declan Kidney generously and realistically accepted that 'we knew we never had a divine right to win all our games at Thomond Park.'

Leicester: G. Murphy, C. Rabeni, D. Hipkiss (L. Lloyd 71), O. Smith, A. Tuilagi (S. Vesty 79), I. Humphreys, H. Ellis, M. Castrogiovanni (M. Ayerza 65), G. Chuter, J. White, L. Cullen, L. Deacon, L. Moody, M. Corry capt., S. Jennings.

Munster: S. Payne, J. Kelly (T. O'Leary 22), B. Murphy, L. Mafi, I. Dowling, R. O'Gara, P. Stringer, M. Horan, F. Sheahan (J. Flannery, 49), J. Hayes, D. O'Callaghan, P. O'Connell capt., M. O'Driscoll (A. Foley 49, J. Coughlan, 80), D. Wallace, D. Leamy.

Referee: Joel Jutge (France).

It was as if that defeat knocked the stuffing out of Munster who were a pale shadow of their true selves when losing to the Llanelli Scarlets in the quarter-final at Stradey Park in Wales. But those who thought all of this signalled the end of the team as a major force had another think coming.

The 2007/08 season was to be Declan Kidney's last as Munster head coach. However, before he took off for the country's top job and Grand Slam glory in Cardiff in 2009, he put plans in place to ensure that Munster's 2006 Heineken Cup triumph would not be a once-off for his native province. By now it was apparent that Europe could not be conquered by home talent alone. South African Trevor Halstead, a key man in 2006, had departed but the brains trust was in overdrive and into the frame in 2006/07 came the richly talented Lifeimi Mafi

Munster's Lifiemi Mafi hands off Bourgoin's Sebastien Laloo to set up a try at Thomond Park, October 2006. (*Irish Examiner*)

to be followed twelve months later by the record All Black try-scoring machine Doug Howlett and a third Kiwi, Rua Tipoki.

While the need for remedial action in midfield and wide out was deemed essential, matters closer to home were left much as they were: Horan, Flannery, Hayes in the front-row, O'Connell and O'Callaghan immediately behind, and Quinlan, Leamy and Wallace in the back row. True, injury had caught up with the great Axel Foley but cometh the hour, cometh the man. Denis Leamy would happily fill any back-row position and having sported the number six jersey throughout the triumphant 2006 campaign, now slotted in seamlessly at number eight. A couple of maestros occupied the half-back positions: Ronan O'Gara, Mr Heineken Cup himself, and his loyal servant Peter Stringer, the little man with the bullet-like pass and a rugby savvy possessed by few other number nines. Conducting the orchestra all the time was Kidney, surely one of the wisest men ever to grace the Irish rugby scene. As we have seen, he was not averse to hiring high-quality players from abroad but he also saw virtue in the likes of wing Ian Dowling, who had come up quietly through the ranks, nor was he afraid to shake things up as the campaign progressed.

Such plaudits would have seemed more than a little misplaced after the first outing in the Heineken Cup against London Wasps at High Wycombe. It was a terrific match in which the English side performed a 'Munster' in that they three times came from behind to win 24–23. There was, of course, the losing bonus point to provide some solace although the result still meant that anything other than a win over mighty Clermont Auvergne in the next game at Thomond Park would more or less spell curtains for the team's European ambitions. It might not have helped that work on the redevelopment of the stadium was under way with a few no-go areas and some doubt as to how it would all impact on the atmosphere and the Munster team. On top of that, injury ruled Paul O'Connell out of the match

The response was typical: the crowd got behind the team as if they were watching in the lap of comfort; as was his wont, Mick O'Driscoll was so good as to almost render O'Connell's absence irrelevant and the French were duly hammered 36–13 and by 5 tries to 1. Bryan Carney (a one-time Rugby League star, now a television pundit), Shaun Payne, Rua Tipoki, Alan Quinlan and Marcus Horan got in on the try-scoring act and as usual O'Gara landed the goal kicks. The crowd loved it and so did fringe players like Jake Paringati, Gerry Hurley and Kieran Lewis, all of whom were given a taste of European rugby off the bench. After that it was off to Llanelli Scarlets and Stradey Park in West Wales where Horan again got on the try-scorers list as Munster claimed the crucial away win by 29–16. Confidence was high that a bonus point could be claimed from the return fixture but the Welsh region is not short in pride; they weren't prepared to roll over and it was not until late in the game when Jerry Flannery followed a powerful burst with a perfect try-scoring pass to Carney that the fans were free to relax.

Even then, the failure to claim more than four points meant they simply had to take something from the away fixture against mighty Clermont Auvergne at Parc des Sports Marcel Michelin. This they managed to achieve even though behind by as much as 23–6 at one stage. They were hugely assisted by the courageous decision of

English referee Rob Debney to send three Clermont players to the bin and a fine try by Lifeimi Mafi enabled Kidney's men to steal a bonus point for finishing within seven points of the French. The French had thrown away a golden opportunity to knock Munster out of the competition. They were made to pay the full price when Munster then defeated Wasps in dreadful conditions and at a Thomond Park that was little better than a building site! The rain poured down not just on the players and the fans in the terraces but also on the ladies and gentlemen in the premier seats in the front rows of the far-from-completed East Stand.

It was a compelling contest and Munster fought all the way to claim the win that left them level at the top of the pool with Clermont but through to the quarter-finals because of their superior points difference in the games between the sides. The much-maligned Wasps number ten Danny Cipriani showed his quality on a day far from suited to his particular talents and it certainly was not his fault that Wasps became the latest to succumb to a fired-up Munster team. Cipriani and Ronan O'Gara exchanged first half penalties before Denis Leamy and Lawrence Dallaglio exchanged 'pleasantries'. The Munster man duly saw yellow on the instructions of referee Nigel Owens. The drenched crowd roared their disapproval only to change tack when the hard man from Tipperary returned without any change on the scoreboard. O'Gara knocked over two penalties while the powerful Wasps second-row Simon Shaw was in the bin. Much to the crowd's undisguised pleasure, Dallaglio was also yellow-carded as the game became more fractious. The Red Army could hardly control themselves when Leamy powered over for the clinching try after a move involving twenty-one phases and remarkable control of the slippery ball.

O'Gara converted to leave the final score 19–3 and the saturated supporters to make their way back to the warmth of Myles Breen's, O'Driscoll's, Quinlivan's, Jerry Flannery's and the other noted rugby watering holes, already planning their trip to Gloucester and Kingsholm for their side's record tenth successive appearance in the quarter-finals.

Throughout the campaign, Shaun Payne and Peter Stringer had been outstanding at full back and scrum half respectively so it came as a shock when Declan Kidney came up with one of his most notable calls, instead preferring Denis Hurley and Tomas O'Leary for the quarter-final game at Gloucester. The move paid off in that a perfectly placed kick by Hurley laid on a try for Doug Howlett and O'Leary hardly put a foot wrong. The other Munster wing, Ian Dowling, also touched down in a superbly controlled performance that created a decisive 16–3 scoreline. After that came wins by two points over Saracens at the Ricoh Stadium in Coventry and by three over Toulouse in the Cardiff climax. Paul O'Connell and Declan Kidney raised the trophy in triumph. They would be back in the Millennium Stadium twelve months later, this time to celebrate Ireland's first Grand Slam in sixty-one years.

17

The 'New' Thomond Park

T he famous deeds of the 2005/06 season only emphasised still further the need for a major expansion of Thomond Park. Thankfully the message was getting through loud and clear to the decision makers at Lansdowne Road that either Thomond Park should be extended and modernised or else a different site had to be located and developed. The many thousands who wished to watch the Munster team in European action deserved to be accommodated comfortably and with every reasonable chance of acquiring the ticket of their choice. Various options were considered. In the end, though, the inevitable call was for Thomond Park to be renovated into the kind of magnificent stadium of which we are so justifiably proud today and was to earn the admiration of visitors from all over the world.

Pat Whelan, hooker on the Munster team of 1978 fame and an influential figure of the International Rugby Board, pressed the issue at every opportunity in his role as a member of the IRFU committee. Whelan had waged many a battle on the field of play at Thomond Park for club and province and now turned his guile and stubbornness to this major issue for Munster and Irish rugby. And when he did so, Whelan was adamant that the atmosphere should be synonymous with the ground's long-established reputation. Terraces on both west and east sides and the north and south ends, he insisted, should be an integral part of the project. He wanted Munster fans to be as close to the action as possible so that they could get their message across to friend and foe alike. With the support of Union honorary treasurer

John Lyons, he made steady progress until in the 2005/06 season, a Thomond Park Development Committee was set up. It consisted of Pat Whelan, chairman; senior Munster Branch officers Ken Lyons, Neil O'Driscoll and John Hartery, and Munster Rugby CEO Garrett Fitzgerald.

The architectural firm Murphy/O Laoire was appointed to present its proposals which duly made a lot of sense to Whelan, the boss of a Limerick building company. The brief included maintaining the atmosphere and close relationship between players and spectators as a key requirement; the capacity was to be 26,000, with 15,000 seated and 11,000 standing positions; site constraints included the retention of both the main and the practice pitches, the Shannon RFC clubhouse and north, east and south terraces. Following successful negotiations with Limerick City Council and the property owners on the east side, the development area extended to Knockalisheen road.

The key design aspirations, in addition to fulfilling the requirements of the brief, were as follows:

- To ensure that a stadium of the scale required had a positive impact on the cityscape and skyline, given its elevated site in relation to the surrounding city.
- The building should integrate with its immediate context. The scale of existing structures in the area was predominantly two-storey with residences located directly to the north and south of the existing stadium.
- The new home for Munster rugby should befit their status as the best-supported and leading rugby club in Europe.
- Every design decision had to be justifiable economically.
- The three-dimensional form of the stands was a direct product of achieving optimum viewing for all spectators. The optimum functional layout of a rugby or soccer stadium is generated by accommodating all spectators within 90 metres of the centre of the pitch and within 150 metres of all four corners of the playing surface. This generates an 'orange segment' profile where the maximum number of spectators is concentrated on the centreline.
- The long arch or rainbow truss solution adopted to support the roof was central to the architectural expression of the building

with the trusses being visible from many parts of the city and on its approach routes.

- The mix of vibrant seat colours in the ratio 60 per cent red, 30 per cent navy and 10 per cent gold corresponded with the colour mix in the Munster logo. This avoided the monotonous effect of single-colour seating. When the seating bowl is not at full capacity the optical illusion generated by the random seating mix makes the stadium appear full.

Quite understandably, Murray/O Laoire, with their strong connection to Limerick (Hugh Murray's father, Cecil, was a member of the Young Munster team that won the first Munster Cup final played at Thomond Park in 1938), were apprehensive as to how the public would react to their design. It was not long, though, before those fears were allayed and they were entitled to proclaim that 'Thomond Park is now a fitting theatre for the many great occasions yet to come. Many new stadiums experience a "bedding in" period in the first season when players and supporters alike adapt to the new surroundings. However, the epic official

An aerial view of Thomond Park a few weeks prior to the commencement of the rebuilding of the stadium in 2006. (*Irish Examiner*)

The colour and drama of Thomond Park, November 2008. (*Irish Examiner*)

opening match between Munster and the All Blacks has demonstrated that the redeveloped Thomond Park can be as intimidating, intense and overwhelming as the more modest venue that it replaced.'

The P. J. Hegarty company was entrusted with the task of building the stadium and tackled the task with enthusiasm, ensuring that it came in on time after twenty months' work and highly satisfactory to all concerned. They reported:

> The Thomond Park redevelopment involved the demolition of the existing stand and buildings and the construction of two new stands (West and East) offering a seating capacity of 15,500. These new covered stands were built either side of the pitch without affecting continuing matches and progress by Munster to a second Heineken Cup victory in 2008. A new terrace was added to the West side, with modifications and part cover carried out to the East Terrace. The North and South Terraces were left untouched with the surrounding lighting and access improved. The new combined terrace capacity is 11,000.
>
> The East Stand contains the main reception, museum, dressing rooms and all corporate facilities including executive boxes and conference suites. The West Stand contains additional

dressing rooms, UL Bohemian Rugby Club and the Supporters Club bar. The stadium has a total of 14 bars and refreshment outlets to cater for the 26,500 capacity crowds while the new conference and banqueting facilities can cater for in excess of 500 people depending on the style of event.

The main iconic feature of the new stadium is the symmetrical grandstands on the East and West sides each supported by a 146-tonne, 150m-long truss, making it a new and unique landmark for Limerick city.

The work began in 2007 and took 20 months to construct from start to finish, and Munster played their first match here on 4 October 2008 against Glasgow.

Unveiling the plaque at the reopening of the Thomond Park stadium, November 2008 (l–r): stadium chairman Pat Whelan, IRFU President John Lyons, Taoiseach Brian Cowen and Munster Branch president Nick Comyn. (*Evening Echo*)

However, the first serious test of any potential teething troubles associated with the venture was the meeting of a near full-strength Irish side and Canada on 8 November in Declan Kidney's first match as Ireland head coach. A very respectable attendance of 21,500 turned up on a wet and windy day, many presumably there to experience on the new stadium for the first time. They saw Ireland run up fifty-five unanswered points in a disappointingly one-sided encounter. Nevertheless, there was plenty for the Limerick crowd to cheer with debutant Keith Earls touching down for the first of Ireland's eight tries as early as the third minute. Two more followed from wings Tommy Bowe and Rob Kearney and one each by Jamie Heaslip and replacements David Wallace and Alan Quinlan. Ronan O'Gara converted five and kicked a penalty and there was also a late conversion for Paddy Wallace.

Ireland: K. Earls, T. Bowe, B. O'Driscoll capt., L. Fitzgerald, R. Kearney, R. O'Gara, E. Reddan, M. Horan, J. Flannery, T. Buckley, D. O'Callaghan, P. O'Connell, S. Ferris, S. Jennings, J. Heaslip. *Replacements* (all used): R. Best, J. Hayes, A. Quinlan, D. Wallace, P. Stringer, P. Wallace, S. Horgan.

Canada: J. Pritchard, C. Hearn, B. Keys, R. Smith, J. Mensah-Coker, A. Monro, E. Fairhurst, K. Tkatchuk, P. Riordan capt., J. Thiel, M. Burak, J. Jackson, S. M. Stephen, A. Kleeberger, A. Carpenter. *Replacements*: M. Pletch, F. Walsh, T. Hotson, J. Sinclair, M. Williams, M. Evans, P. Mackenzie.

Referee: Christophe Berdos (France).

From the perspective of Pat Whelan and his team, the most important thing about the day was that it went without a hitch and the stadium was the recipient of unreserved praise from all quarters. It won the People's Choice in the 2009 Royal Institute of the Architects of Ireland Awards. Hugh Murray said he was delighted to accept the award as 'an architect, a Limerick man and a Munster supporter. We created a landmark for Limerick and we are really pleased that the project is getting the recognition it deserves.'

Now all that remained was to find the €40 million it cost to complete the overhaul. The following fund-raising was put in place: €15 million from ticket sales; €9 million from government (lotto); €5 million private donation; €11 million borrowings. It remains a work in progress.

Typical of the man, J. P. McManus made the private €5 million donation without seeking any plaudits or headlines. It was his latest way of doing

J. P. McManus, the businessman who donated €5 million towards the new stadium. (Courtesy Noel Earlie)

everything possible to help his native place, just as he continues to do for a wide variety of other spheres. The enormous proceeds from his golf pro-ams and other fund-raising ventures have assisted countless worthy causes and provided badly needed facilities in the mid-west, most notably perhaps at the Limerick Regional University Hospital in Dooradoyle.

At the time, moves were afoot to change the name of the stadium in favour of a commercial concern as a means of helping to defray the cost. The idea went far enough for the *Limerick Leader* to believe it was actually a done deal and they duly reported in their issue of 21 June 2007:

> Munster rugby fans are furious about the decision to sell the name of the world famous Thomond Park with Limerick's first citizen Mayor Joe Leddin describing it as a 'retrograde' step, and a former Irish International branding it a 'sell-out'.
>
> 'I would be totally against this', said Mayor Leddin. 'You would have to have the name Thomond on that hallowed ground that is famous all over the world. It was essential, if there were a change, that the word Thomond be incorporated.'

Paddy Reid of 1948 Grand Slam fame described the decision to franchise the brand name of the ground as a betrayal. He said 'It's a sell-out. It's shocking and if the Thomond Park name is removed from the most famous ground in rugby, it will be a major blow to Limerick's rugby image. The venue is an icon of Irish sporting history and nobody has the right to remove it.'

The *Limerick Leader* also noted that 'other areas of the ground are also on the market for franchise, with all the food halls, corporate boxes, stands and terracing attracting lively interest from sponsors'. They added that the Munster Supporters Club PRO Glenn Flanagan had a guarded response to the decision. 'There is such a great folklore surrounding Thomond Park and Limerick rugby that there is sure to be an outcry,' he said. 'It is disappointing but that is the way the professional game is going now. From a Munster Supporters Club point of view, major sponsorship will provide the funding to strengthen the squad and that has to be welcomed.'

The *Limerick Leader* piece ended: 'A Munster source indicated that their aim was to have the new branding of the stadium in place in five months' time. Industry sources indicated that main breweries such as Guinness and Heineken would not be interested but some banking or other commercial interests might take up the offer.'

(L–r): Moss Keane, Declan Smith, Moss Finn and Anthony O'Leary of the legendary 1978 Munster squad enjoy the 2008 celebrations. (*Evening Echo*)

The worst of the fears expressed in the article have not come to pass. It is still Thomond Park Stadium, the stands are the East and the West and likewise with the terraces, although the report was prescient to some extent when observing: 'Selling naming rights is now very much part of major stadium marketing, and if the Thomond Park venture proves successful, there is a strong possibility that Lansdowne Road may follow suit.'

A combination of considerable public opposition and a certain lack of interest from the commercial sector prevented the renaming of the stadium. In the ensuing years, three of the country's other iconic rugby venues, Lansdowne Road, Ravenhill and Musgrave Park, have become the Aviva, the Kingspan and the Irish Independent with hardly a murmur from the cities concerned. But Thomond Park, in keeping with its reputation as a fortress, has stood firm.

All Blacks' Revenge

The outstanding success of the official opening of the stadium on Tuesday, 18 November 2008 was a well-merited reward for the many people who had prepared long, hard and enthusiastically to put on a show that would advise the rugby world of the arrival of another major venue for the sport. Quietly but effectively, plans were put in place that would ensure the 26,500 people inside the gleaming new arena and the many thousands watching on live television would remember every minute for a long time to come. The first basic requirement was something over which Pat Whelan and company had little control: the weather. Fortunately for mid-November, it could hardly have been better: chilly and a little windy, yes, but no rain. After that, everything else slotted into place.

Taoiseach Brian Cowen and IRFU president John Lyons were present to perform the opening honours. As kick-off time neared, the buzz of a helicopter was heard over the stadium and out of the dark sky an Irish army officer was winched down to land on the halfway line and present the match ball to Donal Canniffe, captain of the Munster team that defeated the All Blacks in 1978.

Next on the agenda was a spectacular fireworks display and as that faded away public address announcer Tommy Creamer welcomed the teams onto the pitch, the New Zealanders led by their captain Piri Weepu and Munster by their skipper Mick O'Driscoll.

What happened next electrified everyone. There was a haka, as might be expected, but this time it was performed by four New Zealanders – Doug Howlett, Rua Tipoki, Lifeimi Mafi and Jeremy Manning – all wearing the red shirt of Munster. There had been rumours in the preceding days that this was going to happen and now it was a reality. The

Above and facing page: Two hakas, Thomond Park, November 2008. (*Evening Echo*)

decibel level as the quartet went through their routine rose to anything as great as even this famous ground had previously experienced and undoubtedly set the tone for the heroics that were about to unfold.

In many ways, the evening was a thank-you to the thousands of Munster supporters who over the years had spent their hard-earned cash to stand uncomplainingly in the rain at the old ground and travelled extensively to France, Britain and beyond to cheer the side on. Now, instead of queuing for ages to acquire tickets that often afforded only a limited view of the on-field action, they could pick and choose where they would stand or sit and how much they would pay. We turn now to excerpts from a blog by one of the many female members of the Munster Rugby Supporters Club, Gayl Kennedy from Thurles, for a vivid description of the happenings that evening. Under the by-line 'Gayl – West Terrace View' she wrote:

It was great to see the passion, pride, the determination of all the team as they hustled and hassled and harried the New Zealanders, putting in ferocious tackles, chasing everything,

putting their body on the line and never, ever, giving up.

It was not just defence, they made some great breaks in offence also… Paul Warwick was magnificent, kicking all his penalty goals plus a sublime drop goal. Peter Stringer was his imperious sergeant major self, directing his forwards and providing quick passes to the backs. The score was 9–3 to Munster (2 penalties and a drop goal by Warwick to a penalty by Donald) when the All Blacks finally made a breakthrough as Donald scored under the posts to give them the lead at 10–9.

Munster earned a 5m scrum which lead to a second scrum in that danger zone. Coughlan had moved to number 8 with the departure of the injured Denis Leamy (replaced by Billy Holland). From the base of the scrum he gathered the ball, offloaded to Stringer who in turn passed to Barry Murphy who touched down – the only try conceded by New Zealand on their autumn tour that season.

Paul Warwick converted the try to bring the score to 16–10. So it remained till the NZ full back Corey James ran into touch to end the half and handed the match ball to a surprised and delighted young boy in the east terrace.

The crowd were buzzing during the interval, so far the evening had surpassed our hopes but could we hold onto the lead? Donald scored a penalty to bring the score to 16–13. The Fields of Athenry rang out but did not sway the referee. Romain Poite from France was the man in charge that day and he was certainly not a 'homer' then or indeed on any of his subsequent visits to Thomond Park. It is a pity that the final turning point of the game came from one of his more questionable decisions. Mick O'Driscoll spotted a ball had come out of the ruck on the opposite side to the ref and he pounced on it but was penalised for coming in from the side … harshly, we all thought. New Zealand opted for the line-out which was secured by Brad Thorn, they then mauled up the field as the tired Munster legs tried to halt their progress. The ball was flung out to Rokococo who avoided the tackles of Howlett and Stringer to score and reclaim the lead 18–16. It was heart-breaking and so it finished. The players were shattered to have come so close but not close enough to win, but they created their own bit of history that night and added to the legend of Munster.

The four Munster Kiwis would have happily shed blood for the cause, none more so than outstanding centre Rua Tipoki who, however, picked himself up and said: 'I'm not disappointed at all just because of the way the boys did it – I would have been disappointed if we didn't leave it all out there. But we did everything we could on the day. I'm just so proud to be a Munster man today. I'm still a bit emotional. We said before we went out on the field that we wouldn't trade places with anyone. We were going out to be soldiers for each other, we were going to go to war for each other.'

Captain Mick O'Driscoll got straight to the point: 'There was nothing left in the tank. It was a superb performance by one and all and we probably deserved a little more.'

All Blacks: Cory Jane, Hosea Gear (Richard Kahui 63), Anthony Tuitavake, Isaia Toeava (Mils Muliaina 71), Joe Rokococo, Stephen Donald, Piri Weepu capt. (Alby Mathewson 62), Jamie

Lifeimi Mafi, one of many great centres from the southern hemisphere to prosper in the Thomond Park atmosphere, seen here in action against the All Blacks. (*Irish Examiner*)

Mackintosh, Corey Flynn (Hikawera Elliott 62), Ben Franks (JohnAfoa 54), Ross Filipo (Brad Thorn 70), Jason Eaton, Adam Thomson (Kieran Read 50), Scott Waldrom, Liam Messam.

Munster: Doug Howlett, Barry Murphy, Rua Tipoki (Jeremy Manning 55), Lifeimi Mafi, Ian Dowling, Paul Warwick, Peter Stringer, Federico Pucciariello, Frankie Sheahan (Denis Fogarty 62), Tim Ryan (Tony Buckley half-time), Mick O'Driscoll capt., Donnacha Ryan, Denis Leamy (Billy Holland 22), Niall Ronan, James Coughlan.

Referee: Romain Poite (France).

It was not just Irish writers and observers who were thrilled with the occasion. New Zealand journalist/blogger Martin Moodie typified the Kiwi reaction. Under the headline 'Munster the (real) victors after epic showdown', here is some of what he had to say:

If any Kiwis reading this bump into a Munster man or woman in 2011 during the next Rugby World Cup in New Zealand, invite them back into your home. Tell them you were moved by the respect they showed your nation, your culture, your rugby team. Tell them that the Munster class of 2008 – a supposedly 'second string' team – was every bit as heroic as their proud predecessors of 1978.

Tell them that Munster lost only on the scoreboard but won everywhere that it mattered most – in the hearts, minds and affections of all those privileged enough to be present, including crazily patriotic Kiwis like me who (almost impossibly) would not have been downcast at losing to such a side … Tell them most of all, that the name of Munster, even in defeat, is synonymous not only with the great rugby victory of 1978 but also the magnificence of the players and the crowd who graced the rebuilt Thomond Park some three decades later.

Sometimes, you know, you can rejoice more in defeat than victory.

∽

Declan Kidney was succeeded by Australian Tony McGahan, a member of the back-room team for the previous four years and accordingly well versed in Munster's ways. McGahan set a lofty target of a cup and league double in his first year in outright charge and made a fair shot at pulling it off even if the relatively unheralded French side Montauban very nearly caught the reigning champions napping in the first game of the Heineken campaign at Thomond Park. The French took advantage of an uncharacteristic show of complacency by Munster to lead 17–16 with a mere six minutes remaining. Crucially, they conceded an extra 10 metres for backchat when penalised, thus enabling Ronan O'Gara to land yet another of those priceless goals when the need was greatest.

A relieved but annoyed McGahan read the riot act to his squad after that narrow shave and got his message across. Paul Warwick played the proverbial blinder in an impressive away win over Sale Sharks thereby setting up back-to-back matches against Clermont Auvergne.

The squad was in a confident mood when turning up at Parc des Sports Marcel Michelin for the second successive year. They had

Tony McGahan was appointed Munster head coach in 2008. (Courtesy Sportsfile)

somehow departed with a vital losing bonus point on a 26–19 scoreline in 2008; the following December, it was almost identical, 25–19 to the French, but once again enough was done to take something from the fixture. By now there was little love lost between Munster and Clermont and, sure enough, the return at Thomond Park was a decidedly ill-tempered affair which earned a red card for the visitors' second-row forward Jamie Cudmore after a battle of words and fists with Paul O'Connell. The Munster captain escaped with a ten-minute spell in the sin bin. Ronan O'Gara chalked up his 1,000th Heineken Cup point on a day when Munster started and finished brightly but left something to be desired in between.

There can have been few greater ball carriers in the entire history of the Heineken Cup than David Wallace and he made the point in telling fashion early on as he crashed through for the first of three Munster tries. However, this tremendous score and the departure of Cudmore after twenty minutes did not inspire Munster to the anticipated heights. The crowd struggled to conceal their frustration as a try by Julien Malzieu and two penalties and conversion by Brock James sent the French into a 13–11 lead. It was time for the 'sixteenth man' to play its part and the new stands and terraces rocked as first Marcus Horan and then Niall Ronan went over for tries to clinch a 23–13 victory.

After that, it was pretty much plain sailing as Munster walloped Sale at home and Montauban away before performing to the height of their powers in a 43–9 demolition of a star-studded Ospreys side in a memorable Thomond Park quarter-final. 'The Fields of Athenry' has rarely been sung as musically and enthusiastically all through that Limerick lunchtime as Keith Earls showed off his pace and skill when running in a couple of tries. Paul Warwick gleefully sent two drop goals sailing between the Welsh posts and added a touchdown of his own.

A contretemps beween Jamie Cudmore of Clermont Auvergne (left) and Paul O'Connell (right) results in a yellow card for the former and red for the latter. (Courtesy Sportsfile)

Even Paul O'Connell got in on the try-scoring act, while Ronan O'Gara satisfied himself with three penalties and four conversions. At the time, the watching British and Irish Lions coach Ian McGeechan was close to completing his squad for the upcoming tour of South Africa and was so impressed that he called up Keith Earls, Ronan O'Gara, Tomas O'Leary, Jerry Flannery, John Hayes, Paul O'Connell, Alan Quinlan and David Wallace of that Munster squad. (Unfortunately, and for different reasons, O'Leary and Quinlan were unable to make the trip.)

Munster supporters have long debated as to whether such a runaway scoreline was a good or bad thing. Did another tiny little bit of complacency creep in as they prepared for the semi-final confrontation

with Leinster in front of a world-record attendance for a club rugby match of 82,208 at Croke Park? Perhaps so, perhaps not, but there was no denying which was the better side as Leinster coasted home by 25–9 on their way to the first of three Heineken Cup successes in four years.

It took a fair few weeks for the Munster camp and the fans to get over what was seen as the disaster of Croke Park but it was much to the credit of the players that they were able to regroup sufficiently well to finish the season with silverware of their own.

18

The Celtic League

Initially it was simply the Celtic League. Then it became the Magners League, and then the Rabo Pro12. The next incarnation was the Guinness Pro12. Call it what you like, it's the league championship that annually commands most of the attention of the top sides in Ireland, Scotland, Wales and Italy, even if – inevitably – it has had to accept a secondary role behind the Heineken Cup and more recently the European Champions Cup.

Donncha O'Callaghan, one of Munster's greatest ever and a second-row forward who revelled in the special Thomond Park atmosphere. (Courtesy *Irish Examiner*)

Thomond Park has played a central role in each of Munster's three title successes. The event was first contested in 2001/02 when they lost in the final to Leinster at Lansdowne Road. The following year, the key fixture was the semi-final against Ulster in front of 12,000 spectators at Thomond Park in January 2003 when they were seen at their best in a hugely impressive 42–10 victory. The atmosphere on these Rabo Pro12 occasions has not always been electrifying but as five tries flowed from John Kelly, Mike Mullins, John Hayes, Alan Quinlan and replacement Mick Galwey, the crowd roared their approval. Ronan O'Gara landed three penalties and three conversions; Killian Keane also contributed a conversion. David Humphreys, so often a serious rival of O'Gara for the number-ten jersey with Ireland and later head of rugby at Ulster and Gloucester and always a welcome visitor to Thomond Park, replied with a try, penalty and conversion.

Munster: J. Staunton, J. Kelly, M. Mullins, J. Holland, A. Horgan, R. O'Gara, P. Stringer, M. Horan, F. Sheahan, J. Hayes, P. O'Connell, D. O'Callaghan, J. Williams, A. Foley, A. Quinlan. *Replacements*: M. Prendergast, M. Lawler, K. Keane, M. Cahill, M. Galwey, D. Leamy, J. Blaney.

Ulster: B. Cunningham, J. Topping, S. Stewart, A. Larkin, S. Coulter, D. Humphreys, N. Doak, J. Fitzpatrick, M. Sexton, R. Kempson, G. Longwell, J. Davidson, W. Brosnihan, N. McMillan, T. McWhirter. *Replacements*: S. Young, J. Cunningham, K. Campbell, P. Shields, S. Best, A. Ward, M. Blair.

Munster went on to beat Neath 37–17 in the final at the Millennium Stadium in Cardiff and lifted the trophy. There would be a six-year wait before Munster would be crowned champions in the Magners Pro12 again. The event was played strictly on a league basis in 2008/09 but an April clash of Munster and Leinster in front of a capacity Thomond Park crowd proved pivotal. It was a terrific game that showed off the high standard of rugby in the country and was decided in Munster's favour by a late penalty landed from near the left touchline by Ronan O'Gara. Paul Warwick chipped in with another penalty and although Shane Horgan scored the only try of the game for Leinster and Jonathan Sexton kicked six penalties, Munster still prevailed by the narrowest of margins, 24–23. The result against Leinster put Munster twelve points clear at the top of the table with three rounds still to play, making the remainder of the tournament little more than a formality. It certainly was a satisfactory start to Tony McGahan's reign as head coach and some compensation for their heavy 25–9 defeat by Leinster in the semi-final of the Heineken Cup at Croke Park in 2009.

Munster: P. Warwick, D. Howlett, K. Earls, L. Mafi, I. Dowling, R. O'Gara, T. O'Leary, M. Horan, J. Flannery, J. Hayes, D. O'Callaghan, P. O'Connell, A. Quinlan, N. Ronan, D. Wallace. *Replacements*: D. Fogarty, T. Buckley, M. O'Driscoll, D. Ryan, P. Stringer, B. Murphy, D. Hurley.

Leinster: G. Dempsey, I. Nacewa, G. D'Arcy, S. Horgan, R. Kearney, F. Contepomi, C. Whitaker, C. Healy, B. Jackman, S. Wright, L. Cullen, M. O'Kelly, R. Elsom, S. Jennings, J. Heaslip. *Replacements*: J. Fogarty, R. McCormack, T. Hogan, S. O'Brien, C. Jowitt, S. Keogh, J. Sexton.

Forward then to the 2010/11 season and the renewal of the Leinster v Munster rivalry. The Magners had reverted to a 'top four' play-off format and Munster had done enough to ensure the closing stages would take place at Fortress Thomond Park. This was to prove crucial and was due largely to a mid-season win over Leinster, a game Tony McGahan had described as one they 'couldn't afford to lose'.

While the semi-final win over Ospreys was accurately described by one writer as 'anodyne', the final was completely the opposite, certainly from a Munster perspective. Only a week previously, Leinster had come back from the dead against Northampton in the Heineken Cup final in Cardiff (Munster having bombed in that competition, even losing to Harlequins at Thomond Park in the Challenge Cup). Furthermore, the thought of Leinster beating them at Thomond Park to complete a unique double was enough to inflict a serious migraine on players and fans alike! Nevertheless, those who believed Leinster would be exhausted after their magnificent performance at the Millennium Stadium the previous week and would be happy to rest on their laurels were made to think again. Leinster coach Joe Schmidt felt they could run Munster off their feet and they certainly made a very good shot at it.

Munster had failed to score a try against Leinster in any of their six previous meetings. This time they managed two crackers although the third, which came just before the finish, probably gave them the greatest satisfaction of all. Certainly the smiles on the faces of the front-row trio of Marcus Horan, Damien Varley and John Hayes could hardly have been brighter as the Leinster pack was pushed back yards at a scrum close to their own line and when it went down, the inevitable outcome was a penalty try.

The dynamic stepping of Lifeimi Mafi and the enormous workload carried by man of the match David Wallace were other considerable factors in the Munster triumph. Joe Schmidt had no complaints as Thomond Park celebrated the penalty try along with superb tries by Doug Howlett and Keith Earls and two Ronan O'Gara conversions. This time, it was Leinster's turn to end the game tryless as they relied on three penalties by Jonathan Sexton in a 19–9 defeat.

As this was the last game of the season, Munster paraded the cup around Thomond Park after the presentation before assembling for a group photograph. At this point, the stadium erupted into further applause as Paul Darbyshire was wheeled out on to the pitch along with his seven-year-old son Jack to join the fun. Darbyshire, who had made

Munster – and Paul Darbyshire – celebrate their Magners League Grand Final victory over Leinster at Thomond Park in 2011. (Courtesy Sportsfile)

his name during an eighteen-year spell as strength and conditioning coach with Warrington Rugby League club, took up a similar role with Munster in 2007. In his four years with the squad, he built many close friendships with the players and earned their complete respect until forced to retire in March 2011 after being diagnosed with Motor Neurone Disease (MND). While he was clearly very ill on the day of the final, Paul joined in the celebrations, much to the evident satisfaction of the players. Sadly, he passed away on the following 20 June, on a day when Munster players and management members were involved in a fund-raising cycle for research into MND. Paul was forty-one years of age and is survived by his wife Lyndsay and family Ella, Georgia, Jack and Harry.

'The initial shock when we heard of his diagnosis was frightening because around us Darbs was like Superman,' said Donncha O'Callaghan, one of many who had grown very close to Paul over his four years with the province. 'He brought an unbelievable professionalism to us and the mindset that your body could do anything and would never fail.'

Munster: F. Jones (P. Warwick 76), D. Howlett, D. Barnes, L. Mafi, K. Earls, R. O'Gara, C. Murray, M. Horan (W. Du Preez 53), D. Varley (M. Sherry 58), J. Hayes, D. O'Callaghan (D. Leamy 67), P. O'Connell capt., D. Ryan, D. Wallace, J. Coughlan.

Leinster: I. Nacewa, S. Horgan, B. O'Driscoll, F. McFadden, L. Fitzgerald, J. Sexton, E. Reddan (P. O'Donohoe, 77), H. Van der Merwe (C. Healy, 58), R. Strauss (A. Dundon, 71), M. Ross (S. Wright, 71), L. Cullen capt., N. Hines, S. O'Brien (K. McLaughlin, 58), S. Jennings, J. Heaslip.

Referee: Nigel Owens (Wales).

The respective reactions of the two camps were entirely predictable. Leinster coach Joe Schmidt commented: 'A week after our Heineken Cup win, our energy levels may not have been as high as Munster's. To be honest, I felt that Munster needed it more.'

'It's huge for everyone right across the board here', said Munster coach Tony McGahan. 'From the playing group, the management and the organisation to the development officers and young players coming

Not even a brave and bandaged Brian O'Driscoll could save Leinster from Magners League final defeat, 2011. (Courtesy Sportsfile)

through, and more important to the supporters … they can walk around with a smile on their faces knowing that we have done something very important in the context of the Magners League season.'

On the European scene, keen disappointment was to be Munster's lot in season 2009/10. True, it was a major achievement to beat Perpignan both home and away and to emerge as the number one qualifier. As luck would have it, Northampton Saints, who had been in the same pool, finished eighth, which meant the sides would meet in the quarter-final at Thomond Park. Although the Saints had won the first meeting of the sides at Franklins Gardens by 31–27 and Munster scraped a win in the return, courtesy of four Ronan O'Gara penalties to three, there was a general feeling that the home side would capitalise on the Thomond Park factor and come out with something to spare. That proved to be the case. Munster were not overly concerned by the late withdrawal of skipper Paul O'Connell for whom Mick O'Driscoll made his usual big contribution as replacement. Doug Howlett scored two of four Munster tries, the others coming from Paul Warwick and centre Jean de Villiers, later South Africa captain, who was having his one and only campaign in the Munster jersey. Ronan O'Gara landed three penalties and two conversions as Munster coasted home by 33–19.

Munster: P. Warwick, D. Howlett, K. Earls, J. de Villiers, I. Dowling, R. O'Gara, T. O'Leary, M. Horan, J. Flannery, J. Hayes, D. O'Callaghan, M. O' Driscoll capt., A. Quinlan, D. Wallace, J. Coughlan. *Replacements*: D. Varley, J. Brugnaut, T. Buckley, Billy Holland, N. Williams, N. Ronan, P. Stringer, L. Mafi.

Northampton: Ben Foden, Chris Ashton, Jon Clarke, James Downey, Bruce Reihana, Stephen Myler, Lee Dickson, Soane Tonga'uiha, Dylan Hartley capt., Euan Murray, Courtney Lawes, Juandre Kruger, Phil Dowson, Neil Best, Roger Wilson. *Replacements*: Brett Sharman, Regardt Dreyer, Brian Mujati, Ignacio Fernandez Lobbe, Mark Easter, Alan Dickens, Shane Geraghty, Joe Ansbro.

After that resounding result, Munster set off for San Sebastian and Estadio Anoeta in Basque country as Biarritz decided to move the semi-final meeting there in the hope of making a financial killing. The Munster supporters did not let them down but in the end it was a frustrating trip as their side went down to six penalties by the French scrum half Dimitri Yachvili. Keith Earls scored the game's only try and Ronan O'Gara converted but, in truth, Biarritz were the better side on the day.

Considering how Toulon were to emerge as champions in both 2012/13 and 2013/14, it is interesting to note how little impression they made in their initial forays into European action in 2010/11. They were especially vulnerable on the road and hardly knew what hit them when overrun 45–18 by the Munster Juggernaut in front of a Thomond Park crowd revelling in the discomfiture of the former Leinster number ten Felipe Contepomi. For some reason, the Argentinian had fallen out with a few Munster players and quite a large battalion of the Red Army as well.

Even though Toulon brought on the great English number ten Jonny Wilkinson in a bid to steady the ship and included players of the calibre of French scrum half Pierre Mignoni and southern-hemisphere stars Carl Hayman, George Smith and Joe Van Niekirk, they were made to look very ordinary by the following Munster team:

Munster: Paul Warwick, Doug Howlett, Keith Earls, Johne Murphy, Denis Hurley, Ronan O'Gara, Peter Stringer, Wian du Preez, Damien Varley, Tony Buckley, Donncha O'Callaghan, Mick O'Driscoll, Alan Quinlan, David Wallace, Denis Leamy.

Leamy, Howlett (2), O'Driscoll, Buckley and substitute James Coughlan scored Munster tries and Ronan O'Gara converted all six as well as a penalty. Munster also beat Ospreys 22–16 and London Irish 28–14 at Thomond Park but struggled on the road and the win over the Exiles was only good enough for a place in the Amlin Challenge Cup.

The fire had gone out of the side and even a home game was not enough to see off a spirited Harlequins team that deserved its 20–12 victory. Doug Howlett and Felix Jones were the Munster try scorers but 'Quins held the edge after tries by George Robson and Danny Care who combined with Nick Evans and substitute Rory Clegg to complete the scoring with a couple of conversions and two penalties. It may not have represented a Heineken Cup win for 'Quins at Fortress Thomond Park but it was the next best thing and they were well entitled to celebrate a significant achievement.

Harlequins: M. Brown, G. Carrado, G. Lowe, J. Turner-Hall, Ugo Monye, N. Evans, D. Care, J. Marler, J. Gray, J. Johnstone, O. Kahn, G. Robson, M. Fa'asavalu, C. Robshaw capt., N. Easter.

Munster: F. Jones, D. Howlett, L. Mafi, P. Warwick, K. Earls, R. O'Gara capt., C. Murray, W. du Preez, D. Varley, T. Buckley, D. O'Callaghan, M. O'Driscoll, D. Leamy, D. Wallace, J. Coughlan.

Wallabies Walloped By Warwick

For the second time in two years, Munster were the envy of just about every other leading European rugby nation when they managed to woo a major southern-hemisphere team to Thomond Park for a 'friendly'. It says everything about the reputation the team enjoyed worldwide that Australia were happy to follow in the footsteps of the All Blacks in 2008 by agreeing to play Munster, on 16 November 2010, in a match sponsored by Sony Ericsson. Former Munster captain Jim Williams was by now assistant Wallabies coach and he was thrilled to be back among old friends. He was less than enamoured, however, by the weather that lay in wait. The storm that raged across Thomond Park could not spoil the enjoyment a near full house as a well-below-full-strength Munster team defeated their esteemed visitors. The Wallabies duly became the third major southern-hemisphere team to bow the knee to Munster at Thomond Park.

Since the advent of the professional game, some excellent players from the southern hemisphere had signed for Munster. Several came at considerable expense, some were signed at relatively small cost. Chief among the latter group was Paul Warwick. Back home in Australia, he had played with and captained the Wallabies seven-a-side team and by doing so was precluded from representing any other country on the international stage. A native of Brisbane and an outstanding member of the powerful Manly club, Paul hung around long enough to realise that he would never be capped by Australia. So he looked abroad and attracted the interest of Connacht. He went to Galway in 2004 and rewarded them for their foresight with three good years before heading down the N18 to Munster in 2007. He became an immediate hit with the fans when running up no fewer than twenty-one points in his first outing, against the Scarlets in September of that year. However, Paul's best position was out-half, where Ronan O'Gara was immovably established. Accordingly, Warwick usually wore the number-ten jersey only when ROG was away with Ireland or otherwise unavailable and it was through his outstanding versatility as a full back or centre that he earned his corn.

In the opinion of many sound judges, Paul Warwick was one of Munster's best overseas signings. As an individual and team person, he slotted comfortably into the team ethos. Many would have been aggrieved at having to sit on the bench throughout the 2008 Heineken Cup final without getting the call. Instead he rejoiced in a famous victory, accepted that Ronan O'Gara would always be Munster's first choice for the number-ten jersey and settled down to play a significant role wherever he could prove most valuable.

Along with compatriots Tony McGahan and Laurie Fisher, the numbers one and two coaches, Paul avidly looked forward to the Wallabies visit, little realising the crucial part he was destined to play in the outcome of the game – or the vile conditions in which it would be contested. The rain poured down and the wind blew relentlessly at more than 80 kilometres per hour. Whereas 21,000 people turned up to watch and Munster performed as if this was just another normal early

The gale was so strong that Keith Earls had to hold the ball down for Paul Warwick to kick one of his five penalty goals against his native Australia, November 2010. (Courtesy Sportsfile)

winter's day in Limerick, the Aussies had never experienced anything like it. The exception, though, was one of their own but Paul Warwick was wearing the red of Munster rather than the yellow of Australia. He could do nothing wrong on that wretched evening. He kicked a sweet drop goal to negate an early Wallabies penalty by Berrick Barnes and the pair added one more each before the interval which was reached only after an ugly brawl just before the whistle.

After that, it looked as if the Aussies couldn't take any more. The combination of Munster fervour and the elements had knocked the stuffing out of them. Warwick, however, thrived in the going. Ian Nagle, a youthful second-row forward, turned in a tour de force in the line-out and just about everywhere else and fully earned the man-of-the match award. Those around him also stepped up to the plate and as the game went on, the Aussies were so shattered that RTÉ Radio commentator Michael Corcoran informed his listeners that 'Munster are still going through the phases and are really up for it while the Australians look like they wish they had never agreed to this match'.

Even though the goalposts were swaying in the gale and the rain never relented, Warwick hammered home nail after nail into his countrymen's coffin. He knocked over two more penalties and a second drop goal to put Munster 15–6 in front by the time New Zealand referee Bryce

Lawrence put the Wallabies out of their misery by blowing the final whistle. While he was elated at scoring all his side's points and happy to accept the plaudits, Paul felt a degree of sympathy for his countrymen who had had to endure conditions that were completely alien to them.

'I guess I probably felt for the Australians, being Australian, as we were walking off afterwards because they wouldn't have known much about those conditions whereas we're brought up on them here, me being a Munster man now of course,' he said. 'But I'm also delighted with that performance. It was the younger guys up front who won the game for us and that makes it all the more impressive. People go on about the O'Connells and the Hayeses coming towards the end of their careers but there is depth here that people aren't aware of.'

Tony McGahan concealed any sympathy he might have had for his fellow Aussies, stressing instead that 'our line-out was superb but our breakdown work was really the key. Full credit to Laurie (Fisher) for the work he's done there and the same to Anthony Foley for the tremendous work he has done on our defence. It was certainly well marshalled and tough. If you get those two areas right – and it's built on the back of spirit and passion and determination – you get a great result.'

Berrick Barnes, the Australian captain on the night, was not quite so enthusiastic, saying 'There are a few boys in there suffering from hypothermia so we're definitely not used to that. Maybe Munster can come to the outback some time and we'll give them a bit of heat.'

Munster: Johne Murphy (Scott Deasy 72), Doug Howlett, Keith Earls (Barry Murphy 78), Sam Tuitupou, Denis Hurley, Paul Warwick, Duncan Williams (Conor Murray 67), Wian Du Preez, Damien Varley (Mike Sherry 62), Peter Borlase (Stephen Archer 78), Billy Holland, Ian Nagle (Brian Hayes 78), Peter O'Mahony (Tommy O'Donnell 62), Niall Ronan, James Coughlan capt.

Australia: Lachie Turner (Peter Hynes 57), Rod Davies, Pat McCabe, Anthony Faingaa, Luke Morahan, Berrick Barnes capt., Luke Burgess (Nick Phipps 57), Ben Daley (James Slipper 53), Saia Faingaa (Tatafu Polota-Nau 46), Salesi Ma'afu, Dean Mumm, Rob Simmons, Scott Higginbotham (Pat McCutcheon 41), Matt Hodgson, Richard Brown (Van Humphries 53).

Referee: Bryce Lawrence (New Zealand).

19

ROG Gets The Drop On The Saints

Ronan O'Gara achieved so much in his record 110 appearances for Munster in the Heineken Cup that it would be impossible to single out any particular performance for special mention. However, if you happened to be among the 26,500 wildly animated people in Thomond Park on 12 November 2011, you might well be inclined to give your vote to the drop goal that ROG sent sailing between the Northampton Saints posts in the eighty-fourth minute of a spellbinding contest that ended with Munster in the lead by twenty-three points to twenty-one.

Even today, it is impossible to prevent the goosebumps from bursting out if you watch on You Tube for 7 minutes and 45 seconds as the commentator breathlessly describes the drama. The Saints are leading by a single point, 21–20, with the game in its seventy-eighth minute. Munster have possession but play is on and around the halfway line, Northampton's discipline is above reproach and they would have needed to commit a heinous crime for referee Nigel Owens to award a kickable penalty against them.

Accordingly, it was imperative that Munster retain possession and how they did so is now part of rugby folklore. The commentary picked out Damien Varley, Lifeimi Mafi, Paul O'Connell, Niall Ronan, Peter O'Mahony, O'Mahony again, Will Chambers, Tomas O'Leary, O'Connell again, Chambers again, Denis Leamy, Johne Murphy, Varley again, O'Leary again, John Hayes, Doug Howlett, Hayes again, Howlett again, for getting their hands on the ball and inching their way forward. All the time, the crowd are baying at them to bring play sufficiently close to the posts to set O'Gara up for a drop kick at goal. Somehow, though, they keep their patience. And then Leamy decides they can go for it … calmly and assuredly, the Tipperary man delivers a perfect pass to ROG who gathers it 40 metres out from the Saints' posts and in the twinkle of an eye drops the sweetest goal you have ever seen! Nigel Owens raises his hand and simultaneously blows the final whistle. Cue delirium and absolute bedlam. O'Gara jumps high in the air in triumph, his teammates engulf him and the vanquished Saints look on in disbelief.

The other scores in that game (Varley, Howlett tries, O'Gara 2 penalties, 2 conversions for Munster, Chris Ashton, James Downey tries, Ryan Lamb 3 penalties, 1 conversion for Northampton) have receded very much into the background. Thomond Park had played host to many dramatic finishes over the years but was there ever any more sensational or more memorable finale than this?

Munster: J. Murphy, D. Howlett, D. Barnes (W. Chambers), L. Mafi, D. Hurley, R. O'Gara, C. Murray (T. O'Leary), W. du Preez, D. Varley, B. J. Botha (J. Hayes), D. Ryan (D. O'Callaghan), P. O'Connell capt., P. O'Mahony, N. Ronan, J. Coughlan (D. Leamy).

Northampton Saints: B. Foden, C. Ashton, J. Clark, J. Downey, V. Artemyev, R. Lamb, L. Dickson (M. Roberts), S. Tonga'uiha (A. Waller), D. Hartley capt., B. Mujati, C. Lawes, M. Sorensen, C. Clark (P. Dowson), T. Wood, R. Wilson.

Referee: Nigel Owens (Wales).

Tony McGahan usually maintained a calm disposition regardless of how each match panned out but even he couldn't disguise his elation as he enthused: 'This was something special. The belief in the group, the way they stuck at it for eighty minutes, a lesser side would maybe not have been even in the contest. Ronan O'Gara's kick at the end, he's a special person to do that, to show the bottle to put his hand up and make the kick. This felt like a round-six encounter during the week when it actually was an opening-round game.'

A week later, O'Gara was at it again, kicking yet another drop goal at the death to see Munster home by 27–24 at Castres. Four more

The legendary Ronan O'Gara in a 2009 clash with Leinster. (*Irish Examiner*)

wins followed, by tight-enough margins home and away against Scarlets, and by a remarkable 51–36 in the final qualifier against the Saints at Franklin's Gardens. The much-desired home quarter-final had been achieved and there was an understandable degree of confidence in the Munster camp as they awaited the visit of Ulster to Thomond Park.

The bookmakers, those people who rarely get it wrong, installed Munster as warm favourites. You could hardly blame them. Ulster had hardly been heard of since their European Cup victory in 1999 and were travelling to the stadium where only Leicester had previously won in the Heineken Cup, Munster had two titles to their credit, a succession of near misses and a 100 per cent record of reaching the knockout stages.

However, those who looked closely into the contest noticed that Ulster chief David Humphreys had recruited wisely. South African Ruan Pienaar was regarded as one of the finest number nines in the game when he decided to set up home in Belfast. Towering second-row Johan Muller was another Springbok with an imposing pedigree. All Blacks prop Johan Afoa and South African back-row Pedrie Wannenburg added to the considerable overseas influence. Throw a talented group of home-bred players like Stephen Ferris, Andrew Trimble, Rory Best, Tom Court and Chris Henry into the mix and you had a group of fine rugby players already moulded into a formidable unit under coach Brian McLaughlin. While out-half Ian Humphreys, a brother of David, was not regarded as one of their more potent forces, he was for the second time to inflict serious damage on a Munster team at Thomond Park. As already mentioned, he was also Leicester's number ten when they pulled off the only previous Heineken defeat of Munster at Thomond Park in 2007.

Munster hardly knew what hit them in the first twenty minutes. Thomond Park had never seen anything like it as the outstanding Pienaar took the game under his wing. He used the strong but capricious wind to knock over three long-range penalties as Munster once again fell foul of French referee Romain Poite, who was especially harsh on B. J. Botha, who suffered a difficult afternoon against his former Ulster teammates. On top of that, the team as a whole appeared more than a little rattled and went missing as winger Craig Gilroy raced down the touchline virtually unchallenged and dived over for a try that Pienaar converted from wide out. Twenty minutes played: Munster nil, Ulster 16. Things quietened down a little after that as Paul O'Connell rallied the troops but after thirty-five minutes Ian Humphreys was back to drive home a cracking 35-metre drop goal. Loud and sardonic cheers greeted a penalty decision by Poite, which Ronan O'Gara turned into three points and things began to look bright for Munster when Simon Zebo went over for a seven-pointer that trimmed the Ulster lead to 19–10, at the break. To their great credit, Ulster consolidated in the second half as they withstood a series of fierce Munster attacks to emerge worthy winners. Although Stephen Ferris turned in a world-class performance, Munster wondered for many a day afterwards how they had fallen nineteen points behind before getting down to business while Ulster celebrated fittingly as they looked forward to a semi-final confrontation with Edinburgh. It was a more decisive drubbing for Munster than the 22–16 scoreline might indicate.

'I don't know if we have started a game like that since I have been here,' said a devastated Paul O'Connell. 'It left us with an awful lot to do. Nineteen points is a long, long way to come from behind.'

Brian McLaughlin, the Ulster coach, agreed that 'this was a big highlight in my career, probably the biggest day in my life in rugby terms. Today is the culmination of three years' really hard work. We have been emphasising the whole way through the importance of getting Ulster up the ladder and getting to that top table.' They did not quite reach it, though, for after disposing of Edinburgh in the semi-final, they went down to a heavy defeat by Leinster in the final.

Munster: F. Jones, D. Hurley (J. Murphy, 58), K. Earls, L. Mafi, S. Zebo, R. O'Gara, C. Murray (T. O'Leary, 73), W. Du Preez, M. Sherry (D. Varley, 68), B. J. Botha, D. Ryan, P. O'Connell capt., P. O'Mahony (D. Wallace, 73), T. O'Donnell (D. O'Callaghan, 59), J. Coughlan.

Ulster: S. Terblanche, A. Trimble, D. Cave, P. Wallace, C. Gilroy, I. Humphreys, R. Pienaar, T. Court, R. Best, J. Afoa, J. Muller capt., D. Tuohy, S. Ferris, C. Henry, P. Wannenburg.

~

Not for the first time, Munster were described as 'miracle makers' after the manner in which they once again qualified for the knockout stages in 2012/13. It certainly takes an extraordinary chain of events for a team to get through after losing two matches in the pool stages but that is just what they managed to do in spite of losing to Racing Metro and Saracens. Typically, though, they salvaged a bonus point from each game while they also disposed of Edinburgh and Sarries at Thomond Park. This meant that a bonus-point defeat of Racing in the final game along with a favourable outcome from the Leicester Tigers v Toulouse meeting later on the final Sunday would see Munster rather than Leinster fill the eighth and final qualifying spot.

To achieve all of this, they needed plenty of luck on their side and they got it in spades. Importantly, Racing were already out of the reckoning and were playing only for pride, if even that, when they turned up that Sunday lunchtime at Thomond Park. With the game under way for a mere five minutes, Referee Wayne Barnes red-carded the French back-row Antoine Battut, apparently for kneeing Tommy O'Donnell in the face even if very few in the packed stadium actually saw the incident. Ironically, a sense of injustice seemed to ignite something within the Racing players and they put up a decent performance for a spell before eventually conceding a hat-trick of tries to Simon Zebo and one each to Conor Murray and Mike Sherry. Ian Keatley (standing in for Ronan O'Gara who was under a week's suspension because of an incident in a game against Edinburgh)

Ian Keatley (left), the man entrusted with filling ROG's boots, with Paul O'Connell (right), 2014. (Courtesy Sportsfile)

kicked a penalty and two conversions. After that it was simply a case of waiting to see if Leicester could beat Toulouse and in the process prevent the French side from scoring four tries. The Tigers won 9–5, Munster were through and both Toulouse and Leinster were out.

So Munster emerged as second-best losers and qualified in eighth spot to take on top seeds Harlequins at The Stoop. They were widely regarded as outsiders but revelled in the role. Paul O'Connell reserved one of his extra-special contributions for this game and they ground out an 18–12 victory, six penalties by Ronan O'Gara against four by Nick Evans. Fired up by their best display of the season, Munster again excelled in the semi-final against Clermont Auvergne but it was not enough to avoid a 16–10 defeat at Stade de la Mosson.

Times were changing but not for the better, a point underlined by the sight of Ronan O'Gara walking around the stadium after the game, accompanied by a couple of his children. Many deduced from his body language that the retirement of Munster's greatest ever number ten was imminent and it was duly announced a few weeks later. His name was associated with every conceivable record, most notably a credit balance of 1,365 points in 110 appearances. He made his debut against Harlequins in September 1997 and ever afterwards his level of consistency was nothing short of incredible. Only in 1999/2000 and 2001/02 when he totalled a 'mere' 131 and 129 points respectively did one-club man O'Gara not lead the points-scoring table. Nevertheless, the overall total of 1,365 leaves him a massive 496 clear of Stephen Jones of Scarlets. When it came to kicking a penalty, conversion or drop goal when they were most needed, he was light years ahead of all others.

In 2010 O'Gara was voted the ERC European Player of the first fifteen years of the Heineken Cup. He was out-half on a side that also included his Munster teammates David Wallace and Anthony Foley and two other Irishmen, Brian O'Driscoll of Leinster and Geordan Murphy of Leicester Tigers. And all the time, he was performing similar heroics for Ireland whom he represented on 128 occasions and registered 1,083 points.

A couple of years after hanging up his boots, O'Gara recalled some of those days in a chat with Munster-great-turned-journalist Donal Lenihan in the *Irish Examiner*.

> It was probably new to us all from 2000 onwards but playing in Thomond Park was – and sometimes words don't do it justice – just incredible. It was basically the crowd that drove Munster. There certainly were good players but when you performed with 20,000 people behind you, the power that can generate behind a team is incredible and you get the feeling that you cannot be beaten. That was what usually happened there. The games that spring to mind were against Gloucester … it was usually a cold January evening that you played an English club coming in to Thomond Park. Now that you're finished, you enjoy it and it comes back to you. The match was one thing, it was probably sitting in the Clarion in Limerick listening to Gaillimh, listening to Paulie, to whoever had something to say before the English came to town, they're the things you smile about now. Then you put it into practice on the pitch with people who care really passionately about their team, their local team. If you're part of that, you literally feel ten feet tall. Thomond Park was a fortress and sometimes that's overused but it was very, very hard to lose there.

Quite truly, Thomond Park will never see the like of Ronan O'Gara again.

~

Munster had gone beyond the transition stage by the time the stadium was again hosting Heineken Cup action in the autumn of 2013. True greats of the game like O'Gara, John Hayes, Jerry Flannery, Marcus Horan, David Wallace, Alan Quinlan and Anthony Foley, to name only seven, had retired and Peter Stringer had moved across channel to see action with Saracens, Newcastle Falcons and Bath. The days of coming up with overseas stars like John Langford, Jim Williams, Trevor Halstead, Christian Cullen, Rua Tipoki, Lifeimi Mafi and Jean de Villiers were, with few exceptions, a thing of the past. Replacing players of this calibre, especially now that the province's financial situation was anything but favourable, was proving very difficult.

However, the supporters kept the faith and were again superbly rewarded by a side that punched above its weight and, with a little bit of luck against the champions Toulon in the semi-final, would have battled their way into another final. New Zealander Rob Penney was in his second year as head coach and while he tried to introduce a more creative element to the Munster game, he was only marginally successful. The manner in which Paul O'Connell and his lieutenants approached the 2013 semi-final clash with Harlequins indicated that the players felt there was more than one way to skin a cat. They went back to basics, adopted the forward-oriented game that had served them so well over the years, dominated the 'Quins pack and let ROG do the rest.

They got the 2013/14 campaign off to the worst possible start by losing to Edinburgh at Murrayfield but rectified matters sufficiently to beat Perpignan and Gloucester home and away and Edinburgh back at Thomond Park. This set up a renewal of a rivalry with Toulouse that had begun back in 1996/97 in Toulouse but also included memorable victories in Bordeaux in 2000 and Cardiff in the 2008 final. Not surprisingly, Thomond Park was packed for the semi-final meeting of two of the competition's most successful sides. It was probably one of the few games in which Rob Penney's desire for a more expansive approached gelled perfectly with the traditional Munster way of doing things. A less-than-fired-up Toulouse outfit had no answer as they tumbled to one of their biggest ever defeats, 47 points to 23.

Toulouse's renowned, long-serving coach Guy Noves must have been fearing the worst when a side that included outstanding players of the calibre of Louis Picamoles, captain Patricio Albacete, Luke McAlister, Gaël Fickou, Hosea Gear and Maxime Médard was made to look extremely second rate within five minutes of the kick-off, as twenty brilliantly executed phases

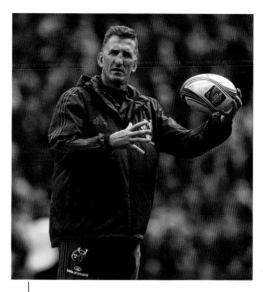

Munster head coach Rob Penney, 2012–14. (Courtesy Sportsfile)

led to a superb try by Keith Earls. Shortly after, Munster suffered a serious setback when a shoulder injury to inspirational captain Peter O'Mahony not only ruled him out of the remainder of the game but the rest of the season as well. Even then and as if to demonstrate that this was going to be Munster's day, C. J. Stander came on as O'Mahony's replacement and slotted in perfectly. It was the South African's twenty-fourth birthday and he celebrated with his side's third try in a man-of-the-match performance. Having led 13–9 into half-time, Munster were even more dominant throughout a second half during which David Kilcoyne, Stander, Casey Laulala and Simon Zebo went over for tries before the stands and terraces shook to their foundations as a massive roar greeted the sixth, touched down by Paul O'Connell two minutes before the final whistle. Ian Keatley landed four conversions and three penalties leaving Toulouse with the consolation of tries by Hosea Gear and Joe Tekori, three penalties by Luke McAlister and two conversions by Lionel Beauxis.

Munster: F. Jones, K. Earls, C. Laulala, J. Downey, S. Zebo, I. Keatley, C. Murray, D. Kilcoyne, D. Varley, B. J. Botha, D. Foley, P. O'Connell, P. O'Mahony capt., T. O'Donnell, J. Coughlan.

Replacements: D. Casey, J. Ryan, A. Cotter, D. O'Callaghan, C. J. Stander, D. Williams, J. J. Hanrahan, G. van den Heever.

Toulouse: M. Médard, Y. Huget, G. Fickou, F. Fritz, H. Gear, L. McAlister, I. Vermaak, G. Steenkamp, C. Tolofua, Y. Montes, Y. Maestri, P. Albacete capt., Y. Camara, J. Tekori, L. Picamoles. *Replacements*: J. Bregvadze, C. Baillie, S. Ferreira, R. Millo-Chluski, G. Galan, J. M. Doussain, L. Beauxis, C. Poitrenaud.

Referee: Nigel Owens (Wales).

Keith Earls shows his class at Thomond Park. (Courtesy Sportsfile)

Munster have rarely been favoured by the luck of the draw in the Heineken Cup and so it was in 2014 when for the second year in a row, they had to make their way to the south of France, this time to Marseilles, for a semi-final clash with Toulon. Even though they scored the game's only try through Simon Zebo, they lost 24–16 to the cosmopolitan stars of the defending champions with many rueing a decision to shun two penalty shots at goal when still only five points separated the sides and with time on the clock. The resultant line-outs yielded no return.

Anthony Foley was chosen to replace Rob Penney as Munster head coach in good time for 2014/15. However, the season was to prove disappointing. The big-money clubs in England and France had their way and the Heineken Cup was replaced by the European Champions Cup. One thing remained the same, however: the draw was as unkind as ever to Munster and they found themselves in the same pool as Clermont Auvergne, Saracens and Sale Sharks. Whereas Clermont and Sarries had the financial wherewithal to recruit some of rugby's finest, it seemed as if Munster were at the opposite end of the monetary spectrum. Of those who had been involved in the glory days only Paul O'Connell remained; lack of funds meant no big-name signings and with injury depriving Foley of key players at crucial stages of the campaign, it would have taken a series of exceptional results to reach the knockout stages for the seventeenth year out of nineteen.

Even though a last-minute drop goal by Ian Keatley snatched a lucky away win over Sale and Thomond Park once again came good with a 14–3 defeat of Saracens, the shortcomings in the squad were apparent, all the more so because of an unprecedented string of injuries. Back-to-back defeats by Clermont in December came as a devastating Christmas present for Foley and his indigenous coaching team of Jerry Flannery, Brian Walsh, Ian Costelloe and Mick O'Driscoll. Clermont followed in the footsteps of Leicester and Ulster by beating Munster in Thomond Park in the European Cup, benefiting from a try by outstanding number eight Fritz Lee after a mere fifty-eight seconds. The brilliant centre Wesley Fofana also scored a Clermont try, Camille Lopez kicked a couple of penalties, while Keatley replied with three for the home side. Seven points separated the sides when Munster forced an attacking 5-metre line-out in the last minute. But Damien Chouly read the call perfectly and Munster's last chance of a draw was gone.

Clermont Auvergne: N. Abendanon, N. Nakaitaci, A. Rougerie, W. Fofana, N. Nalaga, C. Lopez, L. Radoslavjevic, T. Domingo, B. Kayser, C. Ric, J. Cudmore, S. Valaamahina, D. Chouly capt., J. Bonnaire, F. Lee.

Munster: F. Jones, G. Van den Heever, P. Howard, D. Hurley, S. Zebo, I. Keatley, C. Murray, D. Kilcoyne, D. Casey, B. J. Botha, D. Foley, P. O'Connell, P. O'Mahony capt., T. O'Donnell, C. J. Stander.

Munster managed to scrape a losing bonus point in Clermont which just about kept alive their hopes of a place in the quarter-finals, but that was blown out of the water when they suffered a humiliating 33–10 hammering away to Saracens. It was the first time they had lost three successive European Cup games, meaning that the final game against Sale Sharks at Thomond Park was a 'dead rubber'. There was little consolation to be derived from a win by 65–10 although the presence of more than 17,800 spectators indicated that their belief in the Munster team was steadfast.

The point was again well made when Munster returned to Thomond Park on 23 May 2015 for a Guinness Pro12 semi-final against the Ospreys. In the glory years, the Celtic League had taken second place behind the European Cup but times had changed for the worse where the Irish teams were concerned and they were more than happy to make an impression in the secondary competition. Leinster did extremely well to battle their way into the semi-final in Europe and were unlucky to lose to three-in-a-row champions Toulon but even they missed out on the Pro12 semis, a failure that cost Australian coach Matt O'Connor his job.

Foley and his fellow coaches were indebted to a gallant Connacht performance against the Ospreys as it gained Munster the huge advantage of a home semi-final. Instead of having to travel to the Liberty Stadium in Swansea, they had the benefit of performing in front of the Thomond Park faithful, 16,186 of whom turned up.

On the morning of the game, Gerry Thornley interviewed Ian Keatley in an *Irish Times* profile in which the Thomond Park factor came very much under the microscope. Gerry recalled the words of Victor Costello, the former Leinster and Ireland number eight, who had played all his rugby at the venue as a member of the 'away' side – except for one game with Ireland A.

'Having made one of his trademark carries, Victor heard this appreciative roar from the supporters and thought: "Ah, so that's what it's like being a Munster player."' Keatley interrupted the tale by saying: 'He liked the roar? Yep. It's hard to explain, you can just feel their presence. They're an educated fan base and they want to see good, entertaining rugby.' And, remember, Keatley was as much a 'Dub' as Costello, having learned the game at Belvedere College and been a member of the Leinster academy before arriving in Munster via Connacht.

The Munster v Ospreys semi-final was a cracking affair from the outset and, while Munster were the better side, they were very nearly pipped at the post in a truly sensational finish. Tries by Simon Zebo, Denis Hurley and the outstanding Paddy Butler looked to have put the game out of reach of the Welsh. But a succession of missed place kicks, including all three conversions, and a couple of potentially disastrous defensive errors left the Ospreys only three points behind as the game went into stoppage time. At that stage, referee Nigel Owens and both of his touch judges somehow missed an obvious Welsh knock-on by scrum-half Rhys Rees and after two phases the Ospreys centre Josh Matavesi looked to have gone over for a match-winning try. But Owens, widely regarded as one of the best referees in the game, was persuaded to watch the sequence on television replay and spotted the knock-on. He immediately declared the score invalid, leaving a very relieved Munster winners by 21–18.

And then what everybody had assumed beforehand came to pass: Paul O'Connell strode across the immaculate sward to wave to the Thomond Park faithful, clearly indicating that this would be his last game at the venue in the red jersey. There was many a moist eye as Paulie's adoring fans, men, women and children, cheered him before he finally made his way to the sanctuary of the dressing room under the East Stand. All that remained that day was for coach Foley and teammate C. J. Stander to express their admiration for this mountain of a man who will forever hold a special place in the hearts of Munster and Ireland rugby supporters.

'He's been a colossus, any team he was involved with, it's just the manner in which he goes about it, the standards he sets,' Foley said. 'He's the most challenging person that you'll come across in your whole life. He's been a massive influence on everyone who has played with him, coaches that have coached around him and have tried to work with him at times. He's been brilliant for us.'

Stander, the South African who had himself become something of a talisman for the Munster fans after a sequence of man-of-the-match performances, was completing his third season playing with O'Connell. He knew all about Paulie before arriving in Limerick from Pretoria and wasn't disappointed.

> I watched him on television but I never thought I'd play with him. He's a legend in my eyes – in everyone's eyes. You follow him. He's a leader and a real man's man, a man's leader. I look up to him. Playing with him has been one of the highest points of my career, especially to play his last game here at Thomond Park with him. I get emotional talking about it. Before the game, he told us to play in the now and for each other and

Paul O'Connell being interviewed by Des Cahill on stage in Thomond Park at the opening ceremony of the Special Olympics in 2010. (Courtesy *Limerick Leader*)

for our families. You could see it in his eyes. He didn't have to speak. He's the type of guy you follow on the pitch or even after rugby.

However, O'Connell still had another appointment to keep – a journey to Belfast and the Kingspan (formerly Ravenhill) Stadium for the Pro12 final against Glasgow Warriors, who had defeated Ulster in the semi-final. Foley used a lovely phrase – 'I do understand that sport has no conscience and doesn't care who wins and who loses' – to warn that just because this would be Paulie's last appearance in the red jersey that a favourable result would be the inevitable outcome.

Ravenhill nowadays is a fine modern stadium and a long way improved from the grey, uninviting venue that had nevertheless served the game in the north so well for the best part of a century. Indeed, it was there that Ireland defeated Wales to complete the Five Nations Grand Slam back in 1948.

Alas, Munster simply did not turn up on the night. They were roundly beaten 31–13 by a vastly superior Warriors side. It was not the way the 3,000 or so fans who made their way north and the many watching on television wanted to see O'Connell's magnificent career in the red jersey come to an end. It was also a sad end to a season that saw several others leaving the club, including Damien Varley, J. J. Hanrahan, Johne Murphy, Andrew Smith (an Australian centre who scored the side's only try at the Kingspan), Paddy Butler and Sean Dougall, all of whom had played many a fine game for Munster.

Within a few days, all the rumours and reports of the previous several weeks were confirmed. O'Connell's career was not over and he would be on his way instead to European champions Toulon after leading Ireland in the 2015 Rugby World Cup. The whole country reacted with one voice – *bonne chance* and travel well.

20

Schools Rugby

Here's an interesting question for your club's table quiz: can you name the first Limerick side to win the Munster Schools Senior Cup? The answer: Limerick Christian Brothers School (CBS). In 1926, the Sexton Street academy brought to an end the seventeen-year domination of the competition by the County Tipperary powerhouse that is Rockwell College, the Cork schools Christian Brothers College (CBC) and Presentation Brothers College (PBC), and the once-off interlopers, Abbey School, Tipperary. Limerick CBS captured the title again in 1931, 1933 and 1934, the year Thomond Park opened. Only two years later, it housed its first final when CBC Cork defeated Rockwell College.

Mungret were the next Limerick side to win the Schools Senior Cup. A Jesuit college located a couple of miles south-west of the city, which produced several outstanding players and some fine sides until it closed in 1974, they defeated Rockwell in the final in Clonmel. The captain was Cork man Edward Cogan. Interestingly, when Munster completed the Grand Slam in the Schools Interprovincial Championship at Thomond Park for the first time in 1974, Cogan's son Eddie was a member of the side that also included another Mungret representative, Eugene Carley. Two penalties by Peter Ryan gave Mungret their one and only title in 1941, with the *Limerick Leader* reporting that 'in a pack that played well in the loose, Cogan, the captain, was outstanding'. The *Leader* also cautioned that 'several daily papers mentioned that the Rockwell team travelled from Cashel to Clonmel on bicycles. This is not true as

Christian Brothers College, Cork, winners of the 1936 Munster Senior Schools Cup final, the first to take place at Thomond Park. Back row (l–r): T. Keane, J. Shinkwin, T. Twomey, P. Walsh, K. Kearren, V. Richards, N. Barrett, F. Dawson; middle row (l–r): H. O'Shea, S. Sullivan, A. Donovan, M. Forde capt., E. Foley, D. Butler, F. Foley; front row (l–r): B. Kearney and C. Corbett. (Courtesy Christian Brothers College Cork)

Mungret, Munster Schools Senior Cup champions 1941. Back row (l–r): R. Power, A. Farren, K. McCormack, R. Lillis, J. McGarry, S. Goggin; middle row (l–r): J. Tarpey, P. Ryan, O. Lynch, E. Cogan capt., S. Shiel, P. Duffy, E. O'Connor; front row (l–r): P. O'Connor and J. Nestor. (Courtesy *Mungret College Annual*)

they travelled to and from their headquarters per bus. Many of their supporters, however, made the trip on cycles.'

Another Jesuit college, Crescent, looked on with a degree of envy as their 'sister' college Mungret stole a march on them with that victory in 1941 along with capturing the Junior Cup from 1939 through to 1941. The title they so earnestly coveted eluded them until 1947. Fr Gerry Guinane, a rugby man to his fingertips, had become a member of the staff a short few years previously. Recognising that he had a wealth of talent at his disposal, 'the Ginner', as he was widely known, marshalled his forces expertly.

He installed Paddy Berkery as captain and it was an inspired choice. Paddy, a native of Clonmel, came to Limerick in 1940 in time to start his rugby career as an under ten at Crescent. Somewhat on the slight size, he began as a scrum half and played there on the team beaten 6–5 by PBC led by Archie O'Leary in the 1945 Junior Cup decider. However, he was full back and captain by the 1947 season when he was surrounded by a group of high-quality players like Jim Roche, Louis Nestor, Willie Reid, Ivan Harris, John Leahy, Tom Hayes, Goff Spillane and Dermot Molony.

Presentation Brothers College, Cork, 1945/46. Back row (l–r): E. Heaphy, P. Mitchell, J. Crowley, T. Connolly, P. Grant; middle row (l–r): F. O'Leary, A. McHale, A. O'Leary, M. Collins, J. O'Regan, J. Forrest; front row (l–r): D. Bennett, D. O'Donnell, G. O'Connell, N. Nunan capt., C. McCarthy, R. Attwood, D. Dinan. (Courtesy Presentation Brothers Cork)

Crescent were among the short-priced favourites before the campaign began and duly justified that rating in impressive fashion.

They twice made the journey to Cork in vain for the final against PBC: the Mardyke was declared unplayable each time, because of waterlogging. The teams eventually finished level, three points each, leading to a Thomond Park replay well into the month of April. The *Limerick Chronicle*'s rugby correspondent 'Short Pass' noted that 'R. Reynolds, who played in the first game, was unavailable for the replay and was replaced by the then 15½-year-old Richard Harris in the second-row.'

'Short Pass' went on:

> The keen interest in the Munster Senior Schools Cup final replay between Crescent College and Presentation which resulted in an 8–3 win for the former was reflected by the large attendance at Thomond Park. The crowd derived a refreshing tonic from the magnificent display given by two splendid school teams. In the wind-assisted first half, Crescent did all the pressing and their backs were seen in brilliant passing movements and it took sound tackling by the Presentation defence to prevent a score.
>
> After the interval, it was the turn of Pres to pile on the pressure but all attempts to gain ground were frustrated by the impressive full back Paddy Berkery whose safe handling was a feature of the game. Dominating the exchanges in the opening half, Crescent built up a five-point lead when White and Willie Reid created an opening for Molony to dive over for a try that Ivan Harris converted. Early in the second half, Presentation reduced the deficit with a long-range penalty from McHale. But the visitors' delight was short lived and much to the joy of the home support Jim Roche clinched victory with an unconverted try.
>
> After the game, the cup was presented to Paddy Berkery amid scenes of great enthusiasm, this being the first time the famous Limerick college have inscribed their name on the trophy. The winning Crescent College team lined out as follows – Paddy Berkery capt., Willie Reid, Gerry Power, Louis Nestor, Ivan Harris, John Leahy, Jim Roche, Tom Hayes, Michael Keane, Des White, Richard Harris, Michael Collins, M. Fitzgerald, Goff Spillane, Dermot Molony.

Rockwell, Munster Schools Senior Cup champions 1950. Back row (l–r): K. Prendergast, K. Dodd, F. O'Keeffe, D. Bernard, J. Cosgrove, M. McEvoy, S. D'Arcy, G. Bernard; middle row (l–r): J. Manning, P. Casey, J. Burke, M. Brosnan capt., S. F. Gallagher, N. Keane, R. Walsh; front row (l–r): M. English and B. O'Connor. (Courtesy *Rockwell College Annual*)

Presentation Brothers College, Cork, winners of the Munster Schools Senior Cup, 1957. Back row (l–r): A. O'Brien, T. Kiernan, M. Bohane, D. Saunders, J. Murray, D. Lynch, G. Boland; middle row (l–r): J. O'Shea, J. Pyne, K. Canniffe, J. Walsh capt., F. Hegarty, N. Collins, F. McCarthy; front row (l–r): T. O'Leary and D. Bradley. (Courtesy Presentation Brothers Cork)

Two years later, Crescent were celebrating again, with Goff Spillane and Richard Harris still there along with a whole host of promising players like Gordon Wood, Niall Quaid, Noel Harris and Mick O'Donnell. They met the holders Rockwell in the Thomond Park decider and came out on top 8–0 with a try by winger Gerry Murphy and a conversion and penalty by inspirational captain Spillane.

Rockwell were back in Thomond Park in 1950 for a final confrontation with Mungret who were completely outplayed on the day by a powerful side including future Ireland and Lions out-half Mick English and captained by Kerry man Mick Brosnan. They won by six unconverted tries, 18–0.

Crescent were making a habit of winning the Senior Cup every second year at Thomond Park and another seriously talented side struck again in 1951. Noel Harris, one of the stars of the victorious side two years earlier, displayed his wide range of talents as captain and out-half as they defeated PBC 5–3 in the decider. A few days later, a Thomond Park game labelled as an 'Irish schools final' against Leinster Cup winners Belvedere, ended in an honourable draw.

> **Crescent:** N. Harris capt., M. O'Donnell, B. Downes, J. O'Keeffe, N. Heffernan, D. O'Connor, R. Leonard, T. Hanrahan, J. Carroll, D. Foley, C. Finucane, E. Martin, T. Stack, M. O'Brien, S. Meagher.

Gradually, the powerful Cork academies PBC and CBC, and Rockwell in Tipperary were loosening Crescent's grip on the silverware and the careers were launched of players who were to grace Thomond Park many times in the future, such as Tom Nesdale, Tom Coffey, Mick O'Callaghan, Liam Coughlan, Ray Hennessy, Jerry Walsh, Joe Nesdale (a medal winner with PBC and Rockwell), Tom Kiernan, Jerry Murray, Paddy McGrath, Brendan O'Dowd, Jim Molloy, Joe Cumiskey and many others.

Tom Kiernan and captain Jerry Walsh were central to PBC's success in 1957 when they beat Crescent in the Thomond Park final. This was arguably one of the finest Pres teams ever. They went unbeaten throughout the season, playing delightful rugby that showed off the schools game in the best possible light. While Kiernan and Walsh are the names that linger most in peoples' memories, there were a number of others who earned representative honours subsequently, including outstanding second-row Jerry Murray, hooker Kieran Canniffe and prop Jim Pyne while full back Tony O'Brien and scrum half David

Bradley were widely recognised as two of the finest in their respective positions from schools through to senior rugby.

PBC retained the cup in 1958 only to suffer a surprise defeat in the 1959 decider when a penalty by Tadgh Kerins won the day for Rockwell. Kerins went on to enjoy a successful career with Sundays Well, St Mary's College and Leinster, skipper Mick Butler was a member of the distinguished Dublin rugby family, and Paddy McGrath was to wear the Munster and Ireland shirts with distinction. One of those deprived of a third successive Senior Cup medal was Jerry Murray, the outstanding Cork Constitution and Munster second-row forward of the future. Rockwell, however, completed the three-in-a-row in 1960 and 1961 with Tadgh Houlihan a member of each team.

Indications that Crescent were on the way back were provided by their victory in the Junior Cup in 1961. The team was captained by Brian Reddan, brother of Don who played many times for Connacht and Munster, and uncle of multi-capped Ireland scrum half Eoin. Brian was also skipper two years later when the bulk of that side regained the Senior Cup.

Although St Munchin's had never won either of the two major provincial trophies, largely because the school on Henry Street (now the location for the Garda barracks) was short in numbers, they usually provided difficult opposition for the bigger guns while also producing some outstanding players, most notably the great second-row Bill Mulcahy. At the beginning of the 1960s, St Munchin's moved to a new site at Corbally on the banks of the River Shannon and their fortunes took a very definite turn for the better.

When they battled their way into the Senior Cup final in 1968 against Rockwell, past pupils from all over the country and many parts of the world turned up in large numbers at Thomond Park to swell the crowd to record proportions. Larry Moloney, full back on the Munster team that beat the All Blacks at Thomond Park ten years later, lined out in the centre for St Munchin's and grabbed the only score, a drop goal just before half-time after a break by Brian Cox created the opportunity. St Munchin's endured many anxious moments subsequently before they were able to celebrate victory. The presentation of the trophy to captain John Moloney from Clonlara by Most Rev. Dr Henry Murphy, Bishop of Limerick, was an extra source of delight for former students for whom he was a special favourite.

St Munchin's, Munster Schools Senior Cup winners, 1968. Back row (l–r): T. Hayes coach, J. Enright, T. Sadlier, L. Moloney, M. Carroll, N. Noonan, C. O'Connor, P. O'Shea, J. Hennessy; middle row (l–r): B. Cox, G. Rowlands, P. O'Dwyer, J. Moloney capt., J. Bourke, P. Houlihan, M. Hehir; front row (l–r): D. O'Grady and M. Brennan. (Courtesy St Munchin's College)

Presentation Brothers Cork, Munster Schools Senior Cup champions, 1965. Their final victory over Rockwell was bittersweet in that renowned coach Pat Barry suffered a heart attack during the game and died. Back row (l–r): C. Riordan, T. Fitzgibbon, J. Jennings, P. Morehan, K. Creedon, B. McGann, B. Twomey; middle row (l–r): M. Manning, D. Spillane, D. Prendergast, O. Moriarty, M. Buckley, M. Daly; front row (l–r): E. Gamble, P. Sheppard, T. Murphy capt., N. Elliott and D. Coughlan. (Courtesy Presentation Brothers College)

The 1960s had been notable for some great games and outstanding players gracing Thomond Park. Two of Munster's finest out-halves Barry McGann and John Moroney starred there for PBC and Rockwell while the era saw the beginning of the illustrious careers of Donal Canniffe (PBC) and Willie Duggan (Rockwell).

And so to 1970 and one of the most memorable of all Thomond Park finals, not so much for the quality of the rugby but for the fact that Glenstal came within a couple of minutes of their first and only Senior Cup. The superb Glenstal Castle close to the village of Murroe in County Limerick was built by the Barrington family in the 1830s and acquired by the Benedictine Order in 1928. They loved rugby and competed loyally without ever becoming overly serious about making an impression competitively in the apparent belief that their small number of students considerably reduced their prospects of taking on the big guns. However, Fr Peter Gilfedder, an avid and knowledgeable sportsman, saw things a little differently and dreamt that the day might come when the 'Glen' could lay their hands on the coveted trophy.

He genuinely believed that the dream could be realised as he saw a large group of talented footballers come together in time for the 1969/70 campaign. As the weeks went by, very promising results were achieved with Barnaby O'Sullivan a tower of strength at number eight, Michael Kennedy an equally important figure at out-half and Limerick cousins Billy Gabbett and Walter O'Brien two of the most dangerous attacking backs in the competition. The final was always going to be a very tight affair with Rockwell enjoying a massive advantage in tradition and experience, well equipped up front where Billy Cronin and Mick Morrissey were major figures and blessed with an outstanding centre in future Irish international Paul McNaughton. And there have been few better full backs in the schools game than Paul McElhinney.

To their credit, Glenstal quickly shook off the nerves inherent in a team's first cup final appearance and took the lead with a try by Billy Gabbett shortly after half-time. They held on for dear life until stoppage time when Rockwell scrum half Peter Hanahoe dived over for the equalising try. It was a shattering blow for the County Limerick side who, however, responded to the urgings of Fr Peter and again turned up full of confidence and self-belief for the replay. McNaughton gave 'Rock' an early lead with a try converted by McElhinney. Kennedy responded with a Glenstal penalty only for Paul Kane to go over for a second Rockwell try to lead 8–3 at the interval. Glenstal came again with a second half try by James Quigley but the conversion was off target and it was Rockwell's day once again.

Rockwell: P. McElhinney, M. Slattery, A. Hickey, P. McNaughton, P. Lee, M. Ryan, P. Hanahoe, J. Grennan, C. Haydar, D. Ormond capt., M. Morrissey, F. Brady, P. Kane, W. Cronin, V. Lonergan.

Glenstal: F. McElligott, W. O'Brien, G. Bradley, W. Gabbett, F. Corbett, M. Kennedy, J. Hegarty, E. Quigley, R. Deasy, A. O'Sullivan, C. Griffin, J. Quigley, P. Chamberlain, B. O'Sullivan, G. Harvey.

The province had produced a number of outstanding schools interprovincial teams over the years but it was not until 1974 that a Munster side completed the 'Grand Slam' for the first time. They defeated Ulster 12–0 at Thomond Park to complete the deal with the following side:

Michael O'Sullivan capt. (PBC), Denis Toomey (Crescent), Padraig Slattery (Rockwell), Peter Rolls (St Munchins), Jimmy Bowen, Moss Finn (both PBC), Eddie Cogan (Mungret), Brian Clifford (PBC), Eugene Carley (Mungret), Ted Mulcahy and Ted Sheehan (both St Munchin's), Jerry Holland (CBC), Paddy Madden (St Munchin's), Anthony O'Leary and Barry Cogan (both CBC).

Bowen and Finn were members of the Munster team that beat the All Blacks at Thomond Park four years later when O'Sullivan and Mulcahy were among the substitutes. Bowen, Finn and Jerry Holland went on to play for Ireland. Anthony O'Leary enjoyed a highly successful rugby career with Cork Constitution, Wanderers and Munster before becoming one of the country's finest yachtsmen. Padraig Slattery is a member of the renowned Lahinch golfing family and one of Ireland's leading public relations practitioners.

For sheer quality, the best schools game ever played at Thomond Park was probably the international meeting of Ireland and Australia in December 1977. An Australian side containing the Ella twins Mark and Glen and their brother Gary, won 12–10 but those fortunate enough to be present fondly recall the occasion for the superb football produced by the two sides. Australia deserved their win although Ireland missed four first-half penalties that cost them dearly. Peter Nowlan of Wesley

College scored the Irish try and Philip McDonnell of St Mary's College landed a couple of penalties while Glen and Gary Ella touched down for Australia and Tony Melrose converted both tries.

Several members of the teams went on to enjoy successful senior careers, none more so than the brilliant Mark Ella while his brothers, along with a number of others including Melrose, Michael Hawker, Tony Darcy, Shane Nightingale and Chris Roche, also made the senior Wallabies team. Captain Philip Matthews and out-half Paul Dean were key members of the Irish team that bridged a 26-year gap when winning the Triple Crown in 1985. Mick Moylett (Shannon), Paul Collins (UCC and Highfield) and Kenny Hooks of Bangor were also capped.

Australia: T. Melrose capt., Glen Ella, M. Hawker, Gary Ella, P. McPherson, Mark Ella, D. Vaughan, T. Darcy, M. Illett, R. Leslie, S. Nightingale, W. Melrose, I. Millar, G. Bailey, C. Roche.

Ireland: R. Hopkins (Terenure), P. Nowlan (Wesley), P. Bauress (Blackrock), B. Keogh (CBC Monkstown), K. Hooks (Bangor Grammar School), P. Dean and P. McDonnell (both St Mary's College), B. Iveston (Regent House), G. Douglas and M. J. Blair

St Munchin's, Munster Schools Senior Cup champions, 1982. Back row (l–r): S. Conneely coach, P. Danaher, R. Moloney, R. Sheehan, D. Dineen, J. Ahern, G. Moylan, T. O'Connor, D. O'Donoghue, J. Bermingham, Fr F. Duhig; middle row (l–r): L. Looney, D. Hannon, D. Geary, P. Lloyd, P. Culhane capt., P. Murray, P. Craughan, D. Liston, E. O'Sullivan; front row (l–r): M. Walsh, M. Ruschitzko, J. Roche, T. Leahy, P. Kilbridge and W. Quinlan. (Courtesy St Munchin's College)

(both Methodist College), M. Moylett (Castleknock), P. Collins (CBC), A. Blair (High School), C. Jennings (St Gerard's), P. Matthews capt. (Regent House).

The years 1968 to 1981 were a very barren period for the Limerick schools and Thomond Park as CBC and PBC dominated and Musgrave Park staged final after final until St Munchin's again made their mark in 1982, clinching their second title with an impressive win over PBC. Although they could call on several stars of the future, including Philip Danaher and skipper Pat Murray, it was an intimidating match for the Corbally college in that they had never previously beaten Pres in a competitive fixture and would go through almost the entire campaign without captain and influential back-row Paul Culhane because of injury. However, Murray at full back, Danaher at out-half and Liam Looney on the wing gave Munchin's a cutting edge behind the scrum while up front Geoff Moylan and Robert Sheehan were key figures. PBC full back Pat Attridge put his side ahead with a fine early try but Munchin's gradually settled and tries by Moylan and David Dineen and the accurate boot of Willie Quinlan saw them to victory by 14–7.

The following season, the Kelvin Leahy-led Crescent side came out on the right side of a Musgrave Park final against PBC, while they had home support at Thomond Park in 1986 when overcoming CBC with a team captained by wing forward Mark O'Donoghue.

Limerick rugby has been fortunate in the impressive way the various schools in and around the city have supported the game and created a large number of fine teams and players. The now-defunct St Enda's was no exception, especially in the 1980s when Billy Moloney, a teacher at the Galvone school and a keen enthusiast since his earliest days in Nenagh, proved an excellent coach. He guided several Enda's teams with varying degrees of success until he had a squad of players at his disposal good enough to battle their way into the final of the Munster Schools Senior Cup in 1987. They were probably overawed at taking on PBC at Musgrave Park and lost 19–0. However, most of that side were available again in 1988 and they qualified for the final, this time at Thomond Park. The clash with CBC had to be postponed on two occasions because of a waterlogged pitch and so the sides could not meet until 17 April. It was a desperately close affair before CBC triumphed by a penalty goal to nil.

CBC: R. Kelleher, S. Fitzpatrick, B. Smith, A. Roche, A. McGonnell, Donogh O'Mahony (F. Dunne), David O'Mahony, P. Soden, C. Twomey, A. McDonald, R. Healy, H. Twomey, D. Lucey capt., J. Byrne, D. Loftus, M. Creedon.

St Enda's: D. Rooney, P. McNamara, I. Duggan, D. Duggan, I. Cross, M. Kerley, D. Tobin, D. Noonan, T. Murphy, D. Ryan, D. Coll, P. Hastings capt., E. Mason, B. O'Brien, K. McNamara.

Enda's scrum half Derek Tobin went on to play for Munster in their victory over the touring Australians in 1992 and was a key man in the Young Munster team that won the All-Ireland League in 1993.

Crescent's next success came under the leadership of Billy O'Shea and included future Lions prop Paul Wallace who picked up a second medal with Crescent when the trophy was retained with hooker Mike O'Mara as captain. PBC contested five successive finals between 1991 and 1996 and lost just one, to a David Wallace-inspired Crescent at Thomond Park in 1996. Several members of the great Munster senior teams of the late 1990s and the first decade of the new millennium figured in those matches, a healthy breeding ground for the future.

Rockwell bridged a six-year gap in 2001 by beating St Munchin's in the final at Thomond Park before the Corbally college enjoyed a golden spell, capturing the title in three years out of five, getting the better of PBC by margins of as little as one, one and four points in the finals of 2002, 2003 and 2006 respectively. Future Lions Keith Earls and Conor Murray were members of the 2006 group. Castletroy College pulled off the senior/junior double in 2008. Those finals against CBC and PBC took place at Dooradoyle as the new Thomond Park stadium was under construction.

One of the most impressive aspects of the ethos of Rockwell College is the way they have maintained over the years a proud rugby tradition, which was born in the late 1890s by the exploits of the legendary Ryan brothers. They may not have always reached the final or succeeded when they got there but Rockwell loyally maintained their faith in rugby football whether winners or losers. In the 2011 final, they met PBC at Thomond Park with J. J. Hanrahan in his pomp. They played well, J. J. scored a lovely try, but PBC still won the day.

Rockwell were back in Thomond Park a year later as two penalties by Aidan Moynihan against a try by Matthew McSweeney earned them their twenty-fifth title against St Munchin's. They were captained that day by Sean McCarthy, a nephew of Munster great Mick Galwey.

Rockwell: D. Johnston, A. Lynch, R. Jermyn, C. Kiely, S. McMahon, A. Moynihan, D. McGagh, J. McCormack, D. Mulcahy, J. Maxwell, S. McCarthy capt., D. Foley, A. Sweeney, A. Butler, S. O'Dwyer. *Replacements*: R. Maher for Johnston, A. Barron for McGagh, N. Flynn for Foley, J. Feehan for Sweeney.

It was a different story in 2013. As Barry Coughlan put it in the *Irish Examiner*:

Crescent Comprehensive 27 Rockwell College 5.

This remarkable Munster Schools Senior Cup triumph by Crescent at Thomond Park was in keeping with part of the school's name – comprehensive! It was Crescent's first senior

Presentation Brothers College, Munster Schools Senior Cup champions, 2010. Back row (l–r): R. Caplice, J. Kiernan, G. Collins, B. Carroll, S. Glynn, K. Kingston, G. Murray, K. Ryan, A. Hudson, B. Scott, C. Bannon; middle row (l–r): B. Fitzgerald, B. O'Connor, W. Murphy, P. McKeown, R. O'Herlihy, C. O'Flaherty, C. Keane, B. Coughlan, R. Murphy, P. Deasy, W. Foley, R. Scannell; front row (l–r): J. Costigan, E. O'Shaughnessy, E. Dennehy, R. Barry, D. O'Mahony and N. Scannell captains, B. Vaughan, S. Óg Murphy, J. Horgan, J. Duffy and E. Mills. (Courtesy Presentation Brothers College Cork)

title since 1994 but it was one of the school's greatest triumphs, particularly as it will go down as one few expected them to win.

But they certainly delivered, with skipper Gearóid Lyons performing kicking heroics from the tee and from hand, centres J. J. O'Neill and William Leonard causing considerable problems and winger Greg O'Shea a constant danger. That's not to mention the magnificence of a pack that took control from the early stages, with the entire back row grouping of Diarmuid Dee, Jack Dinneen and Jay Kavanagh setting the scene and the standards.

Crescent: J. Frawley, J. O'Sullivan, J. J. O'Neill, W. Leonard, G. O'Shea, G. Lyons capt., G. Fitzgerald, S. McGee, J. Green, L. McMahon, J. Keane, R. Scott, D. Dee, J. Dinneen, J. Kavanagh. *Replacements*: J. Purcell for Leonard (41, injured), C. Blake for McGee, M. O'Donnell for Scott (both 47), G. Mullins for McMahon, E. Casserly for Dinneen, J. Leonard for Frawley, E. Barry for Fitzgerald, C. Rea for Green (all 68).

Crescent duly retained the trophy in 2014 with a side that played some superb rugby and after beating PBC in the semi-final at the Mardyke, won the first all-Limerick final against Ardscoil Rís by 21–7 at Thomond Park. Cormac Blake, Dylan Sheehan and Jason O'Sullivan scored the Crescent tries and Fionn McGibney converted all three, leaving Ardscoil with only a late try by Kelvin Brown converted by David O'Mahoney.

Crescent: D. Sheehan, J. O'Sullivan, J. J. O'Neill (J. Harrington), W. Leonard, C. Nash (J. Hogan), F. McGibney, G. Fitzgerald (E. Barry), M. O'Donnell (M. Rickard), C. Moloney, L. McMahon, R. Scott, R. Noone (C. Guerin), S. Fitzgerald, J. Kavanagh, C. Blake capt.

Ardscoil Rís: S. Fitzgerald capt., B. Moriarty, P. McNamara, J. O'Donnell, L. Brock (L. White), D. O'Mahony, D. Scannell (H. Bourke), J. O'Halloran, S. Fenton, T. Walsh (K. Bracken), D. Ryan, P. Staff, J. Cannon, J. McCabe, K. Brown.

Ardscoil Rís were back once more in 2015, eliminating CBC and PBC on the way to meeting Rockwell in their sixth Thomond Park final in seven years. Bill Johnston from Clonmel, a brother of David who had two medals from the wins in 2011 and 2012, was their inspirational force at out-half and poised to emulate the feats of previous great Rockwell number tens Mick English of former years and J. J. Hanrahan in the modern era. Johnston had another fine match in the final when the Sean O'Connor-skippered 'Rock' inflicted a second successive final defeat on Ardscoil Rís. Coaches Mark Butler and Munster legend Denis Leamy along with Alan O'Donnell and Frank Fitzgerald were rewarded for their dedication on a sunny day at Thomond Park when the crowd exceeded expectations to such an extent that a last-minute decision was made to open the West Stand. While Leamy was celebrating, Mossie Lawler, his former Munster teammate and Ardscoil coach, was downhearted after his team's second successive final loss.

Rockwell squad: Tom McHale, Dearmuid Gallagher, Sean Lanigan-Ryan, Lee Molloy, Conor Cashman, Kieran Moynihan, Bill Johnston, Daryl Egan, Jack Tierney, Niall Campion, James Kendrick, Ben Murray, Diarmuid Barron, Conor Beary, Jack Binchy, Sean O'Connor capt., Bryan McLaughin, Mike Casey, Mikey Wilson, Tommy Anglim, Bill O'Brien, John Power, Josh Pickering, Elliott Stone, Jamie Stone, Kevin Kelly, Philly Ryan, Aerton Griffin, Ashton Griffin.

21

Junior Rugby

In the spring months of 1999, Young Munster, a club with a proud record of achievement when it came to nurturing young talent, were left with a dilemma. They had a nineteen-year-old in their ranks who could be the difference between victory and defeat in the final of the Munster Junior Cup. Would it be fair to the youngster in question to send him out against such tough opposition as Tipperary club Kilfeacle and District in what most people predicted would be a no-holds-barred encounter suitable only for those who had been through the mill many times over? On the other hand, would it be wise of the club to leave out such a talented forward who could swing the balance in their favour, all the more so when the man in question was mad for action?

Paul O'Connell played that day and turned in the kind of performance that revealed his potential as a second-row forward and how difficult it would be to intimidate him on a rugby field. All present at Thomond Park witnessed something special, not just the type of fierce contest for which the competition was renowned, but also a young man replete with ability at the line-out, at the ruck, at the maul, in the loose, with ball in hand, defending and attacking and above all totally at home taking on people older, far better physically developed and just as committed as himself.

The towering redhead from Drombanna on the outskirts of Limerick city was destined to be a sporting prodigy from his earliest days. He was a superb swimmer, an immensely talented golfer and showed promise in the GAA arena with his local South Liberties club, but it was not

Young Munster celebrate with the Munster Junior Cup trophy after their victory over Kilfeacle and District in the 1999 final at Thomond Park. The nineteen-year-old Paul O'Connell is the player extreme right, back row. His brother, Justin, is immediately to his right. (Courtesy Press 22)

Paul O'Connell in the thick of the action in the 1999 Munster Junior Cup final. (Courtesy Press 22)

until Paul went to Ardscoil Rís on Limerick's north side that he turned to rugby. Like just about everything else he turned his hand to, he was an immediate success and was on the road to rugby greatness, having earned his place for two seasons in the Munster and Ireland schools teams. There was also a hint of mischief in his psyche that prompted him to join those who found ways of scaling the boundary walls of Thomond Park to watch Munster on the big Heineken Cup days. But, of course, it was not long before he was strolling casually through the doors of the stadium in his own right, alongside Declan Kidney, Ronan O'Gara and all the other greats of the Munster squad. The rest, as they say, is history. Young Munster duly won the most recent of their seven Munster Junior Cup titles that 1999 afternoon.

Unless you knew what makes Munster rugby tick, you might imagine that a Junior Cup medal was no big deal. In fact, for those who toil away at the coalface, it is a very precious commodity and Paul O'Connell viewed it as such. The medal sits proudly alongside a Six Nations Grand Slam in 2009, captain of back-to-back Six Nations Championships in 2014 and 2015, two Heineken Cups with Munster, more than 100 Ireland caps and countless other honours. And as he never ceases to point out, little or none of this would have been possible without the influence of Young Munster and all he learned among his friends and advisers at Tom Clifford Park.

Since the event was instituted in 1909, the Munster Junior Cup has been regarded as one of the most difficult pieces of silverware to acquire for the junior clubs in the province and the seconds teams of the senior clubs. Teams invariably have needed to play five or six extremely competitive rounds before laying their hands on the trophy, with each demanding much of a man's courage and character.

Shannon were the major force in Junior Cup rugby as Thomond Park became the north Munster 'home' of the competition. Having regained the title at the Mardyke in 1939 with a side containing D. B. (Donogh) O'Malley, later to become a famous politician and government minister and also a keen and accomplished sportsman, they retained the trophy in 1940 in the first Junior Cup final to take place at Thomond Park. They were captained by the formidable Jack O'Flaherty, who later earned a well-merited reputation as a rugby coach ahead of his time.

Clanwilliam proved worthy opponents in a tense decider before Shannon's greater fitness told in extra time when they scored three tries.

They obviously boasted a remarkable squad of players at the time for they also captured the highly competitive Transfield Cup and Charity Cup that season. The final of the Charity Cup was held over until the following September when the Junior Cup champions, Shannon, defeated the Senior Cup holders, Garryowen, at Thomond Park by nine points to nil.

The teams in the first Munster Junior Cup final at Thomond Park were:

Shannon: J. O'Halloran, G. O'Donovan, C. McDermott, J. McCarthy, P. Sarsfield, R. White, J. Coree, P. O'Dwyer, J. Browne, P. Daly, M. Hayes, M. Minihan, T. Moloney, J. Clancy, J. O'Flaherty capt.

Clanwilliam: T. O'Loughlin, T. Davis, E. Kelly, E. Rahilly, J. Fennelly, C. Lehane, J. Carey, J. Gordon, J. Leahy, P. Enright, M. Flynn, W. O'Dwyer, P. Walsh, G. Looby, M. Fitzgerald.

Interestingly, rugby was thriving in some non-traditional areas of the region. For instance, in January 1941 Askeaton won the Transfield Cup, beating Shannon on the way to final victory over PBC. The Askeaton club survived for three years.

The old cliché 'no quarter asked or given' certainly applied in many of these matches. A first-round encounter between a team known as Crescent College Old Boys and Young Munster in 1943 shook rugby officialdom to the core. Their first meeting ended scoreless and, while Crescent cruised to a 16–3 win in the replay, nine players were sent off. The *Limerick Leader* informed its readers that 'in every case, no one could fault referee Mr Paddy Sullivan's decisions'. Paddy Reid accounted for all the winners' points, scoring a try, a drop goal and a penalty. Reid later revealed that, after this game, he had nipped out of Thomond Park on his bicycle as quickly and quietly as possible to make his way home safely.

Around this time the St Mary's club was founded. 'Saints' had their roots in St Mary's Parish. A couple of years later, Thomond RFC from the general Thomondgate area came on the scene. It was in 1944, too, that James Wood of Young Munster was elected president of the Munster Branch. He was father of Gordon and grandfather of Keith, two of the greatest rugby players to come out of Limerick.

A Richmond side captained by Terence O'Brien captured the club's second Junior Cup in seven years with a surprise 8–0 final win over UCC in 1943 and they struck again three years later. However, Presentation were luckless in their pursuit of the title, going down in the 1944 final to Dolphin and to Nenagh Ormond by 5–3 at Thomond Park four years later.

Presentation's run of misfortune in the Junior Cup continued in 1948 when they lost 5–3 in the final to Nenagh Ormond at Thomond Park which also hosted the decider two years later when a Limerick man helped to dash the hopes of Young Munster. UCC prevailed by a try created by Cyril Downes, a tearaway wing forward destined to play many a fine match for Old Crescent and to serve as president of the Munster Branch, and touched down by Mick Buckley, to nil.

UCC: J. Keane capt., J. O'Sullivan, V. Giltinane, J. O'Donovan, C. Wilson, M. Buckley, M. Bennett, F. Hennessy, F. Dowdall, G. Harrington, J. Hindle, P. Long, P. Mitchell, D. McHenry, J. O'Brien, K. O'Connell, C. Downes, C. Busteed, M. O'Regan.

Richmond pulled off the most recent of their four Munster Junior Cups in 1952 but it took three final meetings with Sundays Well before skipper Frank Lynch held the trophy aloft at Thomond Park. The teams had finished scoreless and tied again 11-all before Tom Lillis proved the hero third time around with a penalty and try created by a shrewd kick from Gerry Keyes, who also scored a try.

Richmond: A. Sheedy, F. Sheedy, G. Keyes, T. Lillis, M. Cross, G. Quinn, J. Walters, D. Moore, J. Sexton, F. Lynch capt., D. Howlett, E. Kinnane, M. Hanley, P. O'Connell, G. Keyes, W. O'Brien, J. Williams, G. McNamara, D. Rockett, J. Butler, E. Waters.

Shannon's victory in the Junior Cup in 1954 was a portent of things to come. A team captained by Frank O'Flynn, a much-loved character, and including the likes of Gerry O'Halloran, Bobby Keane, Sean O'Carroll, Mick Crowe, Bill O'Shea, Tommy Creamer, Jim O'Donovan, Ferdie Roche and Tony Sheppard fell behind in the Thomond Park final to a Dan Kennedy try for Cashel but came back on the resumption to prevail by 6–3 thanks to tries by Bob Keane and John O'Halloran. Within twelve months, Shannon were doing battle in senior rugby and the core of that junior side would lead them to a Senior Cup triumph in 1960.

Munster Junior team 1958. Back row (l–r): T. McInerney (St Mary's), R. O'Brien (Dolphin), J. O'Flynn (St Mary's), B. Duffy (Clonmel), H. Coveney (Cork Constitution), B. O'Dowd (Bohemians), P. O'Loughlin (Ennis), T. Sheehan (Shannon); front row (l–r): N. O'Mahony (UCC), G. Reardon (Dolphin), K. Canniffe capt. (Cork Constitution), N. Welton (UCC), B. O'Farrell (Garryowen), J. McNamara (Shannon), J. Gill (Nenagh). (Courtesy *Evening Echo*)

Shannon squad 1954: G. O'Halloran, P. O'Halloran, R. Keane, S. O'Carroll, M. Crowe, M. Kirby, W. O'Shea, T. Creamer, J. Keane, F. O'Flynn capt., E. Browner, J. O'Donovan, C. O'Flynn, M. O'Flynn, C. Ryan, J. O'Halloran, F. Roche, R. McNamara, A. Sheppard.

Shannon's love affair with the Junior Cup ended for a spell when Cork Constitution pulled off a hat-trick of wins. They beat Young Munster in the finals of 1957 and 1958 before Young Munsters, captained by Noel Kilbridge, put an end to their gallop, winning a Musgrave Park final replay following on a 3–3 draw at Thomond Park. Munsters were back in the final for a fourth successive year in 1960 and once again the Cork venue was good to them as they defeated Sundays Well by 16–3. The youthful Christy Carey played a major part in both successes.

When it came to the Junior Cup, though, it was difficult to keep Shannon out of the limelight. Having won the Senior Cup in 1960, they added the junior equivalent in each of the following two seasons. They needed a Thomond Park replay to beat Nenagh Ormond in 1961 when Tommy Creamer proved a true hero. One of two Shannon players to

Abbeyfeale, Munster Junior Cup winners at Thomond Park, 1963/64. Back row (l–r): P. Boucher-Hayes, B. O'Mahony, T. Lynch, G. O'Brien, J. Phelan, F. Kelly, C. McMahon, J. Barry; front row (l–r): L. Walsh, T. Hanley, J. Moynihan, B. Broderick capt., P. Keogh, N. Cotter, M. Shine. (Courtesy *Limerick Leader*)

leave the field injured in the first half, he returned on the wing shortly after the break although hooker Joe Gleeson needed urgent hospital treatment for a fractured jaw. Nevertheless, Shannon ran out worthy winners, thanks to a try by Mick Arthurs created by Tom Dunne and Mick Ryan, and a penalty and conversion by Gerry O'Carroll.

Shannon: Tommy Creamer, Mick Arthurs, Mick Ryan, Paddy Hall, Gerry Boland, Tom Dunne, Sean O'Carroll, Kevin Braddish, Joe Gleeson, Des Gilligan, Bob Ryan, Paddy Healy capt., Tony O'Flynn, Jim Larkin, J. Phayer.

Nenagh Ormond: J. O'Brien, D. White, D. Connolly, N. Hassett, T. J. O' Donoghue, S. Sheedy, N. O'Meara, S. Morrissey, E. McGrath, J. Gleeson, G. Lewis capt., F. Flannery, C. Powell, P. McMahon, T. Morgan.

Referee: Pax O'Kane.

A replay was also required in 1962 to separate Shannon and Nenagh after both again qualified for the final. They drew at Thomond Park before Shannon edged home in the replay. Tommy Creamer won his third medal that year and after hanging up his boots, remained a great supporter of his club and the game in general until he was known as the 'Voice of Thomond Park' when appointed the public-address announcer for the big European games at the venue.

Several rural clubs had won the Junior Cup over the years and in the mid-1960s there were memorable celebrations in west Limerick when Abbeyfeale were triumphant in 1964 and again in 1966. Founded as recently as 1960, largely due to the influence of Dr George O'Mahony, a powerfully built individual who instilled his love for the game not only into his sons Michael and Billy, both of whom played for Munster, but also into a large number of talented young footballers to the oval-ball code. In 1963, Abbeyfeale came up against Nenagh in the first final contested by two county clubs at Thomond Park. Once again, the Tipperary side was out of luck as Frank Kelly's try in the second half saw Abbeyfeale to a remarkable victory only four years after their foundation. Thomond Park rocked that April afternoon as Bernard Broderick lifted the trophy in triumph and George and Betty O'Mahony led the celebrations. Their son Billy was a member of that side and there could not have been two prouder people.

Abbeyfeale lost to Old Christians in the final the following year but regained the title in 1966 when their new pavilion at Abbeyside was officially opened by Dermot G. O'Donovan, president of the IRFU. Billy O'Mahony had moved on to senior ranks by this time and although he turned out for the Probables in a final trial, was never capped by Ireland. Abbeyfeale still packed plenty of talent although even they must have felt a degree of sympathy for Nenagh who once again came up agonisingly short in the Thomond Park decider. A try by second-row Kevin Wynne, converted by John Barry, did the trick for the west Limerick side.

Limerick's St Mary's RFC came up with the ideal way of celebrating their Silver Jubilee in 1968: winning the Junior Cup for the first (and so far the only) time in their history. They had produced many fine teams and players in their first twenty-five years and so it came as no surprise when they finally realised their most coveted ambition. The club had always been associated with the Hayes family, many of whom wore the horizontal blue-and-white stripes with pride and distinction, and the presence of Mick Hayes as coach had much to do with their biggest day of all. The dynasty started with Paddy, who was better known as Bansha, and continued with Mick, Augustine, Joe 'The Dane', Fra and Peter and each enjoyed a degree of fame in their own right in Limerick.

Two youngsters, Brendan Foley and Eddie Price, whose names would ring out loud in Munster and Irish rugby over the following decade or so were major contributors to the 'Saints' triumph in 1968. On the way to the final, they beat Richmond, Thomond, Shannon after a replay and Newcastle West. The rugby season in those days ended officially on the last day of April but the Branch allowed an extension of three days into May for the clash of St Mary's and Waterford City.

Mick Hayes and the 'Saints' think tank were hard at work as the weeks went by and they duly promoted Brendan Foley, Jim O'Dwyer and Noel Ryan from the club's second XV to the the premier side and just as astutely switched the free-scoring Eddie Price from wing forward to the key out-half berth. The masterstroke paid a rich dividend as Price controlled the game brilliantly and landed the three penalty goals that clinched victory. Foley, who was only seventeen at the time and so one of the youngest-ever winners of a Munster Junior Cup medal, went on to enjoy an honours-laden career with Shannon, Munster and Ireland, while his son, Anthony, was regarded as one of the best number eight forwards to pull on the same three jerseys. Eddie Price was to play

Brian Flanagan holds the Munster Junior Cup aloft after captaining Thomond to final success at Thomond Park in 1980. Included in the picture are 'Mr Thomond', Seamus Kiely (centre) and other distinguished rugby personalities including Sean Gavin, Cyril Gallivan, Tom Collery and Eamonn Tobin. (Courtesy *Limerick Leader*)

alongside Brendan in the successful Shannon Munster Cup winning sides of 1977 and 1978 and in many other successes for the club.

The era of Thomond as the dominant force in junior rugby was about to dawn. Like St Mary's before them, the 'Sodacakes', as out-and-out Thomondgate natives were known, had long been looking after the many versatile sportspeople in their native place. They tended to play hurling and football with Treaty-Sarsfields and soccer with Ballynanty Rovers but given that they were located in the shadow of Thomond Park, it was inevitable that they would also try their hand at rugby. And it was in that very ground that they were to achieve many of their greatest successes.

Thomond were ahead of their time in mastering the art of the rolling maul long before it became as fashionable and as potent a weapon as it is today. Success in the Junior Cup was invariably predicated on achieving forward supremacy. While expert coaches like Sean McNamara (who in his playing days had won three Senior Cup medals with Garryowen) and Liam Fitzgerald (who passed away prematurely and after whom the club grounds at Woodview Park are now called) understood this prerequisite, they also believed that what had sufficed previously might not do so any longer. So they set out to perfect the rolling maul which, unlike today, did not stipulate that the ball had to be carried at the back. Thomond implemented it so well that the ball was hidden even from the referee and half the length of the field could be covered before it again saw daylight. It is understood that this eventually led to a law change.

Nowadays, Thomond is a senior club well able to take care of itself in the All-Ireland League. They did not harbour such ambitions back in 1981 when making the big breakthrough by landing the Munster Junior Cup. Beating Garryowen in the final at Thomond Park, considering they were the defending champions and had won the Senior Cup a week previously, was no mean feat and Thomond did so thanks to a penalty by Brian Flanagan and drop goal by a Noel Morgan against a Martin Tubridy try.

Another nine years elapsed before Thomond regained the trophy. Just two of the 1971 team, Brian Flanagan and Dick Smyth, were involved, the former as captain. Seamus Kiely ensured the club was properly run while Declan Cusack proved a canny number ten and a veritable scoring machine. He scored a try in his side's 15–9 win over UCC and was to be central to the club's five subsequent wins in the competition. Cusack and Dick Smyth were outstanding players and tacticians and were again teammates in the Junior Cup successes in 1981, when Declan was captain, and 1985. Cusack was skipper once more in 1989 and still wearing the number-ten jersey when the three-in-a-row was completed in 1990 and 1991 under the leadership of Robert Duggan and Mal Sherlock. One of the key men in the hat-trick was Aidan O'Halloran who in 1993 was a major figure in Young Munster's victory in the All-Ireland League.

The Munster Junior Cup remains as fiercely competitive as ever. The big senior clubs continue to figure prominently but the rural teams are usually there or thereabouts. Clonmel, coached by former Munster star Denis Leamy, beat Clanwilliam in the 2014 decider and Bruff, Midleton, Nenagh Ormond, Clonakilty, Kilfeacle, Cobh Pirates and Cashel have all been successful at least once each in the last twenty-four years.

In 2015, however, the tournament's one-time kingpins Shannon captured the old trophy for the tenth time and the first since 1962. Clonmel, the defending champions under the influence of an outstanding coach in Denis Leamy, had already captured the Munster Junior League and All-Ireland Junior Cup and gone desperately close to achieving promotion to senior status in the Ulster Bank All-Ireland League, when they arrived at Thomond Park for yet another final on a wet Sunday in May. They appeared to enjoy a slight edge with scrum-half Alex Sheehan scoring a brilliant opportunist try but Ronan McKenna ran in an intercept try for Shannon and kicked the goals that forced a sixteen-all share of the spoils. A week later, Shannon's balance of experience in the shape of number eight David Quinlan and youth in the highly promising youngsters Kelvin Brown, Stephen Fitzgerald and Greg O'Shea saw them home by a handsome margin in the Musgrave Park replay.

22

Supporters, Soccer, Springsteen & the Baa-Baas

Supporters Club

One of the great success stories associated with the new stadium has been the creation of the Munster Rugby Supporters Club (MRSC) and one of its most attractive adjuncts is the fifty-strong choir whose members hail from all over the province and further afield. Ever since their first performance at the official opening of Thomond Park Stadium in 2008, the choir has grown in strength to become an entertaining part of every pre-match build-up at the venue.

The extremes to which MRSC members go to acquire tickets for away matches and their willingness to reach their destination by diverse routes have become an integral part of Thomond Park lore. And when it comes to enjoying themselves at Thomond Park, before, during and after the game, they are also without parallel. The choir plays a major role, with all concerned acknowledging the important part played by Anita Mahon as its Musical Director. Anita has worked with the choir since the outset in 2008 and has been instrumental in enabling it to deliver high-quality performances at several prestigious venues.

The reputation of the choir has paved the way for many notable artists including Cara O'Sullivan, The Celtic Tenors, Jean Wallace and Nyle Wolfe to join them in 'Stand Up and Fight', 'The Fields of Athenry' and the other great songs that ring out over Thomond Park on big match days. They have performed at many fund-raising events and concerts in rugby clubs around the province as well as at concerts in Cork

The pride of Cork, soprano Cara O'Sullivan works up the Thomond Park faithful with 'Stand Up and Fight'. (*Evening Echo*)

Opera House and University Concert Hall, Limerick. The choir has also proved popular with a wider audience and has sung live on programmes including *The Late Late Show*, *The Pat Kenny Show* on Newstalk, *Tubridy* on 2FM and *The Ian Dempsey Breakfast Show* on Today FM. They have also performed at Ireland soccer internationals where they sang national anthems for Ireland, Australia and South Africa (which use the five most widely spoken South African languages: Xhosa, Zulu, Sesotho, Afrikaans and English). Other notable performances include Europe's first Sports Tourism summit, Paul O'Connell's Freedom of Limerick City ceremony, the opening ceremony of the Special Olympics National Games and the National Pride of Place Awards.

The importance of enjoying the support of a group of people, male and female, who were not attached to any particular club but who wanted to support the Munster team, was readily recognised. Today, MRSC has a membership of 9,000 adults and 1,000 juniors. There is a members' bar in Thomond Park Stadium that absolutely heaves with passion and excitement on big match days and there are also branches in Dublin, London, Brussels and the US. They have made contributions to the Munster Rugby Academy totalling over €900,000.

Soccer at Thomond Park

The modern Limerick FC played their home games in the Airtricity League of Ireland Premier Division at Thomond Park for a couple of years, 2012/13 and 2013/14, after gaining promotion to the Premier Division. However, Thomond Park was much too spacious for the paltry crowds that attended for the most part – which was in contrast to the occasions back in the 1960s when European Cup games against the likes of Berne Young Boys and Torino of Italy required a ground capable of accommodating 10,000 or more spectators.

Football fans of a certain vintage have especially fond memories of the visit of the Swiss side for a European Cup tie against League of Ireland champions Limerick on 31 August 1960. N. J. (Noel) Dunne in the *Irish Independent* and Vincent Mathers in *The Irish Press* estimated the attendance at 8,000, although 'Onlooker' in the *Limerick Chronicle* added: 'I am told the League champions will lose £500 on this, their initial European Cup venture.' Financial difficulty, then as now, was nothing new for League of Ireland football in Limerick and even though it was a distinctly unpleasant evening, the Berne game remains an occasion fondly remembered and frequently recalled by soccer aficionados. The first half was particularly exciting and entertaining, a point well made by 'Onlooker':

> Some pity there had to be a second half! Without it, we would have had 45 minutes of dream football to treasure for the remainder of our days. However, given that the Swiss did belt in five after the change of ends, they were first to admit at the close that the scoreline 'lied' in a big way. Some 7,000 spectators, many of them rain soaked, stood to a man at the interval to cheer a side who had matched the star-studded visiting eleven in all the finer points of the game.

Noel Dunne was in full agreement:

> Not even a fantastic display of fighting grit by Limerick and the frenzied and continuous encouragement of 8,000 people could halt the inexorable progress of the Swiss champions. The Limerick team were recipients of a well-deserved ovation as

they trooped into the dressing rooms at half-time with the score nil-nil. That in itself was a well nigh incredible achievement by Limerick against a side that has performed with distinction against some of the best sides in Europe.

The writer bemoaned the fact that Limerick captain Leo O'Reilly had to play the game with a broken jaw sustained a few days previously in a game against Shamrock Rovers which was also played at Thomond Park to help to accustom the home players to the venue. He needed a 'pick-up injection' to make it and was back in Barrington's Hospital the following morning for an operation. But just about everyone was proud of the spirit of the home side, with Noel Dunne stressing that 'Limerick need feel no shame in this defeat – a side which plays its heart out as they did need have no worries on that score – but even in that astonishing first half it was apparent that they were out of their class as far as footballing class was concerned.'

However, there were one or two on the Limerick side who measured up and a few from Berne who stood out. Over to 'Onlooker' again: 'I doubt if there is a back in the League of Ireland who would have kept Toni Alleman scoreless. For my money, he was the danger man of the Berne attack – a bundle of energy, a bag of tricks and a sprinter and shooter of the highest order. Clinton played himself to a standstill and Alleman confessed to me afterwards that he was one of the best he had ever faced.'

And then there was Gerry McCarthy, a powerful man and defender:

> The local centre-half defended heroically and, as well, took time off to make the runs of the evening. His first-quarter effort was the piece de resistance of a sizzling first half. McCarthy beat off three would-be tacklers in his passage towards goal, and letting fly with his right, tore down the house with a drive that just topped the crossbar. All through, McCarthy was a dominant figure and one could not escape the feeling at the finish that that he was wasted at centre-half.

All that, along with a typically creative contribution by Donie Wallace, was not enough to prevent the Swiss knocking in five second-half goals by Weechselberger (2), Schneider, Durr and Meler. Berne Young Boys won the return leg by 4–2, the Limerick goals coming from Lynam (with an acrobatic overhead kick) and Leo O'Reilly.

Berne Young Boys: Eich, Fuhrer, Bugler, Schnyter, Walker, Sebneiter, Durer, Schneider, Wechselberger, Meierfi, Allman.

Limerick: Pat Skelly, Willie Clinton, Fergus Crawford, Des McNamara, Gerry McCarthy, Ewan Fenton, Joe Casey, George Lynam, Leo O'Reilly, Donie Wallace, Dick O'Connor.

Referee: Jose Ortiz de Mendivil (Spain).

The second European match to be contested at Thomond Park was a Cup Winners' Cup clash with Torino on 15 September 1971. After more than thirty years of trying, Limerick had won the FAI Cup for the first time the previous season under Ewan Fenton's management. Following a scoreless draw in the final at Dalymount Park, they defeated Drogheda United 3–0 in the replay with two goals by Hughie Hamilton and another by Dave Barrett. The Italians won by 1–0 against the following Limerick team:

Limerick: Kevin Fitzpatrick, Vincent Quinn, Sean Byrnes, Richie Hall, Al Finucane, Joe O'Mahony, Paddy Shortt, Andy McEvoy, Dave Barrett, Shamie Coad, Tony Meaney. *Substitute*: Eddie Donovan for Shortt.

Football continued to be played at Thomond Park from time to time. One of the more memorable games was a pre-season visit in 1982 of a powerful Tottenham Hotspur side for which Glenn Hoddle scored four terrific goals in a 6–2 win. Argentinian World Cup winner Ossie Ardiles was also a member of that side. Ardiles was a prized property in that Spurs side and when Limerick's Tony Meaney was deemed to be paying him overdue attention, he was approached by Tottenham 'hard man' Gareth Roberts and advised that he would be wise to change his tactics – and quickly. Roberts was known as Ardiles' 'minder' and, wisely, Meaney desisted. Des Kennedy scored both Limerick goals in a hugely enjoyable game in which Tony Ward, he of the legendary rugby victory over the All Blacks in 1978, showed off his wide array of tricks in the blue Limerick jersey.

Thomond 'Bossed'

Entertainers of the calibre of Bruce Springsteen are rare and once it was announced that 'The Boss' was on his way to Thomond Park on 16 July 2013, the scramble for tickets immediately got under way. A crowd estimated at between 30,000 and 40,000 turned up on a fine summer's evening and as one commentator put it, 'boy, did he play a blinder'. Springsteen thrilled early birds by kicking off his sound check at 5.30 p.m. before returning and playing for more than 3½ hours, much to the delight of those in neighbouring homes who barbecued and danced the night away.

He provided a particularly poignant moment when singing 'My Home Town' at the request of noted Limerick racehorse trainer Enda Bolger and dedicated to John Thomas McNamara, a Croom jockey who was paralysed after a fall at the Cheltenham Festival five months previously. The Limerick hurlers were going well at the time and Springsteen delighted their fans with a rendering of 'Glory Days' – alas, to little avail.

The *Limerick Leader*'s Alan Owens enthused:

> The reaction was universally, overwhelmingly positive. Springsteen's performance eclipsed that of the RDS last year in this reporter's opinion, the Boss feeding from the energy gleaned from a frenzied crowd. Without any fuss, The Boss performed three songs, including For You and Hearts of Stone, during a ten-minute impromptu sound check. Two hours later, he received a rapturous reception as he emerged on stage for what was the biggest concert ever staged in Limerick. Before his first song, Springsteen told the massive crowd he was thrilled to be performing in the city.
>
> 'Good evening Limerick, we are so glad to be here with you tonight and are here to fill you with the everlasting power of rock and roll', he said.
>
> Opening with This Little Light Of Mine, The Boss was greeted with a roar that shook the very foundations of the stadium. The legendary, sprightly 63-year-old rocker then proceeded to race through some of his biggest hits including American Land, Badlands and Hungry Heart.

Bruce Springsteen thrills the Thomond Park audience during his 2013 concert. (Courtesy *Limerick Leader*)

Thomond Park and its management will take particular pleasure from the concert going off without a hitch. This was the biggest event in terms of numbers – about 15,000 on the pitch and the same in the stands – that it has handled since it opened. A relieved John Cantwell, stadium boss, expressed his delight that it passed off exceptionally well and bodes well for the future. 'This will be a great selling point for Limerick going forward in terms of the profile of the act and the scale of the event,' he said.

James Coughlan, a barber from Kilrush, County Clare, made his way to the stage and presented The Boss with a giant Irish passport, to celebrate Springsteen's Irish heritage through the O'Hagan, McNicholas, Farrell, Sullivan, McCann and Garrity families. Later that night, Coughlan was surprised to receive a phone call. The caller said: 'This is the guy you gave the passport to. You wanna meet up?' The passport is now included in the Bruce Springsteen Special Collection in Monmouth University, New Jersey.

Several other concerts have been held at Thomond Park since the new stadium was opened, led by Elton John on 6 June 2009 and followed a month later by Rod Stewart, then by Pink (with guest Butch Walker) and Funhouse on their summer carnival tour on 20 June 2010; the Cranberries at the Special Olympics opening ceremony for their first appearance in their native city in fifteen years on 9 June 2010; Bob Dylan & Alabama 3 on 4 July 2010; and JLS with guest Olly Murs on 26 June 2011.

The opening ceremony of the Special Olympics 2010 in Thomond Park. (Courtesy *Limerick Leader*)

Thomond Park is a whole lot more these days than a rugby ground. For instance, a stadium tour takes visitors to places usually accessible only to players and officials, from a seat in the home and away dressing rooms to a walk down the tunnel and onto the pitch. There is also a museum with fascinating memorabilia, visual aids and images. Wedding receptions can now be held at Thomond Park or major conferences such as the Keith Wood-inspired Sports Tourism European summit, just one of many such high-profile events that have taken place there over the last seven years.

One of Thomond Park's s finest moments came on Thursday 8 June 2010 with the opening ceremony of the Special Olympics Ireland. From the date early in 2009 when it was announced the games would take place at the University of Limerick, a huge plan of action was put in place. The task of recruiting volunteers to help make life comfortable and enjoyable for the 2,500 athletes met with a generous response with Barbara Cahill, the inspiring leader of the operation. Over 3,000 signed up.

When opening ceremony day arrived, all of the athletes and coaches were transported from the University of Limerick in a fleet of fifty-eight buses using a one-way system at Limerick Institute of Technology from where they were escorted to the back gate of Thomond Park by

Great characters and personalities have the graced the ground over the decades. 'Dodo' Reddan of Young Munster loved to dress herself – and her dogs – in black and amber on Munster Cup final day. (Courtesy *Limerick Leader*)

Munster fans John O'Connor and Marie Rawley enjoy another great day at Thomond Park. (Courtesy *Evening Echo*)

Joe O'Donnell and his team of volunteers and seated in order of region on the pitch. This in turn resulted in a very colourful sight with all the provincial and regional colours. The stands, of course, were packed with families, friends and the general public, all entertained by the Cranberries and others prior to the opening ceremony and afterwards until 10 p.m. Among the attendance were Denis O'Brien, chairman of patrons and outstanding supporter of Special Olympics Ireland, rugby stars Keith Wood and Paul O'Connell, Republic of Ireland soccer legend Packie Bonner and broadcasters George Hook and Mícheál Ó Muircheartaigh.

And still that's not all. Not so very long ago, a Dublin rugby enthusiast who spent a number of years in Limerick and made Bohemians his adopted club, fell in love with Thomond Park to such a degree that before his death, he decreed that he should be cremated and his ashes spread on the famous pitch. His wish was duly granted!

The Barbarians

Alan Quinlan and Malcolm O'Kelly have good reason to remember the game between Ireland and the Barbarians at Thomond Park on 4 June 2010. The Baa-Baas – an invitational team based in Britain – were still finding their way in the world of professional rugby that was a fair distance removed from their ethos and so were delighted to have the opportunity for some game time against Ireland before Ireland took off on a trip to Australia and New Zealand. Quinlan had been omitted from the Irish touring party and it was to be O'Kelly's final appearance in a first-class game. Ireland might not have wanted Quinny and Mal … but the Baa-Baas regarded them as ideal to their requirements and included them in their starting line-up. As far as Quinlan was concerned, nobody was more aware of his presence than his close friend and Ireland captain Ronan O'Gara.

'I was talking to Brian O'Driscoll coming back from training and told him I felt we'd see the real Quinny tonight,' said a worried O'Gara on the morning of the game. 'It's my first time ever playing against him – usually at training for the last thirteen years, we've been on the same side … I think he's very disappointed not to be going on the Irish tour so he has a point to prove as well. There will be a lot of Quinny fans there.'

Nothing transpired to damage the O'Gara/Quinlan friendship in a match that was a lot more than an exhibition with both sides intent on fashioning the desired result. The Baa-Baas raced into an early lead with kicks by Clermont Auvergne out-half Brock James and tries by New Zealander Xavier Rush and Australia's George Smith, against an O'Gara penalty. Ireland hit back with tries by Tony Buckley and Niall Ronan; O'Gara wound up with a total of thirteen points. French wing Cedric Heymans chipped in with a Barbarians try, Jean-Baptiste kicked a penalty, sealing the deal for the visitors: Barbarians 29; Ireland 23.

Malcolm O'Kelly received a warm response from the crowd, a fitting tribute to a man who had made life hard for Munster on many occasions throughout an illustrious career during which he won 92 Irish caps and made 183 appearances for Leinster. Proudly wearing his Templeogue College socks, he said: 'I never thought I'd get a standing ovation at Thomond Park. They're a great crowd and it shows the respect they have and I'm looking forward to coming down here in the future as a spectator. It was fantastic and an unbelievable way to finish my career.'

Ireland: Rob Kearney (Leinster), Johne Murphy (Munster), Gavin Duffy (Connacht), Fergus McFadden (Leinster), Andrew Trimble (Ulster), Ronan O'Gara capt., Peter Stringer, Marcus Horan (all Munster), Sean Cronin (Connacht), Tony Buckley (Munster), Ed O'Donoghue, Dan Tuohy (both Ulster), John Muldoon (Connacht), Niall Ronan (Munster), Chris Henry (Ulster). *Replacements:* Jerry Flannery (Munster), Tom Court (Ulster), Mick O'Driscoll, Donncha O'Callaghan, Tomas O'Leary (all Munster), Tommy Bowe, Paddy Wallace (both Ulster).

Barbarians: Paul Warwick (Munster), Cedric Heymans (Toulouse), Casey Laulala (Cardiff Blues), Seru Rabini (Leeds Carnegie), David Smith (Hurricanes), Brock James (Clermont Auvergne), Pierre Mignoni (Toulon), David Barnes (Bath), Schalk Brits (Saracens), Census Johnston (Toulouse), Jerome Thion (Biarritz), Malcolm O'Kelly (Leinster), Alan Quinlan (Munster), George Smith (Brumbies), Xavier Rush (Cardiff Blues). *Replacements:* Benoit August (Biarritz), Julian White (Leicester Tigers), Rodney So'oialo (Hurricanes), Martyn Williams (Cardiff Blues), Byron Kelleher, Jean-Baptiste Elissalde (both Toulouse), Fabrice Estebanez (Brive).

Man of the match: John Muldoon.

Referee: Romain Poite (France).

Ireland were coming off the back of successive victories in the Six Nations Championship in May 2015 when their highly accomplished coach Joe Schmidt accepted a game for his side against the Barbarians. He saw it as an opportunity to consider the fitness and potential of a few players who were in contention for places in the Irish squad for the World Cup due to take place in England and Wales the following autumn and also to give game time to those who had struggled with injury earlier in the season.

From the perspective of the Limerick rugby public, it did not help that Munster were set to play a Guinness Pro12 final against Glasgow Warriors two days later and so there were no 'home' players in either line-up. Furthermore, the weather was most unseasonable and it is doubtful that Schmidt learned a whole lot from the occasion. Winger Craig Kilroy scored a fine try to push his claims for World Cup recognition and his fellow Ulstermen Chris Henry and Paddy Jackson also went over, the remaining points in a total of twenty-one came from three conversions by Ian Madigan. But the Barbarians managed one more through two tries by Alex Cuthbert, the Welsh winger, and Leinster's South African full back Zane Kirchner along with two conversions and a penalty by Jimmy Gopperth, a New Zealander on the threshold of leaving Leinster for Wasps. To be honest, not one of the most memorable games ever played at Thomond Park.

Barbarians: Z. Kirchner (South Africa), A. Cuthbert (Wales), J. Rokocoko (New Zealand), W. Oliver (South Africa), D. Smith (New Zealand), J. Gopperth (Leinster), R. Pienaar (South Africa), R. Tejeriso (Argentina), D. Fourie (Lyon), A. Jones (Wales), R. Capo Ortega (Uruguay), K. Mitauatdze (Georgia), S. Jennings capt. (Ireland), G. Vosloo (Toulon), R. Holani (Japan). *Replacements*: N. Hines (Scotland), S. Taumoepeau (New Zealand), G. Smith (Australia), G. Apton (South Africa), D. Ward (Harlequins).

Ireland: R. Kearney, D. Kearney, C. O'Shea (all Leinster), L. Marshall, C. Kilroy (both Ulster), I. Madigan, E. Reddan, J. McGrath, R. Strauss, T. Furlong, D. Toner (all Leinster), D. Tuohy, R. Diack, C. Henry (all Ulster), J. Heaslip capt. (Leinster). *Replacements*: M. Bent (Leinster), R. Herring (Ulster), M. Ross, B. Marshall, J. Murphy, L. McGrath (all Leinster), P. Jackson (Ulster), C. Kelleher (Leinster).

Referee: G. Garner (England).

Epilogue Tony Ward

Before 1972 I had passed through Limerick but once. It was about ten years earlier and we were on our way to Kerry for a family holiday (we got a puncture in a summer downpour opposite Cannock's). Little did I realise then the impact this great city and these great people would have on my life.

In 1972 I was in my last year in school in Dublin and although a member of the Leinster Schools' squad of that year my sporting future in my own mind was determined, having already signed the relevant part-time professional forms committing to Louis Kilcoyne and Shamrock Rovers from 1973 on.

I'd like to be able to say my first experience of visiting Thomond was awe-inspiring. It was anything but. For one thing I was, along with John Robbie, one of the replacement Leinster backs for that schools interprovincial in which I think we came second. My only memory is of a physically powerful Munster full back with an equally prodigious boot. Gerry Grant was that young man, brother of Young Munster scrum half and coach extraordinary-in-waiting Tony.

Tony Ward in action for Ireland against England in 1981 (Courtesy *Irish Examiner*)

Despite the mystique and legend, Thomond Park was a tatty ground back then. Fantastic location and soon to become the centre of my universe but, minus bodies, the old stand and terracing (well, concrete steps) made it almost graveyard like for matches of minimal spectator appeal.

Fast forward two and a bit years, perception changed and how. Munster Cup semi-final, my third senior game and my first local derby with Len Dineen and Old Crescent the opposition. The atmosphere was electric. We (Garryowen) went on to win the Cup that year (beating Constitution in Cork in the final) thereby qualifying for the Kevin Quilligan-inspired Bateman Cup sometime around Easter.

In beating Galwegians we qualified to meet St Mary's in the Sunday final. The ground was heaving with bodies and atmosphere as it was for most every game I played there after that. There were cup finals in 1977, 1978 and 1979 against Shannon and Young Munsters, countless interprovincials, Charity Cup finals, touring matches, including *that* game on 31 October 1978.

Well do I recall, too, playing for Limerick United against then FA Cup holders Tottenham Hotspur, again with bodies hanging from rooftops on the popular side and at the Ballynanty end. They were great memories of great matches in a very unique and special place.

Push me as to why and two words trip off the lips: respect and knowledge. Those who dared break the loaded silence offered to goal kickers, whether attempted conversion or penalty shot at goal, did so at their peril. If those in the immediate vicinity didn't get you then Tommy Creamer's less-than-gentle reminder over the PA certainly did. To this day it still leads the way in terms of respect for kickers and as I learned in my time playing for Leinster (following the best part of a decade wearing red) and specifically my only time lining out for the enemy in Thomond, silence can be very far from golden. The sound of silence gets to visiting kickers – trust me! The second reason and definitely the more relevant was in playing at Thomond before people you shared time and space with, day in day out, meant no place for meekness in mind or body once you crossed those white lines. They knew their rugby, you knew they knew their rugby so you delivered or died.

I am on the record so many times over the years emphasising what made beating New Zealand so special over and above the achievement in itself. Quite apart from what it was and where it was, we were at the high altar, the spiritual home before the most knowledgeable rugby folk on this island.

And, sparing his blushes, I was also privileged to play at a time when the doyen of rugby writing down south and the most appropriate author of this work C. N. Mulqueen was covering the game, first for the *Limerick Leader* and then for the *Cork Examiner* as it was back then. On a personal level I can honestly say that only three rugby journalists in the print media at that time got to grips with me and in the process won my trust, Ned Van Esbeck and John Redmond being the other two.

Despite the fact that Charlie and Ned van E. are 'Gooners' while John Red is a loyal and long-suffering 'toffee' (mind you, try Leeds if you really want to know the definition of long suffering) I found in all three a rare and precious trait, given the nature of the business, and that was trust.

Charlie's verdict was the one most eagerly awaited, given his in-depth analysis and freedom of space the national scribes yearned for when reporting. Praise or criticism was earned in equal measure. He was, is and will always be central to Munster rugby, its evolution and by extension Thomond Park folklore.

I feel immensely proud, indeed humbled to have played a small part in helping make this iconic ground the special place it has in the hearts and minds of Munster and Limerick folk everywhere.

Bibliography

Club histories and annuals: London Irish RFC; Shannon RFC; Young Munster RFC; Garryowen FC; UL Bohemian RFC; Old Crescent RFC; Cork Constitution FC; University College Cork RFC; St Mary's College RFC.

Foley, Anthony, *Axel: A Memoir,* Hachette Books Ireland, Dublin, 2008.

Galwey, Mick and Mulqueen, Charlie, *Galwey, the Autobiography: The Story of a Great Irish Sportsman,* Irish Rugby Review, Dublin, 2000.

Kane Cafferty, Ursula, *Suitcase Number Seven: A Rugby Story with a Difference,* Personal Publishing, Dublin, 2005.

Keane, Moss, *Rucks, Mauls & Gaelic Football,* Merlin Publishing, Dublin, 2005.

Mourie, Graham and Palenski, Ron, *Captain: An Autobiography*, Arthur Barker Ltd, 1982.

Mulqueen, Charlie, *Limerick's Rugby History*, Limerick Leader Ltd, Limerick, 1978.

— *The Murphy's Story of Munster Rugby*, Limerick Leader Ltd, Limerick, 1993.

— *Brothers in Sport: Rugby*, Mercier Press, Cork, 2011.

O'Flaherty, Michael, *The Home of the Spirit: A Celebration of Limerick Rugby*, Limerick Leader Ltd, Limerick, 1999.

O'Gara, Ronan, *My Autobiography*, Transworld Ireland, Dublin, 2008.

School annuals. Rockwell College; Crescent College; St Munchin's College; Mungret College; Presentation Brothers College, Cork; Christian Brothers College, Cork.

Stent, R. K. *The Fourth Springboks, 1951–1952,* Longmans, Green & Co., London, 1952.

Van Esbeck, Edmund, *Irish Rugby 1874–1999: A History*, Gill & Macmillan, Dublin, 1999

Index

Note: numbers in *italics* refer to
   photographs

Abbeyfeale *246*, 247
All Blacks 4–5, 27, 38–9, 46, 64–7, 77,
   80–1, 189–94, *190*
   1978 1, 73, 80–101, *81*, *87*, 130–1
All-Ireland Club Centenary
   Championship 75–6
All-Ireland League (AIL) 112, 113, 114–
   17, 118–19, 122–8, 133, 138, 160,
   161–3, 236, 250
Ardscoil Rís 238–9, 242
Argentina 73–4, 147
Army XV 15–17, *16*
Askeaton 243
Australia 27, 39, 48–9, 77, 80, 102, 107–
   8, 132, 143–4, 205–8, 233–5
Auvergne 46

Barbarians 5, 46, 98, 260–3
Barry, Des 60, 82, 130
Barry, Nicky 110, 115–16, 120
Bateman Cup 9, 14, 45, 161, 164
Berkery, Paddy 32, 33, *33*, 226, 227
Bohemians 8–9, *9*, 10, 12, 14, *51*, *60*, 63,
   119, 124
   Munster Senior Cup 49–50, 52–3, 54,
      60, 61, 62–3, 70, 103–6
   pavilion 45, 68, 112, 120, 144
Bowen, Jimmy 83, *87*, 90, *90*, 91, 93, 98,
   103, 233
Bradley, Michael 107, 108, 115, 120
Breen, John 83–5, 101
Brosnahan, Francis *105*, 106, 107, 113,
   119
Bruff RFC 162–4, *164*

Canada 185–6
Canniffe, Donal 73, 74, 77, 83, *87*, 91,
   95, 96, 98, 189, 232
Canniffe, Kieran 60, *228*, 229, *245*
Cantillon, Christy 83, *87*, 90, *90*, 91, 98,
   102, 131

Casey, Gerry *103*, 104, 105, *105*, 106,
   107, 113
Castletroy College 236
Chambers, Donal 60, *60*, 63, 64, 68
Charity Cup 16, 243, 265
Christian Brothers College (CBC) 224,
   225, 229, 235–6, 238
Christian Brothers School (CBS) 19, 39,
   224
Clancy, Eamonn 23, *56*, 57, 58, 130
Cleary, Tom 47, 49, 50, 51–2, *51*, *53*, 54,
   60, 62, 63
Clermont Auvergne 4, 178–9, 194–5,
   214, 219–20
Clifford, Tom 18, 19–21, *20*, 22, 23, *24*,
   28, 29, 30, 32, 46, *46*, 47
Clohessy, Peter 34, 119, 120, 129, 134,
   138, 141, 148
concerts 256–7
Cork Constitution 10, 13, 59–60, 70,
   107, 109, 110, 112–13, 114, 115,
   124, 125, 126, 129, 162, 163, *163*,
   245
Creamer, Tommy 78, *128*, 189, 244,
   245–7, 265
Crescent College (Comprehensive) 18–
   19, 33–4, *33*, 36, *37*, 38, 41–2, 113,
   226–9, 230, 235, 236, 237–8
Cross, Pat 105, *105*, 106, 107, 113
Crotty, Dominic 128, 135, 138, 141, 142
Cuchulainns 44, 45
Cullen, Christian 165–6, 167, *167*, 168
Curtin, Mossy 16, *16*, 17, 22, *23*

Danaher, Philip 115, *116*, 117, 120, 129,
   234, 235
Deering, Shay *74*, 75, 76, 77
Dennison, Seamus *74*, 75, 76, 82, 83, *87*,
   88–9, *88*, 93, 98, 102
Dineen, Dom 27, 28, 29, 33, *42*, 45, *51*,
   53
Dowling, Ian 169, 171, 176, 178, 180,
   193, 200, 204

Earls, Keith 186, 195, 196, 200, 201, 202, 204, 205, *207*, 208, 213, 217, *218*, 236
Ella, Mark 108, 233, 234
English, Christy *46*, *51*, 54, 60, *60*, 63
English, Mick 38, *46*, 47, 48, *48*, 49, 50–1, *51*, *52*, 53–4, 60, *60*, 63, 64, 65, *65*, 66–7, 68, 100, *228*, 229
European Champions Cup 219–20

Fair Green 7
fees, match 133
Finn, Moss 83, *87*, 93, *188*, 233
Fitzgerald, Terry 78, *78*, 79, 106, 109
Flannery, Donogh 56, *56*, 57, 58
Flannery, Jerry 169, 176, 177, 178, 186, 196, 200, 204, 216, 219, 261
Foley, Anthony 34, 123, 124, 126, 127, *127*, 128, 129, 134, 135, 138, 141, 142, 144, 146–7, *147*, 149, 153, 168, 170, 171, 176, 177, 199, 208, 215, 216, 219, 220, 221, 223, 248
Foley, Brendan 74, 78, *78*, 79, 83, 85, *87*, *94*, 101, 102, *103*, 106, 124, 144, 248–9
France 53

Gaffney, Alan 148, 151, 168, *168*
Galvin, Jim 113, 114, 117, 123, *127*, 128
Galwey, Mick 34, 110, 114, 116, 117, 123, 126, *127*, 128, 134, 135, 136, 138, 139–40, 141, 142, 145, 147, 148, 168, 199
Garryowen 8, 13, 17, 18–19, 24, 28–9, 35, 43, 66–7, 75–6, 109, 110, 162, 167, 243
    AIL 114, 115–17, 116, 124, 125, 126, 128, 161
    Senior Cup 21–3, *23*, 24–6, *35*, 38, 59–60, 70, *74*, 77–9, 102–3, 119, 129, *161*, 163–4
Glenstal 232–3
Gloucester 1, 151–9, 166, 169, 179–80, 215, 216
Guinane, Gerry 34, 38, 41–3, *42*, 226

Haden, Andy 4, *87*, 93, 94, *94*, 96, 97
Halvey, Eddie 121, 123, 125, 126, *127*, 128, 134, 138, 142
Harris, Richard *25*, 33–7, *33*, *35*, *36*, *37*, 227, 229
Hayes, John 125, *127*, 128, 141, 148, 149, 153, 176, 177, 186, 196, 199, 200, 201, 202, 204, 209, 210, 216
Heineken Cup 124, 133–8, 148, 215, 219
    1999/00 138–42, 145
    2000/01 144–8
    2001/02 148–9
    2002/03 1, 151–60
    2003/04 165–7
    2004/05 167–8
    2005/06 169–73
    2006/07 174–6
    2007/08 176–80, 184, 206
    2008/09 194–7
    2009/10 203–4
    2010/11 204–5
    2011/12 1, 209–13
    2012/13 213–14
    2013/14 216–19
Highfield 49–50, 53, 70, 109
Hogan, Paul 116, *116*, 117, 128, 129
Holland, Jason 138, 139, 141, 142, 148, 153, 199
Horgan, Anthony 138, 141, 142, 145, 199
Horgan, Jack 24–6, 31, 32
Howlett, Doug 165, 177, 180, 189, 192, 193, 200, 201, 202, 203, 204, 205, 208, 209, 210
Hurley, Denis 179–80, 200, 205, 208, 210, 213, 220, 221

Ireland 23, 53, 61, 64, 70, 71, 108, 147, 149–50, 185–6, 215, 223, 233–5, 260–3
Italy 149–50

Keane, Bobby 46, *46*, *56*, 57, 244
Keane, Killian 128, 129, 135, 138, 141–2, 161, 199
Keane, Moss 74, 77, 83, 85, *87*, 88, *92*, 93–4, 100, 101, *103*, *188*
Keatley, Ian 15, 213–14, *214*, 217, 219, 220–1

Kelly, John 138, 141, 149, 150, 153, *155*, 176, 199

Kidney, Declan 106, 136, *136*, 137–8, *137*, 139, 141–2, 148, 168, 176, 177–8, *179*–80

Kiely, Oliver (Sonny) 106, 109, 110, 117

Kiernan, Tom 56, 57, 58, 64, *65*, 66, 67, 69, 82–3, 85–6, 89, 90, 92, 97, 98, 99, 130–1, *131*, 133, *228*, 229

Lane, Mick 29, 30, 31, 32

Langford, John 138, 140, 141, 142, 145, 148

Larkin, Dan 116, *116*, 117, 120, 129, 134

Lawler, Mossie 68, 153, *155*, 199, 239

league championship (Celtic League/Pro12) 198–203, 220–1, 223, 262

Leamy, Denis 169, 170, *171*, 176, 177, 179, 191, 193, 199, 202, 205, 209, 210, 239

Leinster 5, 6, 7, 10–12, 15, 43, 102, 133, 138, 172, 197, 199–201, 202–3, 213, 214, 220

Lenihan, Donal 108, 120, 215

Leslie, Andy 77, 119, 136

Lions 20–1, 23, 38–40, 53–4, 61, 117

Lourdes 28–9

Lucey, Mick *65*, 66, 67, 68, 70

McCarthy, Jim 17, 28, 29, 30, 31, *32*, 33

McGahan, Tony 194, *195*, 200, 202–3, 206, 208, 210

McGann, Barry 74, 77, *231*, 232

McGrath, Paddy 56, 57, 58, *65*, 66, 67, 68, 69, 229, 230

McLean, Terry 64, 65, 66, 67, 85–6, 88, 98

McLoughlin, Gerry 74, *78*, 79, 83, *87*, 91, 102, *103*, 106, 109

McManus, J.P. 186–7, *187*

McNamara, Sean 22, *23*, 27, 28, *35*, 38, *40*, 249

Mafi, Lifeimi 176, *177*, 179, 189, 193, *193*, 200, 201, 202, 204, 205, 209, 210, 213

Mardyke 27, 46, 81, 227, 238, 242

Markets Field 3, 6, 7, 8, 15, 27, 81

Melville, Nigel 4, 156–7

Moloney, Larry *74*, 75, 76, 77, 82, 85, *87*, 93, 98, 102, 230, *231*

Morgan, Brendan 16, *16*, 17, 22, *23*, *35*, 38

Moylett, Mick 106, 108, 109, 117, 234, 235

Mulcahy, Bill 38, 60–3, *60*, *61*, 69, 230

Mulcahy, Ted 104, 106, 108, 233

Mullins, Mike 138, 141, 153, 166, 199

Mungret 224, *225*, 226, 229

Munster Junior Cup 45, 68, 106, 107, 125, 161, 162, 240, 240–50

Munster Schools Junior Cup 49, 226, 230, 236

Munster Schools Senior Cup 224–33, 235–9

  Crescent College (Comprehensive) 33, *33*, 34, 36, *37*, 38, 41, 42, 113, 227, 229, 235, 236, 237–8

Munster Senior Cup 9, 10, 12, 14, 16, 17, 35, 68, 75, 108–9, 112, 125, 160, 161–2

  1938 12–14

  1947 21–3, 57

  1950 24–6

  1952 38

  1958 49–50, 52–3, 54

  1959 54

  1960 55–9, 130, 244

  1961 59–60

  1962 60, 61, 62–3, 70

  1969 70

  1977 77–8

  1978 78–9

  1979 102–3

  1980 103–6

  1982 106

  1984 107

  1986–88 109–10

  1989 112–13

  1990–92 113–14

  1993 119

  1995/97/98 129

  2011 163–4

Munster Senior League 8–9, 16, 63, 109, 112, 118

Murphy, Barry 169, 171, 176, 191, 193, 200, 208

Murphy, Noel, Jnr 59, *59*, *65*, 66, 67

Murray, Conor 164, 208, 213, 236
Murray, Jerry 60, *65*, 66, 67, *228*, 229, 230
Murray, Pat 117, 123, 124, 125, 126, 134, *134*, *234*, 235

Nesdale, Tom 38, *46*, *48*, 49, 229

O'Brien, Brian 45, *65*, 66, 67, 123, 124, 125, *137*, 138, 142
O'Callaghan, Donncha 148, 150, *152*, 153, 169, 170, *170*, 176, 177, 186, *198*, 199, 200, 202, 204, 205, 210, 213, 218, 261
O'Callaghan, Mick *65*, 66, 67, 68, 103, 229
O'Callaghan, Paddy 45, *51*, 54, 60, 62, 73, 74, 77
O'Connell, Paul 148, *166*, 169, 170, *170*, *171*, 175, 176, 177, 178, 180, 186, 195, 196, *196*, 199, 200, 202, 203, 209, 210, 212, 213, 214, *214*, 216, 217, 219, 220, 221–3, *222*, 240–2, *241*, 260
O'Donovan, Niall 106, 109, 123, 124, 125, 126, 136, 137–8
O'Dowd, Brendan 51, *51*, 53, 54, 60, *60*, *62*, 63, 68, 121, 229, *245*
O'Driscoll, Mick 148, 153, *155*, 176, 178, 189, 192, 193, 200, 203, 205, 219, 261
O'Gara, Ronan 1, 4, 125, 138, 139, 140, *140*, 141, 142, 145, 148–9, 152–3, 159–60, 166, 167, 170, 171, 174, 176, 177, 178, 179, 186, 194, 195, 196, 199, 200, 201, 202, 203, 204, 205, 206, 209–11, *211*, 212, 213, 214–16, *242*, 260, 261
O'Halloran, Gerry *56*, 57, 58, 130, 244
Old Crescent *25*, 38, 41, 42, 43, 46, 62–3, *62*, 70, 110, 118–19, 125–6
Old Wesley 45, 114, 123
O'Leary, Tomas 176, 179–80, 196, 200, 204, 209, 210, 213, 261
O'Loughlin, Dave 11, 12, 17, 28
O'Malley, Desmond 41–3
O'Malley, Donogh 45, 242
O'Meara, John *25*, 29, 30, 31, 32

O'Reilly, Tony 38, 39, 40, 47, 62, 63
O'Shea, Billy 113, 116, 117, 123, 236
O'Sullivan, Eddie 108, 109, 143, 149, 168

Payne, Shaun 166, *167*, 176, 178, 179–80
Prendergast, Kevin 60, *60*, 63, 68, *228*
Presentation Brothers College (PBC) 66, 130, 136, 168, 224, 226, *226*, 227, *228*, 229–30, *231*, 232, 235, 236, *237*, 238, 244
Price, Eddie 8, 13, 14, *14*, *78*, 79, 248–9
Pucciariello, Frederico 169, 193

Quilligan, Kevin 29, *35*, *46*, 75, *81*, 100, 265
Quinlan, Alan 125, 126, *127*, 138, 141, 142, 153, *158*, 173, 177, 178, 186, 196, 199, 200, 204, 205, 216, 260, 261

Reid, Paddy 17, 18–19, 21, 22, 23, *23*, 24, 27, 39, 187
Reid, Tom 22, *23*, 29, *35*, 38, 39–40, 47
Richmond 125, 244
Roche, Con 17, 22, *23*, 38
Rockwell College 49, 70, 130, 169, 224–6, *228*, 229, 230, 232–3, 236–9
Rolls, Peter *103*, 104, 106, 233
Romania 149
Royal Air Force 27–8
Ryan, Johnny *51*, 54, 60, *60*, 63
Ryan, Michael Noel 56, *56*, 57, 58, *81*, 130

St Enda's 235–6
St George, Charlie 9–10, 36
St Mary's College 75–6, *75*, 123, 126–7, 161
St Mary's RFC 247–8
St Munchin's 168, 230, *231*, *234*, 235, 236, 237
Sale Sharks 169–71, 194, 195, 219, 220
Saracens 4, 122, 125, 139–41, 180, 213, 216, 219, 220
schools rugby 39, 168, 224–39
  Crescent College *see separate entry*
Second World War 10, 15–17, 41, 42–3
seven-a-side rugby 121–2, 206